How Science Takes Stock

How Science Takes Stock

The Story of Meta-Analysis

❖   ❖   ❖

Morton Hunt

Russell Sage Foundation

New York

The Russell Sage Foundation

The Russell Sage Foundation, one of the oldest of America's general purpose foundations, was established in 1907 by Mrs. Margaret Olivia Sage for "the improvement of social and living conditions in the United States." The Foundation seeks to fulfill this mandate by fostering the development and dissemination of knowledge about the country's political, social, and economic problems. While the Foundation endeavors to assure the accuracy and objectivity of each book it publishes, the conclusions and interpretations in Russell Sage Foundation publications are those of the authors and not of the Foundation, its Trustees, or its staff. Publication by Russell Sage, therefore, does not imply Foundation endorsement.

Library of Congress Cataloging-in-Publication Data

Hunt, Morton., 1920–
   How Science takes stock : the story of meta-analysis / Morton Hunt.
      p. cm.
   Includes bibliographical references and index.
   ISBN 0-87154-389-3 (cloth)   ISBN 0-87154-398-2 (paper)
1. Science—Methodology. 2. Science—Miscellanea. 3. Meta-analysis. I. Title.
   Q175.H94   1997   97–964
   001.4'22—dc21   CIP

RUSSELL SAGE FOUNDATION
112 East 64th Street, New York, New York 10021
10 9 8 7 6 5 4 3 2 1

to Bernice, meta-mate

"Chaos was the law of nature; Order was the dream of man."

——Henry Adams, paraphrasing Karl Pearson

Contents

ABOUT THE AUTHOR

Morton Hunt writes about the social and behavioral sciences. He attended Temple University and the University of Pennsylvania, worked briefly on the staffs of two magazines, and since 1949 has been a freelance writer. He has written eighteen books and some 450 articles. He has won a number of prestigious science-writing awards.

ALSO BY MORTON HUNT

The Natural History of Love
Her Infinite Variety: The American Woman as Lover, Mate and Rival
Mental Hospital
The Talking Cure (with Rena Corman and Louis R. Ormont)
The World of the Formerly Married
The Affair: A Portrait of Extra-Marital Love in Contemporary America
The Mugging
Sexual Behavior in the 1970s
*Prime Time: A Guide to the Pleasures and Opportunities of the New Middle
    Age* (with Bernice Hunt)
The Divorce Experience (with Bernice Hunt)
The Universe Within: A New Science Explores the Human Mind
Profiles of Social Research: The Scientific Study of Human Interactions
*The Compassionate Beast: What Science Is Discovering About the Humane
    Side of Humankind*
The Story of Psychology

Acknowledgments

The Russell Sage Foundation has supported research into the application of meta-analysis to the social sciences since 1987; many of the findings that have emanated from that support lend themselves to meta-analysis in other fields of science as well.

The publications resulting from the Foundation's grants have been largely technical, intended for scientists and policy analysts interested in learning about and applying meta-analytic methodology. But in 1994 Eric Wanner, president of the Foundation, felt it was time to tell a larger public about meta-analysis—a public comprising any and all persons with a general intellectual interest in science, plus one special audience: members of Congress, state legislators, agency administrators, and their staffs, all of whom might find meta-analyses a swift and effective way to acquire the data needed to buttress decisions about social programs and legislation.

This book is the product of a grant proposed by Mr. Wanner and affirmed by the Russell Sage Foundation's board of directors. I am deeply grateful to Foundation Scholar Robert K. Merton for recommending me to Mr. Wanner, and to Mr. Wanner and the board for entrusting me with the task of authorship.

My special thanks go to Harris Cooper, who read the manuscript and corrected a number of technical errors; any that remain are my responsibility. I am also grateful to all those people who gladly suffered—at least I hope it was gladly—to be interviewed at length and to those others whom I did not interview but who generously furnished me with reprints and other documents: Nalini Ambady, Alexia A. Antczak-Bouckoms, Theodore X. Barber, Betsy Becker, Iain Chalmers, Thomas Chalmers, Eleanor Chelimsky, Graham Colditz, Rory Collins, George Comstock, Thomas Cook, Harris Cooper, David S. Cordray, Elizabeth C. Devine, Judith Droitcour, Daniel Druckman, Alice Eagly, H. J. Eysenck, Chris Fossett, Gene V Glass, Roger Greenberg, Joel Greenhouse, Rob Greenwald, Judith Hall, Eric Hanushek, Larry V. Hedges, Bruce Kupelnick, Richard D. Laine, Joseph Lau, Richard J. Light, Mark Lipsey, Norman Miller, Frederick Mosteller, Ingram Olkin, Michele Orza, Robert Rosenthal, Donald Rubin, Christopher Schmid, William Shadish, Varda

Shoham, Mary Lee Smith, William Stock, Miron Straf, Kenneth Wachter, Paul M. Wortman, Robert York, and Salim Yusuf.

I thank the following for permission to reprint copyrighted materials:

—The American Psychological Association and William R. Shadish: figures 1 and 2 from Shadish and Sweeney (1991). Adapted with permission.

—*The Lancet*: Figure 2 from the Early Breast Cancer Trialists' Collaborative Group (1992).

—*The New England Journal of Medicine and the Massachusetts Medical Society*: Figure 1 from Lau and others (1992). Reprinted by permission; all rights reserved.

—The Russell Sage Foundation: Figures 6.6 and 6.7 from Betsy Jane Becker's chapter in Cook and others (1992).

—U.S. General Accounting Office: Figure titled "Quality of Studies and Credibility of Available Information" from U.S. General Accounting Office (1984).

—John Wiley & Sons and Mark Lipsey: Figures 2 and 3 from Lipsey (1995).

MORTON HUNT

Chapter 1

Making Order of Scientific Chaos

The Explosion of Contemporary Science

"If I have seen further it is by standing on the shoulders of giants," Isaac Newton wrote to Robert Hooke in 1675/6. In assuming this modest pose, he alluded to a fundamental assumption that our culture makes about science, namely, that it is progressive and cumulative, a corollary of which is that forays into the unknown by any researcher, however brilliant, are merely extensions of the knowledge amassed up to that time. For centuries it has been an article of faith that scientists base their research on existing information, add a modicum of new and better data to it, and thereby advance toward an ever more profound, complete, and accurate explanation of reality.

But today we are experiencing a crisis of faith; many of us no longer feel sure that science, though growing explosively, is moving inexorably toward the truth. Indeed, "growing explosively" is an ominous oxymoron: "growing" implies orderly development, but "explosively" denotes disorder and fragmentation. Virtually every field of science is now pervaded by a relentless cross fire in which the findings of new studies not only differ from previously established truths but disagree with one another, often vehemently. Our faith that scientists are cooperatively and steadily enlarging their understanding of the world is giving way to doubt as, time and again, new research assaults existing knowledge.

In recent years, however, methodologists in a number of scientific disciplines have been developing an antidote to the increasingly chaotic output of contemporary research. Known as meta-analysis, it is a means of combining the numerical results of studies with disparate, even conflicting, research methods and findings; it enables researchers to discover the consistencies in a set of seemingly inconsistent findings and to arrive at conclusions more accurate and credible than those presented in any one of the primary studies. More than that, meta-analysis makes it possible to pinpoint how and why studies come up with different results,

1

and so determine which treatments—circumstances or interventions—are most effective and why they succeed.*

To appreciate how anarchic contemporary research has become and how needed this new methodology is, one has only to read the daily papers. Here, for instance, are two typical recent news stories:

NEW STUDY FINDS VITAMINS ARE NOT CANCER PREVENTERS
A new study [reported in *The New England Journal of Medicine*] has failed to find evidence that vitamin supplements protect against the development of precancerous growths in the colon. . . . Many [previous] studies had found that people who eat large amounts of fruits and vegetables had lower cancer rates, and fruits and vegetables are known for providing vitamins C and E.[1]

STUDY SAYS EXERCISE MUST BE STRENUOUS TO STRETCH LIFETIME
Moderate exercise may well be the route to a healthier life, but if living longer is your goal, you will have to sweat. A new Harvard study that followed the fates of 17,300 middle-aged men for more than 20 years has found that only vigorous and not nonvigorous activities reduced their risk of dying during the study period.[2]

In a follow-up, the writer adds: "The new finding . . . has surprised leading researchers in the field. They are striving to reconcile it with many other studies that point to a life-saving benefit from moderate exercise, and they are perplexed that the Harvard study failed to find the expected benefit."[3]

Some other instances of seeming disarray in recent scientific findings:

• Ten studies determine how much the risk of ischemic heart disease (blockage of heart arteries) is reduced when serum cholesterol is lowered by roughly one-tenth of the average levels in Western countries. All ten studies conclude that it does reduce the risk, but the reported reduction ranges from nearly 40 percent in one study to as little as 15 percent in another.[4]

• Twenty-one studies of the use of fluorouracil against advanced colon cancer all find it beneficial, but findings of its effectiveness vary so widely—from a high of 85 percent to a low of 8 percent—as to be meaningless and useless to clinicians.[5]

---

* The method has many other names, among them research synthesis, evaluation synthesis, overview, systematic review, pooling, and structured review. In general, I use the term meta-analysis, since it is the one most often used in journal titles, indexes, and data bases.

- In 1994 a study published by the National Task Force on the Prevention and Treatment of Obesity reported that "yo-yo dieting" (the repeated losing and regaining of weight) poses no significant health risks—a direct contradiction of the findings of previous studies that off-and-on dieting can disrupt the body's metabolism, increase body fat, lead to heart problems, and heighten the risks of suffering other health problem.[6]
- A recent major study of the effects of exposure to the electromagnetic fields that surround power lines and electrical equipment shows a stronger link between electromagnetic fields and brain cancer than any previous study—but also contradicts earlier studies by finding no evidence of increased risk of leukemia.[7]

Such cases are legion not only in medical and biological research but also in behavioral and social science research:*

- Many studies of the treatment of aphasia (loss of speech due to brain damage) by speech therapy find it valueless, while others find it distinctly effective.[8]
- A number of studies of the effect of coaching on Scholastic Aptitude Test scores have shown that it raises them significantly, others that it raises them only trivially.[9]
- A generation ago, the Department of Health, Education, and Welfare asked Richard J. Light, a statistician at Harvard University, to determine whether the Head Start program worked. Light found a wealth of research data in thirteen studies that had already evaluated the program. The first twelve all showed modest positive effects, but the thirteenth, far larger than any of the others, disconcertingly showed no effect.[10] "I had no idea what to do," Light recently told a reporter for *Science*; his bewilderment eventually motivated him to develop a way of combining disparate research results, a precursor of meta-analysis.[11]
- Some studies find school desegregation to improve the academic achievement of black students significantly; others find only modest gains; and still others observe hardly any improvement. Even more confusing, some social scientists present credible evidence that desegregation improves achievement, but others offer equally credible evidence that it diminishes achievement.[12]

---

* For brevity, the behavioral and social sciences are referred to hereafter as the social sciences.

- Do women in management have a different leadership style from men? The question has long been hotly debated: some management experts and social scientists claim the evidence shows they do differ, others that the data yield no clear pattern of differences in supervisory style.[13]
- A massive and influential review of the scientific literature on sex differences assembled during the heyday of feminism by two respected women psychologists found little evidence of such differences in any area of social behavior except aggression. But later studies have furnished experimental and observational evidence of sex differences in many kinds of social behavior, including helping, sending and receiving nonverbal messages, and conforming to group values.[14]
- The Department of Health and Human Services recently ordered a review of studies of the prevalence of alcohol, drug, and mental disorders among the homeless, expecting the information to help in developing sensible policies for reducing homelessness. A reviewer located eighty studies containing an abundance of data—but no answers. The estimates in the studies differed so widely as to be useless: alcohol problems in the homeless population, from 4 percent to 86 percent; mental health problems, from 1 percent to 70 percent; and drug problems, from 2 percent to 90 percent.[15]

And so on.

Why have the sciences apparently degenerated into an intellectual free-for-all in our time?

In truth, there never was a golden era of pure harmony and cooperation among scientists. There have always been and are always bound to be competition, disagreement, and conflict among those pursuing research in any given area, since no two researchers think, perceive, or conduct a study in exactly the same fashion, nor are any two laboratory experiments or field observations exactly alike. Even when two researchers use the same methods to study a phenomenon, normal sampling errors (akin to the chance variations in the sum of two identical dice thrown repeatedly), minor differences in the persons they are studying, and other random factors make it unlikely that they will get the same or even very similar results. Accordingly, comparable and even replicate studies of any subject almost never yield identical findings.

In the social sciences the possibility of disparity is far greater than in the physical and biomedical sciences.[16] So many interacting variables influence human behavior that no two groups of human subjects are identical, even if the groups are large and carefully equated. Moreover, human subjects, unlike cells in vitro or bacteria in a patient's body, often react to experimental situations according to their own volitions and past experiences, thereby adding unique influences to the effects of the variables being examined by the researchers and supposedly under their control.

While discrepancies and contradictions have always existed in scientific research, today they are more numerous, well publicized, and disturbing than before. One obvious reason for the increase is the mushroom-like expansion of the sciences in the last half century. In medicine, for instance, during a single recent year the *New England Journal of Medicine* and the *British Medical Journal* alone devoted some 4,400 pages to 1,100 articles, and currently, throughout the world, over two million medical articles are published each year.[17] With such voluminous output and so many new areas of investigation, it is inevitable there should be more disagreement than ever.

The reward system of science greatly intensifies the potential for disagreement. Career success is contingent on publication, and publishers are most interested in those studies that present news—findings that challenge the previously accepted wisdom. Although the primary motive of researchers is new knowledge, they are bound to hope that the results of their investigations will correct, conflict with, or disprove the results of earlier studies and those of concurrent research by colleague-competitors; such hopes, as a wealth of experimental evidence has shown, often unconsciously affect the researchers' performance in ways that tend to produce the desired result.

The resulting intellectual melee does serious injury to science and society.

For one thing, it impedes scientific progress: As the volume of research grows, so does the diversity of results, making it all but impossible for scientists to make sense of the divergent reports even within their own narrow specialties. In consequence, their research tends to be based less on the accumulated knowledge of their field than on their limited and biased view of it.

For another, when legislators and public administrators seek, through hearings and staff research, to study a pressing issue, they can rarely make sense of the hodge-podge of findings offered them. In the recent congressional debates about smoking in public places, members of Congress were told by antismoking advocates that many studies, including a report by the surgeon general, found "passive smoking" (inhalation of others' smoke) to be a cause of lung cancer. Tobacco-state colleagues and tobacco-industry lobbyists told them, however, of other studies by qualified researchers showing little evidence of such a connection, and even, remarkably, of two small 1984 studies and a larger, more recent one—in the authoritative *New England Journal of Medicine*—that found *less* lung cancer in people exposed to others' smoke in the home than in people not so exposed.[18] Who could blame a legislator for not relying on research to help him or her decide how to vote on the issue?

Lastly, the prevalence of scientific disparities is eroding public belief in and support for research. Many intellectuals see the conflicting findings as justifying "constructivism," a view now popular among the "postmodernist" academic Left that scientific discoveries are not objective truths but only cultural artifacts, not representations of reality but self-serving products of the system.[19] At a different intellectual level, many of the uninformed and gullible see the contradictory outcomes of current research as grounds for broadly rejecting scientific knowledge in favor of simpler and more coherent beliefs—or "faiths"—in the power of prayer, guardian angels, miracles, astrology, past-lives regression, channeling, back-from-death experiences, and assorted New Age psychic phenomena.[20]

The Classic—and Inadequate—Solution

In most fields of science the standard way of dealing with the multiplicity of studies and divergent findings has long been the "literature review" or "research review." Scientific reports customarily begin with a brief résumé of previous work on the problem being considered; in that tradition, for some decades journal editors have published occasional articles summarizing and evaluating recent studies in actively researched areas of their discipline, and nearly every field has a type of annual review journal consisting entirely of such résumés.

Review articles, according to Howard White of the College of Information Studies, Drexel University, "are generally admired as a force for cumulation in science."[21] From the vantage point of meta-analysis, however, that tribute seems unwarranted. It is true that a good review article can marshal and summarize recent work on a particular topic; it is true, too, that one can only admire those who perform the heroic task of reading scores of often dense, technical, and tedious studies and summing up each in a sentence or two. But anyone conversant with meta-analysis will question whether reading the desiccated summaries in such articles—not unlike chewing a mouthful of dry bran—yields a genuine integration of the new knowledge. Consider, for example, the following brief excerpt from a recent review article on individual psychotherapy:

> Some comparisons of psychotherapy and drug treatment have suggested that combined treatment may present definite advantages over either treatment alone (Frank & Kupfer 1987; Weissman et al 1987; Hollon et al 1988), others have shown no differences between psychotherapy and psychotherapy plus medication at termination (Beck

et al 1985), and still others have shown advantages at follow-up for patients who received cognitive-behavior therapy (Simons et al 1986). In the comparison of a cognitive-behavioral (prescriptive) therapy and a dynamic-experiential (exploratory) treatment of depression and anxiety, Shapiro & Firth (1987) found a slight advantage for the prescriptive approach, especially on symptom reduction.[22]

This specimen exemplifies the typical achievement and typical failure of the research review article: Although it offers a handy list of items in a particular area of research, it does little to integrate or cumulate them. Some reviews do offer more combinatory conclusions, but not methodically or rigorously; a recent critique of fifty medical review articles said that most summarized the pertinent findings in an unsystematic, subjective, and "armchair" fashion.[23] In an even harsher appraisal of medical review articles, two leading medical meta-analysts, Thomas Chalmers and Joseph Lau, write,

> Too often, authors of traditional review articles decide what they would like to establish as the truth either before starting the review process or after reading a few persuasive articles. Then they proceed to defend their conclusions by citing all the evidence they can find. The opportunity for a biased presentation is enormous, and its readers are vulnerable because they have no opportunity to examine the possibilities of biases in the review.[24]

Such criticisms apply to review articles in other fields of science. In *Summing Up*, a handbook of meta-analysis, Richard Light and David Pillemer characterize traditional review articles as not only subjective and scientifically unsound but "an inefficient way to extract useful information" because they lack any systematic method of integrating the relationships among the variables in the different studies and of reconciling differences in the results.[25]

Most review articles do not subject the studies they examine to the relatively simple statistical tests that would estimate how likely it is they mistook chance results—chiefly, sampling error—for meaningful ones (a false positive conclusion) or used too small a sample so that chance factors concealed the important results (a false negative conclusion). Review articles, in short, offer knowledge without measurement, the worth of which was famously expressed long ago by Lord Kelvin:

> When you can measure what you are speaking about and express it in numbers you know something about it, but when you cannot measure it, when you cannot express it in numbers, your knowledge is of a meagre and unsatisfactory kind; it may be the beginning of knowledge, but you have scarcely, in your thoughts, advanced to the stage of *science*, whatever the matter may be.

A Radical New Approach

In 1904 the British mathematician Karl Pearson invented a statistical method for combining divergent findings. At that time, the effectiveness of inoculation against typhoid fever was still unclear; not only did the results of different trials vary but the samples were so small that the results of any one trial might be partly or largely due to chance factors. Pearson's simple but creative idea was to compute the correlation within each sample between inoculation and mortality (a correlation is a statistic showing how closely one variable is related to another variable) and then average the correlations of all the samples; the result, balancing out the chance factors and idiosyncrasies of the individual studies, would be a datum more trustworthy than any of the individual statistics that went into computing it.[26]

Seven decades later, when meta-analysis finally caught on, its practitioners developed an array of more complicated and precise computations than Pearson's, but to this day the basic concept behind combining and reconciling studies remains as simple and radical as in 1904. Rather than reaching vague conclusions like those of review articles—"The majority of studies show that . . ." or "While some studies find the treatment effective, most fail to reach statistical significance"—the new approach asks, "How can we produce a precise, quantitative finding representing what the studies show when synthesized into one superstudy?"

Current meta-analytic techniques involve subtle and discriminating procedures, of which Pearson's averaging is one of the simplest. We will look at them later (in verbal, not mathematical, terms) when we peer over the shoulders of scientists as they conduct meta-analyses that resolve the ambiguities in bodies of important research data. For now, however, let us carry out a hypothetical experiment that will give us a first glimpse at how meta-analysts combine data, the central process in meta-analysis.

You are one of a hundred physicians taking part in the testing of a new fever-reducing medication, antipyron. You are to give the same specified dose of the drug to the next eight patients you treat for influenza, and to record their temperatures on taking the dose and again four hours later.

Your first case is a young man who has a fever of 104° F; four hours after taking the drug his temperature has plummeted to 98°, and you, naturally, are delighted and enthusiastic. Your second flu patient is a middle-aged man with a fever of 102°; disappointingly, in four hours the antipyron lowers his temperature only to 100°. You give it to six more patients—with varying results.

What can you conclude about the overall effectiveness of the drug? Can you average the data of your eight cases and arrive at a typical figure for fever reduction for the dosage given? Certainly. Indeed, the researchers with whom you are collaborating might then take your average and mathematically combine it with the averages turned in by the other ninety-nine physicians taking part in the study to arrive at an overall drug effect. They might discover, say, that antipyron reduced fever in flu patients by an average of 2.5° F in four hours, across one hundred medical trials and eight hundred patients. This is a rudimentary meta-analysis, indicating how effective the drug is on average.

But being a well-trained doctor, you do not accept your own finding—or the finding of all one hundred trials—as an adequate guide to treatment, since you know that all patients are not alike. For one thing, the young man who was your first case weighs 150 pounds, the older man who was the second case, 220 pounds, and, typically, the greater the body weight, the less effect a given dose will have, since its effect is more diffused in a larger system. For another, the men also differ in age; perhaps the drug works more swiftly in a young body, with its higher metabolic rate, than in an older one. Of course, the other ninety-nine physicians know this too. So they, like you, not only recorded the change in each patient's temperature but also their weight, age, and possibly some other data. The project researchers might have compiled your data, arranging the patients in the order of their weight:

Patient	Age	Weight	Temp. change
1	20	150	−6°
5	50	160	−5°
4	35	170	−4°
6	60	190	−4°
3	45	180	−3°
7	30	200	−3°
8	25	210	−2°
2	55	220	−2°

With the data arranged in this fashion, you would easily see a clear relationship between the weight of the patient and the effect of the drug; with one exception, patient 6, as the patient's weight goes up the effect gets smaller. It is less clear that age affects the outcome.

Using your data, it is possible to calculate the correlations between the variables of weight and temperature change and between age and temperature change. A correlation will be +1.00 if the relation between two variables is perfect and positive (that is, as one variable goes up, so does the other), −1.00 if it is perfect but negative (as one goes up the other goes down), and zero if no relation exists at all.

When you receive the researchers' report, you learn that in your own set of eight patients the correlation between weight and the drug's effectiveness is −.93 and between age and effectiveness, −.17. But when the researchers meta-analyzed—combined—the correlations for all one hundred data sets, they found that the average correlation between weight and temperature change is −.85, a strong (but not perfect) negative relation. The average correlation between age and effectiveness is only −.13, a weak association. Based on these meta-analytic findings, they conclude that higher doses of the drug may be necessary when treating heavier patients but that age, being largely irrelevant, does not need to be taken into account.

This imaginary experiment is a simplified version of only one process central to meta-analysis, namely, *combining* the findings of different studies. But a second and equally central problem exists: *reconciling* differences among studies. Suppose that nearly all one hundred physicians reported average reductions in their patients' fever of 3° but that one doctor reported an average reduction of only 1° and another an average reduction of 5.5°. How do you reconcile these differences from the more general finding? A little detective work might reveal that the small reduction came from a clinic that treated obese patients while the large reduction involved athletes. The meta-analyst might then suggest that differences among the patients are the clue to reconciling the disparate outcomes.

With that brief rundown behind us, let's return to Pearson's first effort at combining the data of a set of studies. In 1904 the mainstream scientific community expressed little interest in Pearson's techniques. The time was not ripe, and the idea of synthesizing studies mostly languished for the next six decades. Only a handful of avant-garde scientists pursued Pearson's ideas in the first half of the century, sensing the impending need to synthesize studies.

In the first third of the century, for example, agricultural scientists conducted numerous experiments in farming techniques but were unable to draw general conclusions from them since the tests almost always involved differences in soil, agricultural practices, climatic conditions, and so on. The problem was how to reach any useful generalizations from these dissimilar studies. A statistician named Leonard H. C. Tippett found an answer. From each experiment, Tippett obtained three pieces of data: the size of the sample, the size of the difference in crop yield between different farming techniques, and the amount of variation in yield that occurred by chance within any specific technique (for instance, in experiments using the same kind and amount of fertilizer, how much variation in yield occurred without any known cause?).

With this information, Tippett was then able, adjusting for sample size, to compare the difference *between* techniques to the difference *within* techniques, the latter being a measure of how much variation might occur by chance. This enabled him to calculate the likelihood that the difference in yield between farming techniques was due to chance—and conversely, the likelihood that the technique was causing real improvements in yield. He might, for instance, discover that, given a particular sample size and a certain amount of *within*-technique variation, only twelve times in one hundred would a *between*-technique difference of a prescribed size as large as existed in that set of studies occur solely by chance. (Today we call this number the "probability of a chance finding.")

Then Tippett made a notable leap: He worked out a statistical method of combining the probability values of the several studies. This statistic, bypassing all the differences among the studies, showed how likely it was that the results of the whole set of studies were due to chance and, conversely, how likely that the results arose from the new farming technique.[27]

Although a handful of other researchers working with agricultural studies soon used Tippett's method or their own variants of it, scientists in other disciplines did not adopt the approach. Nor did they accept the other methods of combining probabilities constructed by a few avant-garde statisticians working on research in education, psychology, and the social sciences. In 1937 an imaginative biostatistician, William G. Cochran, went off in a different direction and worked out a way of combining the sizes of the effects reported in studies rather than the correlations between treatment and effect; although this approach would become a key technique of meta-analysis, it also attracted little attention.[28]

But by the 1950s the sciences were growing explosively, and scientists increasingly needed to sum up the proliferating studies in their fields and reconcile their differences. A small but growing cadre of researchers began developing methods to combine the results of studies within medicine, psychology, and sociology.[29] By the early 1970s, others were designing methods for aggregating studies of teaching methods, television instruction, and computer-assisted instruction. Robert Rosenthal, a social psychologist at Harvard, was developing a technique for combining the effect sizes of psychological studies at the very same time that Gene V Glass, a professor of education at the University of Colorado, was working out a remarkably similar method of combining studies of the effects of psychotherapy, though neither knew of the other's work.[30]

Finally came the event generally cited as the beginning of the meta-analysis movement. In April 1976, Glass, then president of the American Educational Research Association, delivered his presidential address at the annual meeting, held that year at the St. Francis Hotel in San Francisco. For this important event, he chose to highlight a new and higher level of scientific analysis to which he gave the name "meta-analysis." Glass, then in his mid-thirties and fully aware of the topic's potential importance, had labored and agonized over the paper for two years, during which, he recently said, "I was a basket case."* As the day of his address neared, he was desperately afraid that the audience of a thousand would either drift away, doze off, or deride his ideas. But Glass, who describes himself as a highly competitive person, stepped cockily to the podium and with seeming self-assurance gave a lucid, witty, and persuasive talk. The audience, recalls psychologist Mary Lee Smith (who was then his wife and had worked with him on the meta-analysis paper), was "blown away by it. There was tremendous excitement about it; people were awestruck." His address, published later that year in *The Educational Researcher*, was judged by many who read it to be a breakthrough applicable to all sciences.[31]

The meta-analytic process, briefly sketched in Glass's paper and later spelled out by him and two collaborators, as well as by others, has five basic phases that parallel the phases of conducting a new study. They can be summarized in a few phrases, though the details fill books:[32]

1. Formulating the problem: Deciding what questions the meta-analyst hopes to answer and what kinds of evidence to examine.
2. Collecting the data: Searching for all studies on the problem by every feasible means.
3. Evaluating the data: Deciding which of the gathered evidence is valid and usable; eliminating studies that do not meet these standards.
4. Synthesizing the data: Using statistical methods, such as the combining of probabilities and the combining of effect sizes, to reconcile and aggregate disparate studies.
5. Presenting the findings: Reporting the resulting "analysis of analyses" (Glass's phrase) to the wider research community, providing details, data, and methods used.

That sounds simple; in fact, the process is almost always complicated, tedious, and problematic. "The magnitude of the task cannot be

---

*Unpublished quotations throughout the text are from personal interviews conducted by the author.

overemphasized in my view," writes Nan Laird of the Harvard School of Public Health.[33] Daniel Druckman, an eminent political scientist who devoted three years of his evenings and weekends to single-handedly conducting a meta-analysis, says, "It drove me crazy. Never again!"

Nonetheless, from Glass's 1976 presentation to the present the prestige and practice of meta-analysis has grown steadily—at first slowly, then with increasing speed and spreading from one discipline to another. But not without initially encountering much scornful and even hostile opposition: In an article in *American Psychologist* in 1978, the distinguished English psychologist H. J. Eysenck contemptuously dismissed Glass's work as "an exercise in mega-silliness"; in 1979 a peer reviewer of a meta-analysis by Harris Cooper, which looked at studies of sex differences in conformity, wrote, "I simply cannot imagine any great contribution to knowledge from combining statistical results"; and when social psychologist Judith Hall gave a seminar on meta-analysis at the Harvard School of Public Health in 1980, to an audience made up primarily of natural scientists, she encountered such acerbic criticism and derision that, she recently said, "If they'd had any rotten tomatoes to throw at me, they would have."[34]

None of which prevented meta-analysis, an idea whose time had come, from winning converts in first one discipline, then another. Those who carry out meta-analyses, when asked what draws them to such work, offer a variety of motivations. One sees it as the "cutting edge" of science; another says he is "a compulsive data analyst" who has to solve the puzzles presented by disparate findings; a third calls herself a "neatnik" who likes "to bring order out of chaos, to tidy things up"; and nearly all share a desire to discover patterns in the seemingly hopeless jumble of dissimilar findings.

And so meta-analysis gained currency, with books on its methodology appearing in the 1980s and a few top-notch statisticians, among them Frederick Mosteller of Harvard, Ingram Olkin of Stanford, and Larry Hedges of the University of Chicago, refining the techniques. The best indicator of its success may be the frequency of its appearance in scientific journals. At first, editors, unsure that the method was either scientifically legitimate or a true contribution to knowledge, were reluctant to publish meta-analyses. But each year they published more than the year before. In 1977, five major data bases, ERIC (education), PsycINFO, Scisearch, SOCIAL SCISEARCH, and MEDLINE had zero listings of meta-analyses, but in 1984 they had a total of 108, in 1987, 191, and in 1994, 347, by which time the grand total in those five data bases was 3,444.[35] Recently, some journal editors have even plaintively asked contributors to ease up on submissions of meta-analyses.

A Sampler of Meta-Analytic Achievements

What has this flood of meta-analyses yielded? Not every effort has produced important findings; indeed, many have added little to the world's inventory of scientific knowledge. But a fair share have made important contributions and resolved long-standing uncertainties. In a number of cases, the validity of meta-analytic conclusions has been confirmed by later massive studies or clinical trials—which suggests that the latter were more or less unnecessary. Some of the more noteworthy cases are presented in chapters 2 through 6, but here is a handful of others in capsule form:

- Coronary artery bypass surgery to treat ischemic heart disease has been practiced for twenty-five years, but clinical studies of varied design have yielded widely divergent conclusions about its ability to reduce mortality as compared to medical treatment. There has even been some question as to whether bypass surgery, though it improves quality of life, has any life-extending value. A 1994 meta-analysis, collaboratively conducted by a dozen institutions in five countries, combined seven major trials that compared bypass surgery with medical therapy. It found that five years after treatment, the mortality rate of bypass patients was 10.2 percent while that of medically treated patients was 15.8 percent—half again as high—and that there was a comparable advantage for bypass patients at seven and ten years.[36]
- In the 1980s, calcium channel blockers were among the most commonly used drugs for acute myocardial infarction (heart attack), unstable angina, and certain other cardiovascular conditions. The National Heart, Lung, and Blood Institute and the Bowman-Gray School of Medicine cosponsored a meta-analysis of twenty-eight disparate studies. Its surprising conclusion, published in 1987, was that "calcium channel blockers do not reduce the risk of initial or recurrent infarction or death when given routinely to patients with acute myocardial infarction or unstable angina."[37]
- Between 1965 and 1980 at least fifty clinical trials sought to determine whether there was any benefit in giving preventive antibiotics to patients about to undergo colon surgery, rather than merely requiring the standard bowel-cleansing procedures. The clinical trials reported confusingly discrepant infection and mortality rates; a few even indicated better results for patients not treated with antibiotics. A meta-analysis conducted by a team at New York's Mount Sinai School of Medicine and published in 1981 clarified the issue: Combining the results of twenty-six trials that met the standards for meta-analysis, it showed

that antibiotic therapy reduced infection rates from 36 percent to 22 percent, and death rates from 11.2 percent to 4.5 percent.[38]

- In 1977, cimetidine, an H_2 blocker, dramatically changed the preferred treatment of peptic ulcers from surgery to pharmaceutical therapy, and over the next fifteen years two other H_2 blockers, famotidine and ranitidine, were introduced. Clinical studies differed as to which drug yielded the best results. A 1993 meta-analysis of sixteen trials directly comparing the drugs showed that famotidine taken at bedtime had significantly higher healing rates than either cimetidine or ranitidine and that the three did not differ significantly in terms of adverse reactions.[39]

- For many years researchers have debated whether chlorination of drinking water, which prevents many infectious diseases, is carcinogenic. Studies provided contradictory findings and the issue long remained unsettled. In 1992, however, a team at the Medical College of Wisconsin in Milwaukee meta-analyzed ten studies and reported that chlorination is correlated with slightly higher rates of rectal and bladder cancer but that "the potential health risks of microbial contamination of drinking water greatly exceed the risks" of the two cancers. The team also pointed out that the ten meta-analyzed studies were conducted in the 1970s; since then, federal standards have lowered the permissible level of chlorination, and the risk of the two cancers may now be lower.[40]

- Is intelligence related to the innate quickness of the individual's brain when reacting to external stimuli? The answer would cast light on the long-debated issue of the extent to which intelligence is determined by heredity rather than by experience and social influences. A good index of innate, unlearned mental speed is "inspection time" (IT), commonly measured by flashing two lines of different lengths on a screen immediately followed by a pattern to overcome the brief residual image in memory. An individual's IT is defined as the minimum time of exposure he or she needs to reliably discriminate between the two lines. Dozens of studies have yielded a mish-mash of answers, but a recent meta-analysis by psychologists John Kranzler and Arthur Jensen of the University of California–Berkeley found a strong negative correlation of about −.54 between IT and adult general IQ; that is, the longer the IT, the lower the individual's IQ.[41]

- Does alcohol cause aggressive behavior? Most studies have provided only correlational evidence—that is, alcohol and aggression tend to co-occur—but while correlation suggests some kind of link between the two, it does not prove causality; something else may cause the correlation. The amount of time spent watching television, for instance, correlates with ill health, but TV watching does not itself impair health; sicker people watch more because they are less able to do other things.[42] Or, back to our example, it might be the case that people who lack the ability to control their impulses are more likely both to drink and to behave aggressively.

Experimental studies have yielded evidence for several competing causal explanations of the alcohol-aggression correlation. Among them: alcohol causes cognitive and emotional changes resulting in aggression; drinkers deliberately use alcohol so as to have an excuse for aggressive behavior; alcohol psychologically disinhibits persons who are predisposed to aggression; alcohol directly and physiologically causes aggression by anesthetizing the part of the brain that normally prevents such responses. Brad Bushman and Harris Cooper of the University of Missouri meta-analyzed thirty experimental studies in which the behavior of different kinds of drinkers was observed either after drinking alcohol, after drinking a placebo they thought was alcohol, or after drinking nothing. The meta-analysis revealed little or no support for any single causal theory but, synthesizing the results of the studies, Bushman and Cooper did conclude that alcohol definitely causes aggression, possibly through a combination of some of the hypothesized causal factors.[43]

- The extent to which violence on television stimulates aggressive, antisocial, or delinquent behavior has been a matter of controversy for over three decades. More than two hundred studies have yielded an array of answers; over the years, that lack of agreement has undoubtedly strengthened the hand of television programmers and weakened that of government regulators. A meta-analysis recently conducted for the National Research Council finally furnished a definitive answer: Viewers are more apt to commit aggressive or antisocial acts after seeing violence on TV (particularly violent erotica), the most common kind being physical violence against another person.[44]

- As mentioned earlier, the findings of studies of the prevalence of alcohol, drug, and mental health problems among the homeless have been extraordinarily inconsistent, ranging from 4 percent to 86 percent for alcohol problems, 2 percent to 90 percent for drug problems, and 1 percent to 70 percent for mental health problems. A meta-analysis by Anthony Lehman of the University of Maryland and David Cordray of Vanderbilt University made sense of these vast discrepancies, their synthesized findings being that 28 percent of the homeless have alcohol abuse problems, 10 percent have drug abuse problems, anywhere from 23 to 49 percent have mental disorders (depending on the category of disorder), and 11 percent have various combinations of the three. The figures represent the current prevalence of these problems among the homeless; far larger numbers have had such problems at some time in the past and presumably could have them again.[45]

- Fluoxetine (Prozac) came on the market in 1987, swiftly became the most prescribed antidepressant in the United States, and was hailed by the media as a wonder drug. Scores of studies said that it was far more effective than the tricyclics, the previous standard antidepressants. A team composed of researchers from the State University of New York at Syracuse and several other institutions carried out two meta-analyses of studies comparing the effects of Prozac with those of tricyclics and placebos under double-blind conditions (that is, with neither patient nor physician knowing what the patient was being given). The meta-analytic findings were illuminating: In many ostensibly double-blind trials, Prozac has less noticeable side-effects than tricyclics, which tend to cause dry mouth, blurry vision, and other obvious symptoms; as a result, patients and doctors were often able to guess correctly when Prozac was being administered and wishfully overevaluated its antidepressant effect. Correcting for this error and aggregating the results, the team found that Prozac was only a half to a quarter as effective as previously reported and no better than the tricyclics, except for the diminished side-effects.[46]

- A staggering amount of research is churned out annually on agricultural issues—far more than growers or agricultural administrators can master. An example: In 1992 alone, the National Agricultural Library added 363 new research items about strawberries. To demonstrate that meta-analysis can present both growers and administrators with easily comprehensible summary findings, Douglas Shaw, a professor of agriculture at the University of California–Davis, and statistician Ingram Olkin of Stanford University meta-analyzed a group of studies of chemical control and a group of studies of biological control that focused on the important strawberry pest *Tetranychus urticae* (a spider mite). The original studies in each group differed in their findings, but the meta-analysis clarified the matter: Although biological controls had a statistically significant effect, chemical controls were nearly four times as effective in terms of increased strawberry yield. The meta-analysis did not look at other benefits and harms that might be associated with yield.[47]

The Value of Meta-Analysis

Despite the track record of meta-analysis, a number of scientists still scorn and belittle it. Some deride it as "garbage in, garbage out," arguing that combining studies, even using fancy statistics, merges trashy research with sound research and therefore degrades the whole exercise. Others say meta-analysis "crowds out wisdom," since assistants usually do the tedious work of evaluating and compiling the data, and although they lack knowledge and mature judgment; the senior researchers, however, then meta-analyze the data as confidently as if they had compiled it themselves. Still others see meta-analysis as a fancy set of techniques for achieving ever greater precision in answering questions of possibly dubious merit.

David Sohn, a psychologist at the University of North Carolina, is even more caustic and rejecting. Asserting in a recent issue of *American Psychologist* that primary research is the only valid method of making discoveries, he ridicules the claim that meta-analysis is a superior mechanism of discovery:

> It is not reasonable to suppose that the truth about nature can be discovered by a study of the research literature. . . . Meta-analytic writers have created the impression, with a farcical portrayal of the scientific process, that the process of arriving at truth is mediated by a literature review. . . . After some critical mass of findings has been gathered, someone decides to see what all of the findings mean by doing a literature review, and thereby knowledge is finally established.[48]

Such is the minority view, however. The majority, as already documented, see meta-analysis as an important, even historic, advance in science. Below are a few of the major benefits that meta-analysis is widely agreed to yield:

- Physicians can now make decisions as to the use of therapies or diagnostic procedures on the basis of a single article that synthesizes the findings of tens, scores, or hundreds of clinical studies.
- Scientists in every field can similarly gain a coherent view of the central reality behind the multifarious and often discordant findings of research in their areas.
- Meta-analysis of a series of small clinical trials of a new therapy often yields a finding on the basis of which physicians can confidently begin using it without waiting long years for a massive trial to be conducted.
- In every science, meta-analysis can generally synthesize differing results, but when it cannot, it can often identify the moderator and me-

diator variables (about which more later) that account for the irreconcilable differences. By so doing, the meta-analysis identifies the precise areas in which future research is needed, a function of considerable value to science.

• On the pragmatic level, meta-analyses of a wide range of social problems have profound implications for social policy; their findings about such issues as the value of job training for the unemployed, the effects of drinking-age laws, and the rehabilitation of juvenile delinquents offer policy-makers easily assimilated syntheses of bodies of research they have neither the time nor the training to evaluate on their own.

Whether one sees meta-analysis as a set of recondite techniques for getting precise answers to irrelevant questions or as an epochal advance in scientific methodology, it unquestionably has come to occupy a major place in contemporary scientific research. Yet it is not itself a science and does not embody any scientific theory. It is, rather, a method or group of methods by means of which scientists can recognize order in what had looked like disorder. As Ingram Olkin writes, "I like to think of the meta-analytic process as similar to being in a helicopter. On the ground individual trees are visible with high resolution. This resolution diminishes as the helicopter rises, and in its place we begin to see patterns not visible from the ground."[49]

To use a different image, meta-analysis is a tool used by scientists. Far from being a belittling characterization, this is high praise, for as the illustrious physicist Freeman Dyson, a member of the Institute for Advanced Study at Princeton, recently commented, "The great advances in science usually result from new tools rather than from new doctrines."[50]

Chapter 2

Settling Doubts About Psychotherapy

Attack, Counterattack, and Stalemate

By 1952, the "talking cure"—psychoanalysis and related forms of psychotherapy—was nearly six decades old, highly esteemed by the avant-garde and intelligentsia, and rapidly growing in popularity.[1] Its healing power had been proclaimed by such distinguished intellectuals as André Breton, Thomas Mann, and Arthur Koestler and popularized by Moss Hart in *Lady in the Dark*, a success on Broadway in 1941 and later on the screen. New forms of dynamic psychotherapy, related to psychoanalysis but briefer and less costly, appeared almost yearly, and, *mirabile dictu*, nearly all were said by their practitioners to benefit a high proportion of patients—usually two-thirds, but sometimes more than nine-tenths.[2] Psychotherapy, which the medical establishment long resisted, seemed to have broken through and overrun America.

But in 1952 there came a sudden violent counterattack. An article in the American Psychological Association's *Journal of Consulting and Clinical Psychology* compared the results of nineteen studies of neurotic patients treated by psychotherapy with those of two samples of neurotics who received no treatment and delivered a shocking verdict: "Roughly two-thirds of a group of neurotic patients will recover or improve to a marked extent within about two years of the onset of their illness, whether they are treated by means of psychotherapy or not. The figures fail to show any favorable effects of psychotherapy."[3]

Who would so boldly attack the cherished belief in an established healing art—and do so in an official organ of the psychological establishment? He was H. J. Eysenck, 36, a German-born British psychologist on the staff of the Institute of Psychiatry, University of London.[4] He had early developed an antipathy toward Freudian psychotherapy and its offshoots, as had some other British psychologists, but where they were soft-spoken about their reservations, Eysenck was, by nature, the very opposite. A tall, well-built, strong-featured young man, affable and mannerly in person, he was—and still is—intellectually a brawler and dissident; indeed, he titled a recent autobiographical essay "Maverick Psychologist" and a full-length autobiography *Rebel with a Cause*.

As a schoolboy in Germany, Eysenck had been headstrong, flippant, and outspoken, infuriating a key teacher by describing the esteemed Frederick the Great as "an autocratic, warmongering homosexual." In his teens he held socialist views and, although not Jewish, so detested Hitler and Nazism that at age eighteen, when Hitler became chancellor, he chose exile, leaving his parental home and settling in England, where he studied psychology at the University of London. At the time there were two main schools of psychology in England, the psychometrists (measurers of individual differences) and the experimentalists; Eysenck found each of them too narrow and, always blunt and forthright, made himself persona non grata with the leaders of both. Nonetheless, thanks to his considerable research abilities, he was beginning to advance up the academic ladder when he suddenly became famous (or infamous) as a result of his 1952 denigration of psychotherapy.

"The sky fell in," Eysenck has written of the reaction to his article. "I immediately made enemies of Freudians, of psychotherapists, and of the great majority of clinical psychologists and their students."[5] Within a short time, many replies ranging from the icily analytical to the hotly abusive appeared in professional journals. Of the numerous flaws their authors found in Eysenck's article, two were predominant. First, his recovery figures for untreated patients were based on the release rate of psychoneurotic patients from state mental hospitals in the United States and on Equitable Life Assurance disability claims filed by neurotics who had been treated only by general practitioners; neither of these, Eysenck's critics said, could legitimately be compared with the patients in the nineteen studies of treated neurotics. Second, although the nineteen dealt with many dissimilar patient groups and treatment methods, Eysenck had lumped all 7,293 patients together and offered a single overall figure (64 percent) as the cured-or-improved rate.[6]

Eysenck, of course, counterattacked; the other side replied; and for the next twenty-five years the defenders and critics of psychotherapy carried on a polemic and often nasty debate. The latter included not only Eysenck and certain sympathizers but the behavioral therapists, a new breed who, from 1958 on, derided the psychodynamic therapies and said they were ineffective compared with "desensitization" methods, derived from Pavlovian experiments in conditioning and deconditioning.

Although the attacks on Eysenck's 1952 study pointed out its defects, Eysenck had put the burden on therapists to prove that the talking cure and its variants did work. In the fifteen years following the publication of his paper, hundreds of "outcome studies" were conducted, some of them rigorously controlled. (In a controlled study, researchers compare treated patients with "controls"—untreated persons who suffer from the same kind of ailment and are drawn from the same population, such as the same hospital or clinic.) By the early 1970s, a few researchers began collecting some of this mass of material and making statements about the overall weight of evidence. One review summarized the findings of twenty-three controlled studies and concluded that, in general, therapy was effective. Another and more comprehensive review reported that for both individual and group therapy, about 80 percent of controlled studies showed mainly positive results.[7] Other reviews came to similar conclusions.

That might seem like enough to settle the matter, but these analyses also failed to resolve the conflict because they relied on a common faulty premise, asking, What do the majority of studies say? If most found that psychotherapy worked, it worked; if not, it failed. This method, known to statisticians as "vote-counting," may seem eminently reasonable but statistically is about as water-tight as a sieve.

Vote-Counting—A Plausible but Unreliable Way to Sum Up Research

A 1971 article in the *Harvard Educational Review* on methods of "accumulating evidence" said that of four general approaches to combining studies, vote-counting was "the best and most systematic."[8] Better yet, it was quick and simple: In effect, the researcher had only to divide a heap of studies of some treatment or experimental condition into two piles, those showing that it worked and those showing that it did not, the bigger pile being the winner. The method is intuitively so appealing that it is still used: a recent review of forty-three studies of yo-yo dieting in the *Journal of the American Medical Association* concluded, "The majority of studies do not support an adverse effect of weight cycling on metabolism . . . [or] find a higher prevalence of unfavorable fat distribution among weight cyclers."[9]

But by the 1970s, researchers who wanted to combine the evidence of diverse studies, especially of psychotherapeutic outcomes, were becoming more knowledgeable about statistics and recognized that this simple method would not do. "It doesn't seem to be all wrong," says Frederick Mosteller, "and it seems to be unbiased, but it's inefficient; it doesn't use the data well."

For one thing, in vote-counting every study counts as much as every other, even though one might be based on twenty cases, another on two thousand. Common sense as well as elementary statistical theory tells us that we cannot have as much confidence in the findings of a small sample as those of a large one, since the likelihood of sampling error is higher for small samples.

A simple thought experiment will make this clear. Imagine that you have a large sack of marbles, some red and some white but in an unknown proportion. You reach in without looking and bring out a small handful of six marbles; four are red, two are white. You reach in again, this time with both hands, and scoop up a batch of thirty marbles; sixteen are red, fourteen are white. Which ratio is more likely to be correct or nearly so? It takes no mathematical expertise to sense that 16:14 is closer to the mark than 4:2.

A second major flaw is that vote-counting does not take into account the varying strengths of results across different studies. One might show that twenty-six patients benefited more from a new kind of therapy than they would have been expected to from traditional therapy, while twenty-four did not; that would put it in the positive pile. Another might show that twenty benefited more, thirty did not; that would put it in the negative pile. The problem, obviously, is that the second study reveals a more strongly negative effect than the first study does a positive one, but the vote-count overlooks this fact.

This last flaw had long been correctable, however. Since early in the century, statisticians had known how to evaluate the findings in terms of "statistical significance." Very small differences are nonsignificant (that is, sampling error or chance cannot be ruled out as the cause), while larger differences are significant (that is, it is implausible that all of the result is due to chance).

Researchers can rather easily calculate the probability that the results of an experiment occurred only by chance, a probability designated as "p". The element of chance is related to the number of trials or tests involved. For example, suppose a magician claims he can mentally control how a flipped coin will land and in a simple trial produces heads each time in a series of three flips. Is it impossible that the result was due to chance? Not at all; as everyone knows, there is a one-in-two chance that any flip will land heads, one-in-four chance that two successive flips will both be heads, and a one-in-eight chance that three successive flips will all be heads. Flipping heads three times consecutively is not significant because it will happen by chance once every eight attempts ($p < .13$); flipping five heads consecutively is, by contrast, a much rarer occurrence because it happens by chance only one in thirty-two times (p < .032, that is, there is only about a 3 percent likelihood that any such series of heads happened by chance).

Among scientific researchers, the usual boundary between significance and nonsignificance is p < .05, meaning that there is less than a 5 percent possibility that the result is due to chance.* This limit is based on tradition rather than some statistical arcanum or tradition; in 1926 it simply seemed a handy number to the leading statistician Ronald Fisher, who wrote, "It is convenient to draw the line [of significance] at about the level at which we can say: 'Either there is something in the treatment, or a coincidence has occurred such as does not occur more than once in twenty trials.'"[10] Researchers are content when their findings have a p < .05, better pleased when they fit with a p < .01, and delighted by a p < .001, signifying that their results would occur by chance only once in a thousand times.

By means of significance testing, researchers can refine vote-counting: Rather than saying merely how many studies have positive or negative findings, they can say how many revealed statistically significant positive findings, how many were not statistically significant (and therefore do not count either way), and how many revealed significant negative findings.

Significance testing represented a great improvement: if p < .05, the researcher knows that there is less than 1 chance in 20 that the observed difference between the experimental and control groups occurred by chance. Another way to think about it is that the true underlying means of the two groups do differ. But estimating the exact value of the difference between two means, or for that matter any population value based on a sample, is always just that, an estimate. Any such "point estimate" may, due to sampling error, be somewhat larger or smaller than the actual difference; in fact, the point estimate is the meta-analyst's best guess of the value at which the chances are even that the real value is either higher or lower. How much higher or lower? The range of possibilities is known as the "confidence interval." The smaller the sample, the wider the confidence interval. Within a larger sample, the confidence interval

---

* Statisticians will find this explanation oversimplified. A more precise one (which readers can skip without harm): The test of significance in research starts with a "null hypothesis" that the results are exactly equal across all conditions—a hypothesis the researcher hopes to prove false. P is the probability that this null hypothesis is true; if p is ≤ .05, the researcher can reject it and attribute the results to other causes. See discussion by Becker in Cooper and Hedges (1994) p. 217.

is narrower and researchers can be more confident that the true value is closer to their finding. Thus, even when a vote-count is based on statistical significance, if some of the studies are small it yields only a fuzzy, inconclusive verdict.

Nor is vote-counting statistically "powerful." If a treatment produces only a small positive effect, vote-counting will fail to spot it if most of the studies have small samples; the effects are lost in the uncertainties of their wide confidence intervals. The cumulated results, therefore, may fail to reveal that most of the studies show a positive effect; the overview sees only the few large positive results and accordingly reaches the false negative conclusion that the treatment generally does not work.[11]

Finally, vote-counting does not measure the size of the effect in the studies. If sample sizes are large, it may correctly conclude that taken together the studies reveal a statistically significant positive effect but fail to show how great the average effect is; the benefit of the treatment might be trivial. As one authoritative manual of meta-analysis puts it, "To know that televised instruction beats traditional classroom instruction in twenty-five of thirty studies—if, in fact, it does—is not to know whether television wins by a nose or in a walkaway."[12] All of which became academic in 1976, when Gene Glass, in his presentation of the concept of meta-analysis, sketched a far better method of combining the results of studies.

Genesis of Meta-Analysis: Part I

Anger at H. J. Eysenck rather than dispassionate scientific interest drove Gene Glass to devise the basic methodology of meta-analysis. "I demonized Eysenck in my fantasies," Glass told me when I visited him not long ago. "I revelled in the thought of really destroying him."[13]

He says such things with a chuckle, a twinkle in his blue eyes, and a broad smile that produces a dimple in his round, cherubic face. Glass laughs easily, talks like a whirlwind, uses elegant technical language but tosses in an occasional Bronx cheer or an expletive like "Nuts!" to show disdain. He appears genuinely good-natured although he says he is "extremely competitive," "self-promoting," and "a Type-A personality." He is definitely not a good person to anger.

Glass came across Eysenck's work in his early thirties, when he was training to practice psychotherapy. He himself had been in therapy for a decade, though he is utterly unlike the Woody Allen image of the neurotic New York intellectual in perpetual therapy. Born in Lincoln, Nebraska, in 1940, Glass had a Midwestern upbringing and in his teens was a high-school jock addicted to sports; he claims that he never read a book and graduated from high school at the bottom of his class. In view of his subsequent academic record, this must be hyperbole: He was graduated cum laude from the University of Nebraska, earned a Ph.D. in psychometrics and statistics at the University of Wisconsin in a mere three years, was immediately appointed an assistant professor at the University of Illinois, and within five years, at age thirty, was a full professor of educational psychology, specializing in statistical methods, at the University of Colorado.

Clearly, a driven man, but in pain. "At twenty-four," he says, "as I was getting my doctorate, the torments and conflicts I was in spurred me into psychotherapy for the first time." It helped him so much that he stayed in treatment year after year; later, in his early thirties when his first marriage broke up, he returned to it and, he says, "it was especially important to me and got me through tough times." Like many people who have benefited from psychotherapy, he began to think of practicing it himself. A psychologist on the faculty gave him some training and directed his reading. Among the books he studied was *The Evaluation of Psychotherapeutic Outcomes* edited by Allen Bergin and Sol Garfield, and although much of the material took a positive view of psychotherapy, the book included a chapter by Eysenck that considerably expanded upon his 1952 therapy-bashing paper. Glass vividly remembers his reactions of more than twenty years ago:

> I was trained as a methodologist and statistician, and I was just outraged. It had no serious substance or content to it, nothing but rhetorical games and Jesuitical spinning out of specious arguments. He did unbelievable things with the data. My training was in statistics but my real interest was in psychotherapy and psychoanalysis, and I *had* to respond. Just about then, in 1974, I became president-elect of the American Educational Research Association (AERA) and I knew that in two years I would have to give a presidential address. I put these two things together and came up with the meta-analysis stuff out of my interest in refuting Eysenck, and decided it would be the topic of my address.

The basic method, though not how it would be implemented, was obvious to him from the start: It would be "research of research"—a translation into higher-level terms "of exactly what you'd do in a single research project where humans are the subject." Specifically, (1) formulate the hypothesis (already done in this case), (2) define the "population" being studied (research studies of psychotherapy outcomes), (3) sample it, (4) evaluate the items in the sample and discard what was untrustworthy, (5) statistically combine the findings of the qualifying items, and (6) report the method and results.

Glass had recently remarried, and his wife, Mary Lee Smith, was as professionally motivated as he to see Eysenck debunked. A tall, handsome blonde, as reserved and cool as Glass is exuberant and intense, she had been trained in counseling psychology and done student counseling—essentially, psychotherapy—at the University of Colorado in Denver for four years and later at the Boulder campus. "The analyses by Eysenck and others of that viewpoint were very distasteful and unfair," she says. "I didn't know how Gene's project would come out, but if there were positive evidence about the benefits of psychotherapy, that would settle a lot of disputes and make a big contribution. Even if the evidence were negative and Eysenck seemed to be right, it wouldn't change my personal underlying belief in the effectiveness of psychotherapy—I'd been through it, I practiced it, and I knew it works. Still, I'd keep a very detached and objective stance toward the outcomes evidence and we'd report whatever we found." Originally meaning only to assist Glass, she ended up sharing the work, later co-authored a longer treatment of the subject with him, and still later co-authored the first manual of meta-analysis.

The first order of business for Glass and Smith was to locate and collect the studies to be combined. Glass's guiding principle was to cast a wide net, sampling all sorts of studies on the outcomes of psychotherapy and counseling, since any advance decision about what kind to collect would bias the findings. He would winnow out the unsuitable ones later.

Glass and Smith spent countless hours in the library, painstakingly poring through many annual volumes of two ponderous, small-print indexes, *Psychological Abstracts* and *Dissertation Abstracts*, in search of promising titles. Each time they found one, they copied the citation by hand (in 1974 the indexes had not yet been converted to searchable computer data bases). Next, they prowled the stacks to find the bound volumes containing the articles and scrutinized their bibliographies for potentially useful titles not listed in the two indexes; this is often called the "ancestry method" of adding to a collection of studies. The whole process sounds dreadfully tiresome, but as every scholar and researcher knows, the tedium is offset by a burst of exhilaration at every find; it is somewhat like panning for gold and every now and then coming up with a nugget. Glass actually found the library search exciting, he says, because with his intensely competitive nature and his goal of bashing Eysenck, "It had the thrill of battle and competition."

Eventually, he and Mary Lee Smith amassed a thousand titles—a sample of a wholly different magnitude from any review of psychotherapy up to that point. As they constructed the sample, they also undertook the monumental chore of obtaining physical copies of the articles. They photocopied scores of articles in the library, a dreary, fatiguing job, wrote hundreds of letters to authors for reprints and to library services for microfilm copies of unpublished dissertations, and hunted for and bought books. The documents, books, and 150 boxes of microfilms and microfiches all wound up in crammed file cabinets and in heaps in a large office in the home they had just built in Boulder.

The third phase, evaluating the materials and extracting the data, went on concurrently with the continuing search. Even though every title Glass and Smith jotted down sounded promising, when they actually got hold of the documents and read them it was disheartening to find that about half of them were useless for meta-analytic purposes because of the lack of any control or comparison group. The same was true of dissertations. Smith: "We'd have a box of ten microfilms come in—for which we'd paid good money—and, always hoping to find something wonderful, I'd put each one in the microfilm reader only to find that three or four, contrary to what the abstract said, weren't comparative studies at all and another one or two didn't have any quantitative data. So all those would be out. I developed a very jaundiced view of the state of research reporting."

They then carefully read every study that did have a control or comparison group and weeded out all those that lacked usable data. Many studies reported only a p value, or, even worse, offered a purely qualitative (and hence useless) statement such as, "Although treatment effects did not reach the level of significance, the majority, compared with the control group, showed a tendency toward positive effects." Other studies gave a variety of statistical data—such as ratios of one group to the other—but no actual numbers; these, however, Glass could transform into numbers that could be analyzed. "It was hammer-and-tongs statistical work," he says.

> I dug up, invented, or reinvented about every technique you can think of to turn some of their esoteric reporting into usable measures of the impact of therapy. But sometimes there was just no way to use their results. Carl Rogers, whose work I admire, published a whole book on his client-centered therapy, but there was not one quantitative report in it except that results were significant at the 5 percent level. It killed me! I couldn't use it, because the differences between the treated group and the control group, though they were significant—they hadn't occurred by chance—could have been niggling and of no importance, and I had no way to tell.

Next, the information in the 375 studies that survived the screening to this point had to be numerically coded so that the computer could understand the information and analyze it. Every piece of information that would play a part in the meta-analysis had to be entered by hand, in the form of a number, on a three-page form; later, employees of a computer service would punch holes in IBM cards to represent those codes—a method that sounds antediluvian today—and an IBM machine would then mechanically read the holes in the cards and transfer the data onto a tape that the computer could read.

A number from 0 to 5, for instance, signified the amount of training the therapist had had (0 for a lay counselor, 3 for a Ph.D. candidate in psychology, 5 for a well-known Ph.D. or psychiatrist, and so on); 1 to 5 designated the kind of therapy used, or none if none was used; 1 to 8 specified the outcome measured (anxiety level, self-concept, school or work achievement, blood pressure or other physiological indicators, and so on).

Both Glass and Smith did the coding, and since many of the choices in assigning numbers were somewhat subjective, they took time at several points to check that they were coding alike: Each coded the same subsample of studies, and they then compared their codings. This, a common procedure in many kinds of psychological and social research, is known as checking on "intercoder agreement" or "interrater reliability." Glass and Smith found their codings gratifyingly similar—perhaps because they were both therapists, or perhaps because, as husband and wife, they shared so much of their thinking and daily experience.

Shared, indeed, to an extreme—they worked much of the time at the same large table in their home office and discussed at breakfast, lunch, and dinner, and almost any other time when they were together, the incoming material and all the manifold problems of working out the first full-dress meta-analysis in history. Such an intense working partnership has wrecked some marriages, but that was not the case here. "Far from causing any friction," Glass says, "it was sort of a high, really." The marriage did dissolve some years later, but for reasons unrelated to their working together.

The crucial step in all this was evaluating the outcomes in the different studies in order to have a basis for combining them. Glass, a proficient and advanced statistician since his graduate school days, regarded the method of evaluation used in almost all psychological research—the measure of statistical significance—as worth little, especially when trying to synthesize studies. "It's ridiculous, this business of combining the p values of studies," he says. "Statistical significance is the least interesting thing about the results. You should describe the results in terms of measures of magnitude—not just, does a treatment affect people, but how *much* does it affect them? *That's* what we needed to know."

Their sample did have a wealth of data on how greatly treatment had affected clients; in fact, Smith and Glass found a total of 833 effect sizes (measures of change) in the 375 studies. Some have been listed above; others included the degree of neuroticism before and after treatment as measured by the MMPI (the Minnesota Multiphasic Personality Inventory, a standard test), palmar sweating, the clients' own appraisals of how they felt before and after therapy, the therapists' appraisals of their clients' condition before and after therapy, and many more.

But does it make sense to try to combine such different measures of change? Is it legitimate to combine palmar sweating and success at work? "Mixing different outcomes together is defensible." Glass and Smith wrote later. "All outcome measures are more or less related to 'well-being,' and so at a general level are comparable."[14] Yes, but how *can* one combine such diverse and differently measured results and arrive at a combined measure of change? What possible statistical legerdemain could combine a $20 raise on the job, a ten-point decrease in blood pressure, a client's own statement that he felt much more at ease in social situations, and any of the hundreds of other outcomes cited, into a single, synthesized measure of effect?

Glass's solution was to "standardize" the many different measures of effect: transform them into common coin, or the same statistical terms, so that they could be added, averaged, divided, or otherwise manipulated. He did so by converting the measures of effect from their reported form to a common form, namely, how many "standard deviation units" separated the treated group from the control group. Standard deviation (sd) is not a difficult concept. Within any group, say, all first-grade boys in a city school system, there is a distribution of IQs: These scores, plotted on a graph, take the form of the familiar bell curve, the high center being the most common IQ, 100, with the curve sloping down on both sides. Similarly, the heights of the boys would also take the form of a bell curve, though it might have a taller and narrower shape than the boys' IQ curve, since heights at any age do not vary as widely as IQs. The sd of any group is simply a measure of the spread on either side of the mean (central) score in the distribution: It is a measure of how far from the mean one must go to encompass about a third of all the scores. Some curves are tall and narrow, like that for boys' heights, and have a small sd, while others are more spread out, like that of IQs, and have a larger sd. But in any case, sd units, like percentages, are a standardized and combinable "metric."

Glass's breakthrough was to turn his hundreds of incompatible measures of effect into compatible and combinable sd units. To understand his method, consider the following three hypothetical studies testing whether psychotherapy improves "well-being." In each there is a treated group and a control group, but the studies measure the effect of therapy in different ways: Study A presents the psychologist's assessment of the client's functioning; study B uses the client's own rating of life satisfaction; and study C uses the client's job performance as rated by a supervisor. Figure 2-1 depicts the distribution of scores for the treated clients and the controls in each study. The vertical lines mark the centers (means) of each distribution.

Can we average the results from the three studies to get an overall sense of the efficacy of therapy? Not yet. Nor can we say that therapy had more effect on patients' self-ratings than on psychologists' ratings, because the psychologists' ratings were made on a one-hundred-point scale and the self-ratings on a seven-point scale. Thus, while a fifteen-point difference on the psychologists' scale might look bigger than a two-point difference on the self-rating scale, it may actually be smaller.

By turning the different units of measurement into a common metric (sd units), we can overcome problems of incomparability. Suppose that in study A, about one-third of the controls had scores ranging from forty to sixty; that difference of twenty points represents roughly one sd. Next, suppose that the psychologists' mean rating for the control group is forty and for the treated group is forty-eight; to express that difference in sd terms, we divide eight by twenty—the treated group is 8/20ths of an sd better than the control group; in other words, therapy resulted in an average difference of .40 sd.

In study B, suppose that about a third of the control subjects have scores between three and five, meaning that the sd is two. Suppose, too, that the average self-rating of the controls is 3.00 (on a scale of zero to seven) and of the treated group is 4.70. The groups are 1.70 scale units apart; in terms of sd units—1.70 divided by 2.00—the difference is .85 sd.

In study C, there is no difference between the control group and the treated group; the difference in sd units is zero.

Now the results of all three studies have been translated into a common metric. Glass called this metric the "effect size" because it is a way of expressing the effects that treatment had on scores; it is represented in statistics as "d". Using his method, it is now possible to compare the effect sizes of the three studies (in study A, $d = .40$; in study B, $d = .85$; and in study C, $d = 0$). To combine the results of the three studies take the average of the effect sizes across the studies—add the effect sizes,

Figure 2-1   Three Hypothetical Studies of Psychotherapy

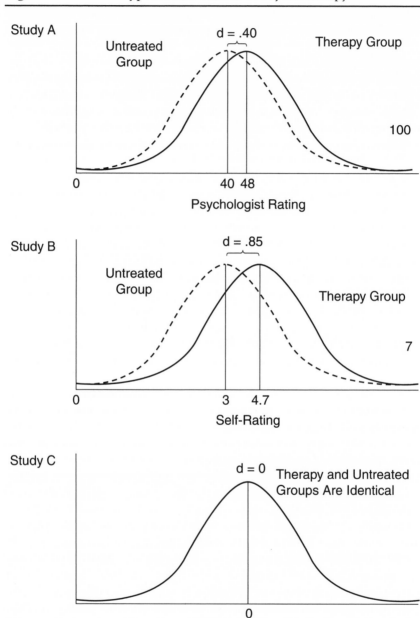

Note: The letter d stands for effect size.

then divide by three—which is d = .417. In other words, the well-being rating of the average treated client was about .42 sd higher than that of the average untreated control.

As logical, and even obvious, as all this sounds now, it was not clear to Glass, in 1976, that his colleagues would see his meta-analytic approach that way. "I thought maybe I'd get laughed at for suggesting such an idea," he recalls. Smith, too, because she would be mentioned as Glass's coworker, recalls having "a lot of fear. At the time, this was the most out-there-on-the-edge kind of analytic activity for anybody to be in. I was afraid it would be badly criticized, or just rejected as insane. I think Gene's real contribution was the courage to do something so completely different from what was then standard accepted practice."

Many meta-analysts have said that the concept of effect size is Glass's deserved claim to fame and his central methodological contribution to meta-analysis. Glass, ever the nonconformist, snorted when I quoted a distinguished statistician to this effect. "That kills me!" he said. "It's a nothing idea, an obvious thing. I'd known about it since graduate school." (Indeed, the psychologist Jacob Cohen and several statisticians had already written about effect size analysis.) "The overall idea of meta-analysis, the whole process, first to last—*that* was my contribution."

Both Smith and Glass calculated the effect sizes as part of their coding. Doing so was no routine matter: the 375 studies reported their findings in an exasperating variety of ways—sometimes as correlations, sometimes as t-ratios, sometimes as regression coefficients and other arcana—and it was often necessary to turn these into standard differences so Glass could combine effect sizes, the major goal of the project. He minimizes the difficulties of this part of the work—"mostly it was like solving a little algebra problem"—but in actuality, in addition to using standard algebraic procedures, he had to invent at least a dozen different new formulas for solving the different data problems.

After nearly two years, and with the AERA convention looming ever closer, Glass and Smith were finally ready to feed their data to the mainframe computer at the university and see what they had found. Actually, they did not expect to be greatly surprised, only enlightened as to the specifics. "I already had some idea," Glass says, "from working with all the studies and sort of tallying it up in my mind." Such a tally was, of course, only a subjective and possibly very distorted impression; as psychologist George Miller had much earlier shown, the human mind can pay attention to only about seven things at any one time, so that an effort to see scores of results in the mind is impossible. The results would become clear to Glass only when the mainframe computer processed the tape in response to the complex instructions he had given it about how to combine the basic data and what cross-tabulations to make. (The latter are computations of the relation between any one feature of a study, such as some client characteristic, and another feature, such as the outcome of therapy.)

The process of inputting the data took place in batches, with Glass and Smith taking material down to the computer center as it was ready. There they would load the reel of tape in the machine, type in a stack of specific instructions, and push the button. Then came the nail-biting wait, usually late at night, as the big reel, locked into place, spun back and forth and a high-speed printer spat out sheet after sheet of results.

It took months before they had all the meta-analyzed numbers in hand. Neither of them recalls any moments of epiphany, although Smith says that in a way everything was a surprise. "You can't look at that many points of data and get any sense of the whole. That's why you do the data analysis." Glass has a rather different recollection; he felt sure that the result would firmly establish the effectiveness of psychotherapy.

And it did so to an extent they might have hoped for but not really envisioned. In simplest terms, the combined effect of psychotherapy in their 375 studies, comprising about forty thousand treated and untreated subjects, had an effect size of .68—over two-thirds of a standard deviation. This meant, as Glass wrote for his AERA address, that "[on average], slightly under twenty hours of therapy, by therapists with two-and-a-half years experience . . . can be expected to move the typical client from the fiftieth to the seventy-fifth percentile of the untreated population." In lay terms: While the median treated client (at the middle of the curve) was as mentally ill before therapy as the median control individual—healthier than half of them, unhealthier than the other half—after therapy, the treated client was healthier than three-quarters of the untreated group. In the social sciences, so large an effect of any intervention—such as a new educational program, or one to rehabilitate criminals, or one to retrain the unemployed—is almost unheard of. Glass and Smith were deeply fulfilled; the two years of effort, the laborious details, the countless frustrations had been worth it.

Among the many other findings of their meta-analysis, one was particularly gratifying. Eysenck had long since become an ardent advocate of behavioral therapy, which he, like other behavioral therapists, claimed was far more effective than other forms of therapy, especially the psychodynamic. The meta-analysis, which included some studies directly comparing behavior therapy with other kinds, showed otherwise. As Glass would say in his AERA address. "The findings are startling. There is only a trivial .07 σ_x [standard deviation] superiority of the behavioral over the nonbehavioral therapies. . . . The available evidence shows essentially no difference in the average impact of each class of therapy."

Mining and Smelting the Data

Selecting the data in the collected studies to be meta-analyzed—the fourth major phase Glass outlined in his AERA address—is somewhat like the mining of stubborn raw materials; extracting and combining their data, the fifth major phase, is analogous to smelting or freeing the valuable material from the often recalcitrant ore.

MINING   The first step in extracting the data from a group of studies is deciding which items of information to code and which to bypass. A study's conventional introductory material and literature review does not affect its results and can be ignored, but a great many other kinds of information are relevant. Among them are the "independent variable"— (the type of intervention or condition being tested), the characteristics of the subjects and those of the researchers (even their sex, since male and female researchers sometimes get different results)—and the "dependent variable" (the outcome or result).

The task of coding consists of reading each study word by word, searching for each item of information called for by the code sheets (or code book, since some meta-analyses call for fifty or more pages of coded data), and writing on the coding form the number that represents that item. To code a simple study may take two or three hours of intense and unflagging attention, a complicated one as long as two days. John Hunter and Frank Schmidt, a team of meta-analytic statisticians, estimate that coding can be 90 to 95 percent of the work of synthesizing data.[15]

Researchers and their assistants are apt to sigh or groan when asked about coding. Judith Hall, a social psychologist at Northeastern University who has coded a number of her own meta-analyses, says, "It's the most *laborious* task. Every time you get halfway through you say, 'Why am I *doing* this?' It really wears you out." But that is true of almost all scientific research. In a movie, it may be presented as a white-knuckle race to discover some remedy before a lethal plague does away with humankind; in a book it may appear as a sweaty, sleepless effort to be first with a great breakthrough, as in James Watson's autobiographical *The Double Helix*. But the reality is closer to what the scholar Richard Altick has written about literary research: "The researcher pays for every exultant discovery with a hundred hours of monotonous, eye-searing labor."[16]

What is most fatiguing about coding is not its tedium but the frequent need to make Solomonic decisions. An example: A study tested
the effectiveness of a particular form of psychotherapy used with one
group against two other groups, one receiving a placebo and the second
receiving no treatment. Several participants in the psychotherapy group
missed a number of sessions, a few missed as many as four in ten. The
coder's problem: Should such participants be included among those having received treatment or would doing so unfairly dilute the effect size
of the treatment? If they should not, what should be the cutoff for participation in the study? Another example: Three forms of therapy to reduce fear of snakes were tested and their results compared, but the research on one form was conducted by a psychologist who had previously
published articles on one of the other therapies being tested. The coder's
problem: Is that researcher's conflict of interest likely to have distorted
his results, and if so, by how much should his or her data be adjusted?[17]

Next comes what is often a very difficult but potentially the most exciting step of coding, the part that sometimes yields what Altick called
an "exultant discovery." This is the calculation of effect sizes, particularly when the results were not given in terms of standard differences but
as medians, correlations, F-ratios, and so on. Many of these data can be
transformed into effect sizes by formulas that statisticians have devised
in the years since Glass's initial presentation. But for some kinds of data
no ready-made procedures exist: they are puzzles the coder must solve
by finding some crafty way of converting them into effect sizes. "What's
fun about data analysis," Robert Rosenthal, a long-time meta-analyst and
the Edgar Pierce Professor of Psychology at Harvard, told me, "what I really enjoy about it, is playing this detective game. There are moments of
sheer delight when I invent a one-time procedure—I may never see this
particular constellation of givens again—and come up with a sensible
solution to this particular problem. That's exciting!"

Less exciting but equally problematic is deciding what to do when a
study yields more than one effect size—when, for instance, several different treatments or different groups of subjects have been used and the study
consequently has a number of outcomes, each of which can yield a valid
effect size. How valid is it to combine results when one study is the source
of half a dozen effect sizes and another is the source of only one?[18] Some
meta-analysts use every effect size when combining findings even though
several come from a single study; others, when a study has multiple effect
sizes, aggregate them and use the average so that every study in the meta-
analysis has an equal input. Each approach has its hazards and costs, the
details of which are beyond the scope of this book.

With so many decisions to be made in extracting the data, it is of vital importance that the coders reach similar judgments about the raw data; the more they agree, the less error gets built into the data. Glass and Smith, as already mentioned, compared their figures to make sure their coding was compatible; without some test of intercoder agreement, readers cannot be sure how reliable the conclusions of a meta-analysis are. The most widely used and simplest measure of compatibility is the agreement rate (AR), or percent of agreement, the formula for which is as follows:

$$AR = \frac{\text{number of observations agreed upon}}{\text{total number of observations}}.$$

Generally, an agreement rate of 80 percent is considered acceptable but 90 percent or higher is preferable.[19]

Although this method of measuring agreement is simple, it has statistical shortcomings. If, for instance, only a few studies of a smoking-cessation program report weight gain, coders might differ in their interpretation of the data in those studies but still have a high agreement rate because they reliably agree about all those other studies in which weight gain is *not* reported. Some meta-analysts have therefore recently devised more trustworthy, but mathematically more complicated, ways of measuring intercoder agreement.[20]

SMELTING   Gene Glass, scorning statistical significance as a measure of what an intervention achieves, based his meta-analytic findings in his AERA address on the 830 effect sizes that he and Mary Lee Smith extracted from the 375 studies in their sample. It is hardly possible to overstate the importance to meta-analysis of the concept of effect size; one recent authoritative overview of the method called it "the key variable in meta-analysis, the hub around which the whole enterprise revolves."[21]

The critical step in the analytic phase of meta-analysis is combining the data—smelting all the effect sizes into one summary effect size. As already described, Glass achieved this by transforming all the varied measurements of effect into standard deviation units, a commensurable metric. In the two decades since Glass introduced meta-analysis, a good deal of careful examination of his method—simple adding and averaging of effect sizes—has revealed certain weaknesses in it and led to the development of more advanced and reliable techniques. The details are beyond the ken of the nonstatistician, but at least two of the major improvements are easy enough to understand.

The first: Because the chance of sampling error in a small study is greater than that in a large one, adding and averaging effect sizes with every study on the same footing can distort the overall result. Formulas have therefore been developed to "weight" the effect size for each study according to the size of its sample; this gives small samples less input and so corrects for their greater sampling errors.[22]

The second: Because the information from which effect sizes are calculated may incorporate errors due to unreliable measurements and other methodological factors, a number of statisticians, Glass among them, have worked out ways to adjust the raw effect sizes that are less vulnerable to such distortions.

As we have seen, Glass was averse to using statistical significance to appraise the effects of any intervention and so included no combined significance data in his 1976 presentation. Nonetheless, combined significance testing has remained a major method of aggregating data ever since it was first used by Tippett in 1931, and by one authority's reckoning there are now nine methods for doing so.[23] It remains an important tool in the meta-analytic workshop because some studies do not report enough information for an effect size to be calculated; research reports often give group means but no standard deviations. Other times p values are given without accompanying test statistics. In such cases, a significance approach can at least combine the p values of the findings.[24]

Much as researchers performing original studies use p values to test the null hypothesis (that any observed effect happened by chance), so meta-analysts use combined p values to determine whether the combined result of a group of studies may be only a chance result. Take a hypothetical example: We want to know whether a particular kind of psychotherapy is effective and find sixteen studies that compare a therapy group to an untreated group. Ten report that the therapy did not significantly affect the patients' well-being but unfortunately give no information on the exact p level associated with this result; they also fail to give the means and standard deviations from which one could calculate effect sizes. The other six studies report a significant positive effect of the therapy, four finding it significant at the $p < .05$ level, one at $p < .01$, and one at $p < .005$. Given these results, can we conclude that the therapy has an effect?

First, the data needed to calculate effect sizes is missing from too many of the sixteen studies to permit a confident overall estimate of effect size. Failing that, we can conduct a simple vote-count, concluding that, since studies finding no significant result outnumber those that do, the therapy has no effect. But for reasons discussed earlier, we prefer to ask a more precise and trustworthy question of our data, namely, "What is the likelihood that we would find sixteen studies with these p levels if the therapy is ineffective?"

To answer this question, we have to assume that the ten studies with nonsignificant findings have exactly equal results for both the therapy and nontherapy groups (that is, we assume these ten have a p level of .50). Next, we combine the p levels by the "adding-Zs method," a statistical procedure that converts the p levels to another statistic (Z score), which also expresses how unlikely it is that no difference exists but further permits the results to be combined. When we carry out this procedure, we get a combined level of $p < .02$, from which we confidently conclude the results were not due to chance alone; the patients in the therapy groups scored reliably higher than patients in the control groups.

Thus, even when effect sizes cannot be calculated, combining p levels can lead to a finding in which researchers can place considerable confidence. An extreme example: A 1995 meta-analysis synthesized eighty-eight studies on the long-debated issue of whether attitudes predict future behavior and reported the combined probability of the null hypothesis as $p < .0000000000001$, a figure that would convince even Doubting Thomas that attitudes do predict behavior.[25]

On the other hand, even the most extreme combined p value tells nothing about the *magnitude* of the effect. According to a monograph by the American Statistical Association, combined p values make no use of the "information content" of the separate data sets and, considered by themselves, can be remarkably misleading. If the effect of a new treatment is statistically highly significant but trifling in actual size, policymakers and physicians may be misled into using it although a more precise analysis would have guided them away from it.[26]

The two meta-analytic methods are thus complementary and serve best to reinforce each other. A combined significance test of $p < .05$ supports the hypothesis that the combined effect size is not a chance result, while the larger the effect size, at any given level of confidence, the more important the finding.[27] Combining significance levels and combining effect sizes are therefore the two principal ways of synthesizing the results of a group of studies, although several other methods, more complicated and less often used, are also presented in books of meta-analytic technique.

Genesis of Meta-Analysis: Part II

In his 1976 AERA address, Gene Glass presented the meta-analysis of psychotherapy outcomes briefly—in about 1,100 words—and only by way of illustration. But he and Smith were already busily reanalyzing their 375 studies with an eye to publishing the first full-blown meta-analysis.

Based on what they had learned and what they had not, they developed a considerably longer and more detailed coding form. It called for nearly one hundred items of information, some of which required the coder to choose among ten or twenty options. Coding the effect size was the most difficult and time-consuming part of the work; it necessitated any one of a dozen different computations for each of the 833 reported treatment effects. Despite Glass's poor opinion of significance ratings, the new coding form also required the calculation of the statistical significance of each effect size. Four graduate students helped with the coding but Smith did much of it. I asked her how she managed to stay in good humor during that arduous process. She sighed, "Let's just say I didn't. It was *incredibly* tedious and I would never do it again." (She did take part later in a few small meta-analyses, then stopped doing them altogether.)

Glass, along with his solution to the problem of converting effect sizes to a commensurable form, also resolved, at least in his own view, another issue of equal magnitude, namely, whether it was legitimate to combine measures as dissimilar as self-esteem ratings, anxiety, sobriety, disruptive behavior, job achievement, dating, galvanic skin response, and others. With his experience both as a therapy client and as a therapist, Glass was certain that the answer was yes; as he and Smith wrote in their report of the second version of the meta-analysis:

> Mixing different outcomes together is defensible. First, it is clear that all outcome measures are more or less related to "well-being" and so at a general level are comparable. . . . [Moreover,] each primary researcher made value judgments concerning the definition and direction of positive therapeutic effects for the particular clients he or she studied. It is reasonable to adopt these value judgments and aggregate them in the present study.[28]

This justification notwithstanding, the combining of different effects would become a major bone of contention between the advocates and the critics of meta-analysis. It is often referred to as the "apples and oranges" problem, which we look at more closely in the next chapter.

Despite the finer-grained analysis Glass and Smith performed in the expanded version of their study, their major finding was consistent with that of the first: "On average, the typical therapy client is better off than 75% of untreated clients." And although their second version sorted out and evaluated the effectiveness of ten forms of therapy—the first version did so for only four—their conclusion was, again, that "few important differences could be established among many quite different types of psychotherapy." They stressed that they found virtually no difference in effectiveness between the behavioral therapies and the nonbehavioral ones, a conclusion certain to infuriate all partisans of behavior therapy, Eysenck in particular.

Their report of the meta-analysis was immediately accepted by *American Psychologist*, a principal journal of the American Psychological Association, and appeared in its September 1977 issue. In this medium, the methodology of meta-analysis and the findings about the outcomes of psychotherapy reached a far wider audience than had Glass's 1976 address; it had a major impact on the worlds of psychotherapy and the social sciences, and to a lesser extent other sciences.

Clinical psychologists and other psychotherapists were deeply gratified. "I was thrilled by it," Robert Rosenthal told me, "I was doing therapy at the time and I felt sure I was benefiting people, but"—and he chuckled disarmingly—"I wasn't at all sure that any other therapists were. It was wonderful to learn that they were."

A number of people in other disciplines were impressed by the methodology of meta-analysis and saw its applicability to their own fields. An exemplar is the case of Larry Hedges, whose life course was determined by the 1976 and 1977 papers. As a graduate student in statistics at Stanford University, he read Glass's presidential address and, the following year, Smith and Glass's meta-analysis and saw his own future. He explains:

> I was struck by the argument that so much of the equivocation about research findings in the social sciences is due to a failure to apply quantitative methods to summarize the research. When you do so, as Glass did, the picture often gets strikingly clearer. I was convinced that meta-analysis was ultimately going to prove absolutely fundamental to scientific work—and that there was a terrific opportunity for me to do something in this new and unplowed field.

Hedges soon became a leading developer of the statistical methods and theory of meta-analysis, and as a full professor in the department of education at the University of Chicago has conducted his own meta-analyses of educational research.

Although most reactions to the Smith and Glass article were highly favorable, some were harshly critical. This was to be expected; academics often disagree for good and honest reasons but also because one way to get one's name known in academia is to vigorously attack a new and highly regarded piece of research. One or perhaps both of those motives inspired a vitriolic attack by Philip Gallo, a professor at San Diego State University, in the May 1978 issue of *American Psychologist*; he reworked certain Smith and Glass data and proved to his own satisfaction that psychotherapy has a "quite weak effect." He thereupon summarily dismissed the whole Smith and Glass meta-analysis: Their findings, he said, were based on aggregating a great many different measures of effect (the apples and oranges argument) and "any attempt to extricate meaningful information from such a hodgepodge is impossible."[29]

Other critics carped about other aspects of the meta-analysis, often in caustic terms, as has become the norm for academic disagreements in recent years, but Eysenck outdid them all. Understandably nettled that Smith and Glass had called his papers on psychotherapy "tendentious diatribes" and said that the "Eysenck myth" was thoroughly disproven by later studies, he waded in like a street fighter. In the May 1978 issue of *American Psychologist*, as already noted, he called their meta-analysis "an exercise in mega-silliness" and, characterizing their inclusion of both high-quality and lesser-quality studies as "garbage in, garbage out," said that if their analytic methods were to be taken seriously "it would mark the beginning of a passage into the dark age of scientific psychology." He was optimistic, however, that that would not happen:

> The notion that one can distill scientific knowledge from a compilation of studies mostly of poor design, relying on subjective, unvalidated, and certainly unreliable clinical judgments, and dissimilar with respect to nearly all the vital parameters, dies hard. This article [Smith and Glass, 1977], it is to be hoped, is the final death rattle of such hopes.

As to their findings about the effectiveness of psychotherapy*: "It would be highly dangerous to take seriously the 'results' reported by Smith and Glass. . . . I must regretfully restate my conclusion of 1952, namely that there is still no acceptable evidence for the efficacy of psychotherapy."[30]

---

* Eysenck and some other British psychologists use the term "psychotherapy" to mean nonbehavioral techniques but not behavioral treatment; in America, behavioral treatment is considered a form of psychotherapy.

For more than a decade after the appearance of the 1977 Smith and Glass paper, other researchers reanalyzed their data or subsets of it, either working from the published paper or obtaining copies of the data tapes from Smith and Glass. To say whether more of these studies backed Smith and Glass or rebutted their conclusions would be to fall into the trap of vote-counting. But perhaps two other observations are pertinent. First, those who selected special portions of the Smith and Glass data and used statistical techniques different from theirs were likely to arrive at conclusions differing from, or amending, Smith and Glass's; those who used their entire body of data or their methods almost always confirmed their findings.[31] Second, a vast 1993 study meta-analyzed 302 meta-analyses—yes, you read that correctly—of a total of nearly five thousand primary studies and came to "a strongly favorable conclusion about the efficacy of well-developed psychological treatment."[32]

An authoritative comment on the matter appears in the scholarly volume *Meta-Analysis for Explanation: A Casebook*. In the introductory chapter, an advisory committee of experts in meta-analysis writes:

> The achievements of meta-analysis have been considerable for a method with such a short history. Some practical questions that formerly fomented wide disagreement now seem to have been resolved by the method. Gone, for instance, are the days when a conference on individual psychotherapy would devote many hours to discussing whether it was effective in general. Since the work of Smith and Glass (1977), and its follow-up by Landman and Dawes (1982), among others, the debate is stilled.[33]

That is not to say that no die-hard dissenters remain; Eysenck and a handful of others continue to denigrate meta-analysis and to assert that psychotherapy is ineffective, and a new book by William Epstein, a professor of social work at the University of Nevada, *The Illusion of Psychotherapy*, says flatly that there is no credible clinical evidence of its effectiveness.

As Jonathan Swift said long ago, "There's none so blind as they that won't see."

A curious postscript: Although Glass and Smith co-authored a book in 1980 meta-analytically demonstrating the benefits of psychotherapy, and another in 1981 on methods of meta-analysis in social research, the two of them lost interest in the subject thereafter. Glass, who has switched from one major interest to another several times in his life, simply had enough of meta-analysis; these days his primary interest is editing a journal of education policy analysis on the Internet. Smith, divorced from Glass for some years, says that her interest in meta-analysis was fulfilled by the psychotherapy study; she is happy to have played a part in the development of a new methodology but has no continuing interest in it, and in recent years has been studying the effects of testing on various aspects of schooling and teaching. In their different ways, both Glass and Smith seem a trifle amused and perhaps rueful at how distant they now are from the thing they gave birth to and which has grown and flourished without their further care.

IN BRIEF . . .

To illustrate the subsequent wide-ranging use of meta-analysis to resolve other issues about psychotherapy, here are short accounts of two other, quite dissimilar, case histories.

Does Marital and Family Therapy Work?

"For years, researchers have debated whether marital and family therapies are effective," began a 1993 paper in the *Journal of Counseling and Clinical Psychology*. This was a low-key restatement of an issue that had long troubled the study's primary investigator, William Shadish. In 1985, when he was a young research associate at the University of Memphis (where he is now a professor of psychology), he got into a heated argument with a colleague, a marriage and family therapist, who claimed that research showed that his form of therapy worked better than any other and with any kind of problem. Shadish's own experiences as a patient in individual psychotherapy during his twenties and a psychotherapist for a few years afterward made him feel certain his colleague was wrong— but the colleague felt just as certain that he was right.

The research literature, which Shadish browsed through for an answer, proved a vast jumble out of which one could pick whatever results one preferred. Exasperated, he decided to do a meta-analysis to wring some sense out of the untidy mess although he had no training in the methodology. "I had become aware of meta-analysis when it was invented," he says. "I thought the 1977 article by Gene Glass and Mary Lee Smith was a stupendous achievement. But I didn't try to do any meta-analysis myself until that discussion with my colleague." To train himself, Shadish studied two books on the subject by Glass, Smith, and co-authors, and once, when the 1989 San Francisco earthquake kept his plane grounded, he spent two whole days in a hotel room beating his way through Hedges and Olkin's dense and difficult *Statistical Methods for Meta-Analysis*, a feat comparable to the mortification of the flesh practiced by early Christian anchorites.

Shadish, already skilled at writing grant proposals, won a substantial grant from the National Institute of Mental Health, and later another from the Russell Sage Foundation. He needed them: The project, even with the help of more than half a dozen graduate students, lasted nearly ten years.

In collecting references, he and his graduate students had an advantage over Glass and Smith: By the mid-1980s *Psychological Abstracts, Dissertation Abstracts*, and three other major indexes were available on-line and could be swiftly and efficiently searched by computer. The team also read, the old-fashioned way, the bibliographies of relevant articles and the tables of contents of journals, hunting for items not contained in the on-line indexes; they also wrote hundreds of letters to specialists asking for yet other suggestions. A year and a half of such efforts netted Shadish a mighty haul of roughly two thousand references.

On examination, however, it turned out that fewer than 10 percent met his requirements. He wanted only studies that specifically employed a form of marital or family therapy, randomly assigned subjects to treatment or control conditions, and dealt with subjects who were actually distressed rather than merely seeking marital enrichment. "We tossed out more than half the references immediately either on the basis of the title or the abstract," Shadish recalled, "things with titles like 'A case study of' and so on. Then we read the remaining ones and again eliminated most of them. I still have two boxes of dissertations"—he waved toward a far corner of his large, cluttered office— "that we couldn't use and that cost me forty dollars each." In the end, from the two thousand references he had distilled a set of 163 studies that met all his conditions.

Shadish and a student assistant then developed a code book. The art of meta-analysis had advanced so much in a decade that the book ran to twenty-three pages and well over two hundred items. The coding, done primarily by students, was considerably more complex and time-consuming than it had been for Smith and Glass. To answer some questions, the coders had to search for clues and judge what to make of them. One question, for instance, asked whether the researcher was blind to the condition (that is, knew whether the subject was being treated or was a control, since knowing might have influenced his or her observations); many studies did not explicitly say, and only a painstaking reading might find hints.

The most difficult part of coding was the calculation of effect sizes. Shadish taught his coders to use several methods, developed after the 1977 Smith and Glass meta-analysis, that, among other refinements, corrected for small-sample bias. This, too, put a burden on the coders. "If the study gave the actual number of subjects, calculating effect size was easy," says Ivey Bright, a young psychotherapist who, as one of the coders, spent twenty hours a week at it for a year. "But sometimes we'd read that maybe ten subjects dropped out before the end, and the study didn't say when they did, and we'd have to figure out from one clue or another how many subjects there were at any point in the study. It was really hard."

When it came to combining the data, Shadish again benefited from a decade of statistical innovation. "I followed the Hedges and Olkin procedures because they weighted for sample size," he says. "I used outlier techniques to check the central tendencies in the effects." (Outliers are atypical cases, far from the median, that distort the averages; sometimes a truer picture emerges when outliers are dropped.) He continued:

> I looked at moderator variables to see if they, rather than the kind of treatment, accounted for differences in effect size, and found that a number of them did. For instance, effect sizes were higher if they were based on behavioral measures rather than nonbehavioral measures, and higher if based on ratings by others rather than self-reports. And if variables in a study were correlated, I used regression techniques to sort out and measure the effects of each one separately.

When Shadish put all this through the computer—not once but several times, refining and reworking the project over the years—he got a number of clear-cut and gratifying results:[34]

- The average effect size was roughly half a standard deviation, which meant that the typical client of marital and family therapy was better-off than 70 percent of control clients. But, according to a subsample of studies that compared marital and family therapies with individual therapies, the former work no better than the latter, as Shadish had thought from the start.
- Marital therapies had higher effect sizes than family therapies, though not to a significant degree; this minor difference was probably due to the fact that the problems requiring family therapy are more difficult than those requiring marital therapy.
- Some types of marital and family therapy appeared to work better than others, but when the differences in the quality of the methods used were eliminated by regression analysis, the differences in effectiveness disappeared. Humanistic therapies—Rogerian "client-centered" ther-

apy and others emphasizing such 1960s values as "authenticity," "self-actualization," and "personal growth"—showed no positive effects in any analysis, however, a bit of a disappointment to Shadish, whose original training in psychotherapy had been Rogerian.

- The meta-analysis also yielded some valuable methodological findings. First, effect sizes were larger when researchers were not "blind" to treatment; apparently, if they knew what was going on, they unwittingly saw more improvement. Second, results reported in dissertations, most of which had not been published, were nearly 40 percent smaller on average than results in published reports; whatever the reason, it meant that meta-analysts who ignored unpublished studies would likely overestimate effects.

Shadish's meta-analysis, listing five graduate students as co-authors, was published in 1993 in the *Journal of Consulting and Clinical Psychology* and won the 1994 Outstanding Research Publication Award of the American Association for Marriage and Family Therapy.

Second-Level Meta-Analysis

Although the primary goal of meta-analysis is to combine studies, its secondary goal, one of increasing importance in recent years, is to disentangle the knotted skein of causal influences in a set of combined studies in order to find out *why* they differed in their results. This is what Shadish was doing when he analyzed the "moderator variables."

Moderator variables are any characteristics of the studies that are associated with differences in effect size. Year of publication is one: Recent studies of a particular subject may, for various reasons such as changes in methodology, tend to report larger—or smaller—effects than earlier ones. The measure (criterion) of effect is another: As mentioned above, self-reports of changes brought about by marital and family therapy yield smaller effect sizes than reports by observers. Race, ethnicity, and IQ of school children can importantly influence the effects of programs meant to improve teaching and learning. The sex of the researcher can make a difference: Many studies have shown that women are more easily influenced than men by persuasive arguments, group pressure, and so on, but a meta-analysis has revealed that male researchers regularly find a larger effect of this nature than female researchers.[35]

Correlations between moderator variables and effect size sometimes point to associations that are of little or no interest, such as when they indicate that studies appearing in journals reveal different effects from those appearing in books. But in other cases, the analysis of moderator variables enables the meta-analyst to judge how much of the effect is due to substantive issues—the treatment itself, the setting, the kind of outcome observed, and the like.[36] In still other cases, it yields crucially important information about how and when the treatment works best; indeed, meta-analysis can reveal such interactions far more effectively than a single study.[37] This is perhaps most easily seen in medical research. "Meta-analysis gives you answers at a first level," says the eminent statistician Ingram Olkin.

> That level says, for instance, lumpectomy plus drugs is as effective as radical mastectomy. But that's only a general, overall statement. Now we have to go to a second level and find out if it is as effective for heavier women as for lighter women, for younger women as for older women, and so on. We have to go into what the medical people call subgroups and statisticians call covariates—other variables that affect the situation.

Among other covariates, in medical meta-analyses, are factors such as when and how a medication is used, as a recent discussion of the treatment of heart attack spells out:

> Meta-analysis should not be regarded simply as a "pooling process" of available trials that address a similar question. Specific questions (e.g., Do β-blockers, when started in the acute phase, reduce mortality after myocardial infarction?) are much more useful for patient care than broader ones (e.g., What are the pooled results of the available trials of β-blockers in ischemic heart disease?).[38]

Searching out such information is done by analyzing the relationships between moderator variables and effect sizes. Meta-analysts do this primarily by means of special statistical techniques that test variables to see how they are associated with differences in effect sizes from study to study. The standard methods of looking for such relationships—analysis of variance and multiple regression—are prone to certain kinds of error when used in meta-analysis, but techniques analogous to them have been developed by statisticians for meta-analytic use.[39]

Trying to Stay Sick in Order to Get Well

Not all successful meta-analyses examine hundreds or even scores of studies. One that was sufficiently meritorious to have been published in the *Journal of Counseling and Clinical Psychology* in 1989 was based on only ten studies. In turn, those studies contained a dozen data sets, all of which lent themselves to partial meta-analysis but only two of which were suitable for full meta-analysis.

The principal researcher was Varda Shoham*, then a postdoctoral fellow working with Robert Rosenthal at Harvard and now a professor at the University of Arizona. Shoham, a tall, dark, intense Israeli, had earned her doctorate in clinical psychology at Tel Aviv University in 1982, and by training and preference was a psychodynamic therapist. But during her internship in 1977–78 at the Mental Research Institute in Palo Alto, psychologists Paul Watzlawick and Carlos Sluzki introduced her to the bizarre, noninsight, short-term form of therapy known as paradoxical intervention, used by some therapists since the mid-1960s to treat a limited number of disturbing symptoms or conditions and reported by them to be highly effective with some patients.

What makes this technique bizarre is that in one way or another, the therapist encourages, praises, or prescribes the very behavior the client is seeking to change. Typically, the therapist will tell an insomniac to stay awake, a procrastinator to put things off, and a depressed person to stay depressed.[40] Remarkably, this often has the opposite effect and the client ceases to suffer from the symptom.

As improbable as the outcome seems, Shoham experienced it personally the first time she used it. She was treating a couple who chronically fought with each other, and she was supposed to tell them to go ahead and fight.

> But I felt that it was a form of trickery, and it went against all my training and values. I just couldn't do it. My supervisor, John Weakland, was watching through a one-way mirror, and finally he called me on the telephone and said, "Okay, don't do it"—and suddenly I was able to do it. His call had acted as paradoxical intervention with me! He told me it was all right for me to be unable to use paradoxical intervention— and that was just what made me able to use it.

This is only one of many ways in which paradoxical intervention can be applied. The therapist can tell the client to do just what the client wants to stop doing, or merely tell the client not to change; in either case, the therapist can directly prescribe the bothersome behavior ("Do this!") or can reframe the symptom as a good and useful thing. There are different explanations of why the method works. One is that the client's effort to continue having the problem redefines it in his mind as controllable behavior.

---

* At that time Shoham-Salomon.

Another is that the client resists and defies what he takes to be the therapist's attempt to control him. A third is that if the client cannot produce the symptom on demand, the problem is lessened, while if he can, he gains a sense of mastery; as Shoham and two colleagues titled an article they wrote on the subject, "You're Changed if You Do and Changed if You Don't."

Shoham, despite her experiences at Palo Alto, remained unconvinced, however, that paradoxical intervention was as effective as other forms of treatment and unsure it worked. In 1983, when she was a post-doctoral student at Harvard, she suggested a meta-analysis of the matter to Rosenthal, her mentor, who enthusiastically agreed to work with her on it. After the usual efforts to collect and screen studies, Shoham found herself with twelve usable sets of data, from which, with Rosenthal's help in data analysis, she and he were able to draw a number of worthwhile meta-analytic conclusions:

- Overall, paradoxical interventions were as effective as a large variety of other therapeutic procedures.
- The phenomenon was robust: The method worked as well in real clinical settings as in university research settings.
- A "positive" approach to paradoxical intervention (changing the meaning of the symptom) was more effective than the more commonly used "neutral" approach (telling the client to experiment by deliberately producing the unwanted symptom).
- Paradoxical interventions remained more effective a month after treatment than other treatments.
- Finally, and most interestingly, only two studies (an earlier one of Shoham's and one by Michael Ascher of Temple University) provided correlations between symptom severity and treatment effectiveness. Although Ascher's data were given in a raw form, Shoham and Rosenthal were able to use the data to compute correlations that could be compared with hers—and, in fact, turned out to be virtually identical. Using these two sets of findings, they performed a mini-meta-analysis; though it consisted of only two studies, it lent important strength to the conclusion that severe cases benefit more from paradoxical intervention than mild cases—a paradox piled upon a paradox.

The data on hand did not permit Shoham and Rosenthal to reach any firm conclusions about how and why paradoxical intervention works, but perhaps their most interesting finding was that paradoxical intervention does not *directly* change the patient's behavior; rather, it produces a change in the patient's situation—his perception of the meaning of the symptom, his feeling of resistance to being manipulated, or his sense of his own ability to produce the symptom. They hypothesized that one or more of these changes *mediates* the therapy; that is, these situational changes, resulting from the therapy, become the cause of behavioral change in the client. (Shoham later put this and other hypotheses to the test in further investigations, with confirming results.)

As Shoham and Rosenthal conclude:

> This small-scale meta-analysis is not designed to reach firm conclusions on the state of the field. Rather, its purpose is to provoke future research to ask more focused questions. . . . In addition to further study of resistance as a potential mediator and moderator for the operation of paradoxical interventions, the time is ripe for the study of other process variables that can provide more understanding of the way these frequently applied but little-understood interventions operate.[41]

Between Treatment and Effect: A Rube Goldberg View

Finding the average effects of any form of treatment is the primary goal of meta-analysis, but this reveals nothing about when, where, and how the treatment works.[42] For that vital information, researchers must turn to the analysis of moderator and mediator variables.

Moderator variables, as we have seen, may either accentuate or minimize the influence that the independent variable (treatment or intervention) exerts over the dependent variable (outcome). Mediator variables, though less obvious and less often studied, play a role that is just as significant, if not more so. They are *effects* of the independent variable which become *causes* of change in the dependent variable.[43] Shadish and a collaborator, Rebecca Sweeney, offer an example: A therapist treating a troubled couple may, because of his or her therapeutic technique (the independent variable), choose to assess how they communicate (the assessment is a first mediator) and decide to change some aspects of it (a second mediator); the result is an increase in their level of marital satisfaction.[44]

Most meta-analyses of psychotherapeutic outcomes hypothesize that there is a direct relationship between the therapeutic orientation (technique) and the outcome; this is a moderator-variable view of the matter. But Shadish and Sweeney argue that mediational models of the process are far more realistic and plausible. By "mediational models" they mean verbal or diagrammatic schemes showing how the several variables are linked. In a simple nonmediational model (see figure 2-2a), the variables are portrayed as boxes with arrows leading directly to the outcome (effect size); the strength of the connection between each vari-

Figure 2-2a   Model Without Mediating Variables

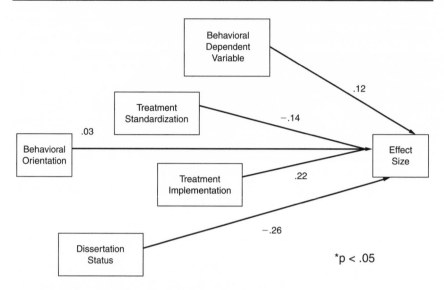

Figure 2-2b   Model with Mediating Variables

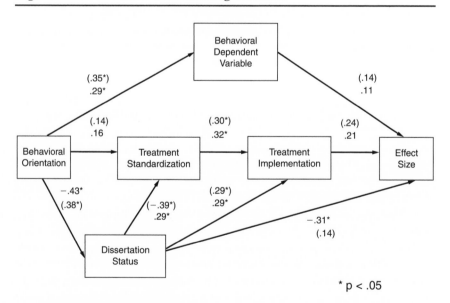

Source: Shadish and Sweeney (1991).

Note: Numbers next to arrows are path coefficients, a form of correlations that have been "partialled out" or computed with other variables held constant.

able and the outcome is a correlation derived by regression analysis and other methods.

In contrast, a "path model" is a sort of Rube Goldberg scheme showing how some variables influence other variables, then the latter influence still others, and those still others that eventually affect the outcome (see figure 2-2b).

Many scientists—social scientists in particular—are hesitant to call such correlational chains causal pathways. Too often they have seen correlations merely turn out to be co-occurring effects of some other cause. Even more confusing, a correlation does not always specify the direction in which the process is taking place; marital conflict, for instance, may be correlated with inability to communicate, but whether faulty communication produces conflict or conflict produces faulty communication is often unclear, and sometimes the process appears to be a reciprocal interaction—in common terms, a vicious circle. Nonetheless, path models are possible *explanations* of how the treatment is related to the effect; the crucial question is whether the explanation can be construed as a causal one.

The question is not only crucial but highly arguable. We will therefore return to the matter of explanations and causality in the next chapter.

Chapter 3

Clarifying Murky Issues in Education

Is it True That "Throwing Money at Schools" Does No Good?

Eric A. Hanushek, professor of economics and political science at the University of Rochester, had written technical studies on sundry public policy issues for fifteen years without making any great stir until, at age thirty-eight, he hit on a topic that made his name in the world of educational policy. In 1981, at the beginning of the Reagan administration, he wrote an article, "Throwing Money at Schools," published in the *Journal of Policy Analysis and Management*. In it, he maintained that although citizens' and teachers' groups constantly urge government bodies to increase school budgets, empirical studies show that more spending does not increase student achievement.

This startlingly counterintuitive finding was catnip to conservatives, who favored scaling back taxes, budgets, and government control over public processes. Hanushek soon became an expert witness for the defense at hearings and court cases brought by citizen groups against school boards they accused of miserly budgeting.

Having hit upon a good thing, Hanushek continued to research the issue and to lecture and write about it. In 1989, using data from 187 studies published in thirty-eight articles and books over the years, he wrote his most influential article yet, "The Impact of Differential Expenditures on School Performance," which appeared in *Educational Researcher*. Repeatedly stating that the available evidence fails to support conventional wisdom, Hanushek bluntly summed up his findings:

> Two decades of research into education production functions have produced startlingly consistent results: Variations in school expenditures are not systematically related to variations in student performance. . . . The concentration on expenditure difference in, for example, school finance court cases or legislative deliberations, appears misguided, given the evidence.[1]

Not surprisingly, Hanushek's notions distressed and angered parent groups, educators, and education policy-makers. One of the latter was Richard Laine, a tall, serious, mature-looking man in his late twenties who, (after serving as an aide to California's Democratic delegation to Congress), started graduate school in 1990 at the University of Chicago. Once in Chicago, Laine became involved with several school reform organizations and began working with them to increase funding for Illinois's public schools through legislative pressure and a lawsuit against the state.

From his graduate studies and work with the school reform organizations, Laine soon became aware that Hanushek exerted a major influence on school finance policies. "He had not only published influential articles stating that money does not matter," Laine told me, "but had been the expert witness for the state in many school finance lawsuits. He was the brick wall I kept running into. So I read his work, and my reaction was that at the gut level it just didn't make sense. But I needed a better statistical background to deal with it, so in the spring of 1992 I enrolled for a seminar with Larry Hedges on research synthesis."*

The dozen seminar students used as their textbook the page proofs of *The Handbook of Research Synthesis*, then in press, of which Hedges was a co-editor (with Harris Cooper). Within the first two weeks of the seminar Laine learned from the *Handbook* that meta-analysts view vote-counting, the method used by Hanushek, as simplistic and apt to produce wrong conclusions, and that the statistical techniques of meta-analysis were far more trustworthy and informative. Galvanized, Laine persuaded three friends in the seminar, Rob Greenwald, Bill McKersie, and Rochelle Gutierrez, to collaborate in a meta-analysis of Hanushek's data as their required course paper. Greenwald recalls Laine's compelling plea:

> Rich said, "Hanushek has been getting away with this for a long time. He's been saying money doesn't matter, and [Secretary of Education] Bill Bennett has been saying, 'Hanushek shows that money doesn't matter and don't throw more money down the drain.' But there's got to be something wrong with this idea; it doesn't make sense. Maybe meta-analysis can determine what the data really show." We were all friends, we'd all worked in groups with policy applications, and we were easily sold on the idea of coming in with Rich.

---

* "Research synthesis" is synonymous with "meta-analysis" as the latter term is used in this book. Hedges and some others, however, use meta-analysis to mean only the statistical, data-analyzing phase of the process.

First, however, they had to get Hedges' approval. "At one seminar session," Hedges told me, "when I asked the students what they planned to write about, Laine said that he, Greenwald, McKersie, and Gutierrez had read Hanushek's work, and Hanushek had used *vote-counting!*—and wasn't that a *terrible* thing to do, and wouldn't this be a great opportunity to carry out one of the first meta-analyses in education and see whether Hanushek's findings would hold up or not?" Hedges, youthful and fit in appearance but judicious and thoughtful in manner, expressed his concern that it would be too tough a job; he warned them that carrying out a meta-analysis was very difficult and that they had only ten weeks to do it. But Laine laid out the enticing challenge: In the 1989 article, Hanushek had written that of sixty-five studies for which per pupil expenditure figures were computable, thirteen showed a statistically significant positive relationship with pupil achievement, three a significant negative relationship, and forty-nine a nonsignificant relationship. From this vote-counting Hanushek had concluded, "There is no strong or systematic relationship between school expenditures and student performance."[2]

Hedges, who was not particularly familiar with Hanushek's work, was intrigued. "It was clear," he said, "that what Hanushek had done wasn't sound and that the four students were deeply interested in the substantive issue. So was I, as a professor of education. I asked them to write me a memo of their plans and advised them not to tackle all seven factors that Hanushek analyzed but to limit themselves to the single most important resource variable, 'per pupil expenditures.'"

What made it feasible for the team to attempt the project in the time allotted was that they would do only a fragment of a meta-analysis: They did not need to formulate the problem (it was implicit from the start) and, far more important, they did not have to conduct a literature search, since, as they said in their memo to Hedges,

> In order to do a research synthesis of high quality with the utmost reliability, it is necessary to undertake an exhaustive search of the literature in order to fully define the universe of research studies which can be synthesized. . . . Fortunately, this project's initial scope will focus on a limited and previously defined universe of studies . . . [those] used by Professor Eric Hanushek in his articles. . . . [Each was] 1) published in a book or refereed journal, 2) relates some objective measure of student output to characteristics of the family and schools attended, and 3) provides information about the statistical significance of estimated relationships.

To which they added, with a touch of hubris:

> While it is this group's belief that Hanushek's definition of his universe was adequate, we believe that the methodology he used to synthesize his universe was flawed. It is upon this premise that we are limiting our universe in this research synthesis project to that used by Professor Hanushek. It is our intention to replicate his work with more emphasis on the methodology of synthesizing the studies, rather than on achieving a preconceived conclusion.[3]

Of Universes and Their Boundaries

The term "universe"—some methodologists prefer "population"—has a special meaning to meta-analysts: It signifies the total body of studies of a subject about which the researchers wish to make generalizations.[4] But is it actually possible to assemble such a universe? Many studies are published in obscure journals or books and difficult to locate except by onerous, time-consuming processes. Others, never published, do not appear in indexes and exist only in file drawers, unknown to outsiders and virtually undiscoverable.

Even assuming all the relevant studies could be found, it might be a ruinous waste of time, energy, and money to collect them all for a meta-analysis. In surveys, polls, and many census studies, researchers rely on scientifically gathered samples, maintaining that a properly gathered sample represents the universe they are studying (within a known, narrow margin of error) and that one can therefore draw from it generalizations that can be validly applied to the universe. Frequently, however, it is not certain that a sample accurately represents the universe because its boundaries are vague; when that is the case, researchers can make generalizations from the sample only at a lower level of confidence.[5]

Not only for that reason but also because every sample involves the possibility of sampling error, some researchers prefer to try to collect everything relevant. Yet even if they more or less succeed in that aim, what they assemble is a *universe of studies* of a phenomenon, which may not be identical with the *universe of actual instances* of that phenomenon. If, for instance, a researcher collected all studies ever conducted of the outcome of psychotherapy with neurotics, would that universe of clients be identical with the universe of all neurotics? Surely not; the universe of studies deals with neurotics in treatment, and they may differ in some way from neurotics who do not seek or cannot obtain it. Further, the types of therapies, therapists, and clients who take part in research may be different from the entire universe of all therapies, therapists, and clients.

One solution to this difficulty is to define the universe of studies narrowly so that it is small, distinct, and more likely to be coterminous with the universe of reality it is said to represent. Hanushek had done so in his study, and Laine and his team accepted Hanushek's defined and bounded universe for their experimental meta-analysis.

Meta-analysts who conduct their own document search start by defining the boundaries of the universe they mean to meta-analyze. They may choose to include case histories in which subjects serve as their own controls, or to limit their universe to studies with separate control groups, or more narrowly to controlled studies in which subjects were randomly assigned either to treatment or control, or still more narrowly to studies meeting these conditions that were also published by a leading journal in the field.

But although such criteria can bound the universe, almost every universe grows the longer the meta-analysts press their search. Some years ago, William Stock, an educational psychologist and methodologist at Arizona State University, was asked by a gerontologist colleague to join him in a meta-analysis of a subject whose literature, he assured Stock, consisted of about ninety articles. Stock was willing but said they had better do a comprehensive search to make sure. The more widely and deeply they searched, the more studies they found; their search dragged on for years and eventually netted over eight hundred items.

Whether to sample or to try to collect the whole universe of studies is the question that bedevils meta-analysts. Some cannot rest until they have found everything; others consider completeness unnecessary and misguided. "Why are we trying to get all these data?" grumbled the Harvard statistician Frederick Mosteller at the 1986 National Research Council workshop on the future of meta-analysis. "Why shouldn't we have some statistical device that tells us when we've got enough? Or tells us we've got the core of it which is important?"[6]

Whatever meta-analysts decide, some basic rules must be followed. The search must be systematic to avoid gross errors due to biases of one sort or another. "Those planning to undertake meta-analyses," writes a research team in the *British Medical Journal*, "should not underestimate the difficulty or expense of performing a well conducted systematic review. There is no question that the choice of methods used for data collection is the key to the validity of such a review."[7]

The Nobel Laureate Linus Pauling claimed in his 1986 book *How to Live Longer and Feel Better* that vitamin C prevents colds and cited some thirty studies, nearly all of which reported that it does. But Pauling said nothing about how he had collected the studies; it was unclear whether his sample genuinely represented the universe of such studies or comprised those he found within easy reach. Paul Knipschild, a Dutch epidemiologist who was interested in the question, undertook a systematic search; he and several associates started with MEDLINE (the on-line medical data base), went on to other indexes, pored through textbooks, contacted researchers in the field, and visited special medical libraries. They gathered sixty-one studies (including Pauling's thirty), graded them according to methodological soundness, and discovered that five of the best fifteen had not been mentioned by Pauling. The fruits of this systematic search led them to a conclusion very different from Pauling's: "Vitamin C, even in gram quantities per day, cannot prevent a cold."[8] Knipschild's result may be disappointing, but it is almost certainly closer to the truth.

"Dollars and Sense: Reassessing Hanushek"

Returning to the reworking of Hanushek's research: Richard Laine and Rob Greenwald located Hanushek's thirty-eight sources in several university libraries, photocopied them, and divided up the copies among the four members of the team. The first task was to comb through the 187 studies encompassed in these sources, extract the information from which Hanushek had calculated the per pupil expenditures, and check his figures. The team members, having few clues as to how Hanushek had derived per pupil expenditures from such data as budgets and school enrollments, had to work out the calculations for themselves, an arduous chore. Their aim was to take nothing for granted but to replicate Hanushek's data extraction as closely as possible; in the end, their figures differed only minimally from Hanushek's.[9] Similarly, they also extracted pupil performance data from the studies.

Then, having both sides of the equation—money input and student achievement—they were ready to put Hanushek's findings to the test. Greenwald, a lean, clean-cut, highly charged young man, practically bounces out of his chair as he recalls the experience:

> We knew fairly early that combined significance testing would be the first leg. If Hanushek's conclusion, based on vote-counting, was correct, our conclusion, based on combined significance methodology, should be the same as his. That was the first question. But if our con-

clusion differed from Hanushek's—if we found that there *was* a significant relationship—this would lead to the second question: If there *are* effects, how big are they? Big enough to really count? Effect-size estimation would allow us to answer that question.

Laine had a computer at home into which he fed the per pupil expenditure figures and the pupil performance data the team had compiled. He was proficient in the spreadsheet program Lotus 1-2-3 and was able to compute the combined significance figures following a procedure given in *The Handbook of Research Synthesis*. His recollections:

> Once we had dumped all the data into the computer, the actual run was pretty quick. Almost as soon as we put the data in, calculated the p values, and started combining them, we could see that Hanushek's data didn't support his conclusions. With our meta-analytic methods, we were getting findings different from his and that really spurred us on. We worked day and night. Hanushek's stuff had been carrying a lot of weight, and it was exciting to see that using *his own* data and better methodology, we could rebut his argument that money doesn't matter.

Combining the p values showed that the overall relationship between PPE (per pupil expenditure) and pupil achievement was positive, and significant at the .05 level—that is, there was only a 5 percent likelihood that the result was due to chance and a 95 percent likelihood that increasing PPE does bring about an increase in pupil achievement.[10]

But how great an increase? That was the crucial question, since rebutting Hanushek would mean little if the effect was trivial. In the original studies the output variable, student achievement, was given in many different forms, so the team used the standard meta-analytic method introduced by Gene Glass in 1976 to standardize the different forms, converting them into units of standard deviation. As for the input variable, PPE, Hedges pointed out that the data were all given in dollars—and thus already standardized and usable as is.

When the data were digested by Laine's computer, the emerging effect sizes were dramatic: An increase of $100 spent per pupil per year (in 1989 dollars, the year of Hanushek's analysis) would raise pupil achievement by one-fifth of a standard deviation. Put another way, such an increase would reduce by almost half the number of students whose achievement was in the lowest tenth of all students.[11]

"We were amazed at the relationship between PPE and effect size," Greenwald says. "I was even afraid at times that people in the field would think we had cooked the books. We said to each other, 'We don't *believe* this!—yet this is what the data *say!*' We kept telling each other that Hanushek's data don't support his conclusions but exactly the opposite."

Armed with these results, the team drafted their paper, "Dollars and Sense: Reassessing Hanushek," each of the four students writing a section and editing the others' contributions. Making no effort to be tactful or diplomatic, they concluded,

> Falling victim to three of the main weaknesses of vote counting, Hanushek failed to identify an existing significant and positive effect between student performance and expenditure levels. . . . He stated that he did not believe that a more sophisticated analysis would alter his findings. Our preliminary meta-analysis shows that he was mistaken: three different meta-analytic techniques refute his central conclusion about the lack of a connection between expenditures and achievement.[12]

Apples and Oranges

Although Laine and his colleagues accepted Hanushek's universe as suitable for meta-analysis, a critic of the new methodology might scoff at their combining results from so diverse a collection of materials. Some of the studies in the sample dealt with single school districts, others with multiple districts; half were based on data from primary schools, half from secondary; most of the figures on student achievement were derived from students' individual scores but others from data aggregated at any one of three levels—the school, the district, or the state.

In short, the universe would seem to exemplify the "apples and oranges" criticism of meta-analysis: If you add apples and oranges and then average their weights, sizes, flavors, and shelf lives, you get meaningless figures. Eysenck, who is still attacking meta-analysis as vigorously today as in 1978, recently wrote, "Meta-analysis is only properly applicable if the data summarized are homogeneous—that is, treatment, patients, and end points must be similar or at least comparable. Yet often there is no evidence of any degree of such homogeneity and plenty of evidence to the contrary."[13] He added, using his favorite whipping boy, the Smith and Glass psychotherapy study, as an example: "The resolute search for some general effect for psychotherapy appears fruitless; the data used are too heterogeneous to be analyzed."

Gene Glass has impatiently dismissed such criticisms by saying it is a good thing to mix apples and oranges when we are trying to generalize about fruit.[14] (One might, for example, generalize that fruits are the results of pollinated ova, about where fruit seeds are located, how the edible parts attract creatures who will distribute the seeds, and so on.) Glass has also faulted the apples and oranges criticism for being at odds with the very nature of research:

> The claim that only studies which are the same in *all* respects can be compared is self-contradictory; there is no need to compare them since they would obviously have the same findings within statistical error. The only studies which need to be synthesized or aggregated are *different* studies. Generalizations will necessarily entail ignoring some distinctions that can be made among studies. Good generalizations will be arrived at by ignoring only those distinctions that make no important difference. But ignore we must; knowledge itself is possible only through the orderly discarding of information.[15]

It is when meta-analysts incautiously combine studies in which the differences in the raw data are very great that they may produce meaningless or misleading findings. Judith Hall and three co-authors of a chapter in *The Handbook of Research Synthesis* rebut the apples and oranges criticism but go on to warn:

> Synthesists must be sensitive to the problem of attempting aggregation of too diverse a sampling of operations and studies. Combining apples and oranges to understand something about fruit may make more sense than combining fruits and humans to understand something about organic matter. The synthesist must ask, "Does this level of generalization add to our explanation and understanding of a phenomenon?" Too diverse a sampling of studies could obscure useful relationships within subgroupings of the studies and not provide information at the level of the more abstract categorization.[16]

By paying attention to the narrative and qualitative aspects of individual studies, meta-analysis can avoid lumping together those that are excessively diverse. There are, moreover, precise ways of evaluating the diversity of any group of studies, the most common being a statistical tool known as "the homogeneity test." Before combining the effect sizes of a group of studies, the researcher checks their variability—how widely the effect sizes in the studies differ. The homogeneity test compares the variability in the effect sizes to the variability that would be expected if sampling error alone were responsible. In essence, the homogeneity test asks, "What are the chances that this much variation in effect sizes is due to sampling error?" If that probability is $p = .05$ or more, it becomes necessary to look for other factors—moderator and mediator variables—

that might account for the excess in variation. If such factors can be linked to the disparities in effect sizes, a combined effect size may be meaningless and misleading; the meta-analyst would do better to divide up the studies into subsamples and process each for a more meaningful meta-analytic finding.[17]

Apples and oranges are manageable; apples, raspberries, watermelons, kiwi fruit, seedless grapes, and strawberries generally are not.

Going Public Against Hanushek

As the seminar paper took shape, Laine and Greenwald began talking about a grander goal, a full-scale meta-analysis of Hanushek's work. (The other two students, preoccupied with work on their dissertations, dropped out of the project.) After Hedges read the paper, he encouraged Laine and Greenwald to go ahead with the larger effort and, when they asked whether he might join them, agreed to do so. It was a golden opportunity for them: two graduate students would be joined by an eminent professor in producing a controversial study with direct policy implications. For Hedges, it was a fine chance to apply his methodology to a critically important issue in education.

In a memo dated June 16, 1992, Hedges outlined for Laine and Greenwald the analyses they were to perform: They would do for each of Hanushek's seven variables what previously they had done only for per pupil expenditures. The project, he told them, had the potential to be important. This was no routine compliment; Hedges considered it so significant that he discussed it with Eric Wanner, president of the Russell Sage Foundation, which awarded him a $44,000 grant for salaries and expenses.

During the summer, the three worked separately, Laine in San Diego, Greenwald in Chicago, and Hedges in New York, and conferred regularly by phone. By fall, they had completed 90 percent of the coding, but what was left was the hardest part, requiring high-order statistical skills. Laine recollected,

> Larry was the driving force on methods. He had an amazing knowledge of how to pull the data we needed out of what was there but not obvious, and to fill in data where there were gaps. He could pull out standard deviations where we had different subcategories of kids but needed standard deviations by overall categories; for him, that was simple. Or he could show us in minutes how to extract standard deviations by separating different means from an aggregated mean.

Hanushek had investigated seven cost variables—per pupil expenditures, teacher-pupil ratio, teacher education, teacher experience, teacher salary, administrative inputs, and facilities—and by means of vote-counting found that only teacher experience had a possibly significant positive effect on pupil achievement, although even that was doubtful.[18] Hedges, Laine, and Greenwald would retest the relationships of all seven variables to pupil achievement by meta-analytic methods.

As the work got under way, they felt obliged to inform Hanushek of the project. Hedges wrote him that he, Laine, and Greenwald were attempting to duplicate Hanushek's table showing how many studies yielded statistically significant positive, negative, and nonsignificant relationships between each of the seven variables and pupil achievement: they also asked for his help in resolving a few discrepancies. Hanushek replied by letter and phone; he provided some help, but perhaps sensing trouble ahead asked Hedges to send him copies of their work sheets.

None were ready until late September, by which time exciting data were emerging from the computer. (The team, now meeting regularly in Hedges' office to review their results, were using a work station tied to a university mainframe equipped with high-powered statistical programs.) When they began assembling the data, Hedges alerted Hanushek to their progress and offered him the opportunity to criticize and correct their preliminary findings:

> We would like to carry out a "reanalysis" or a resynthesis of the studies that you have examined. One reason is that while vote count or box-score reviews of the type you did are certainly sensible, we do know that they can sometimes be misleading.
>
> Thus we were interested to see what might be found if a different statistical analysis strategy were used to summarize the results of the studies. We want to try two things: formal combined significance tests and some summary of an index of effect magnitude.

He then hinted at what was coming by adding that "very preliminary analyses on the relation between PPE and outcome seem interesting," that combined significance testing showed at least some positive relations and no negative ones, and that effect size analysis indicated "a typical effect that may be big enough to have practical significance."

Not unexpectedly, his letter and the accompanying preliminary draft of the article elicited a bristling reply. Hanushek objected to their analysis of his data on a number of highly technical grounds and was dismissive of the entire proceeding:

I realize there is a market for strong conclusions, but at least the exposition of your current draft seems to go beyond the evidence and data you describe. I presume that part of this is [due to] the exuberance of graduate students.

While you may be completely comfortable and confident that the results will hold up under full analysis, it seems that this draft piece is a bit premature. I personally think that you are putting out some potentially misleading conclusions that you would want to be very confident of before publishing.

The correspondence continued but led to only minor modifications of the article, and by May 1993, Hedges, Laine, and Greenwald crossed the academic Rubicon and submitted their article to *Educational Researcher*. After receiving the criticisms of peer reviewers, they revised it, and it was accepted and published in the April 1994 issue under the title, "Does Money Matter? A Meta-Analysis of Studies of the Effects of Differential School Inputs on Student Outcomes." The article reviewed Hanushek's work in detail, discussed the shortcomings of vote-counting, and presented the results of the meta-analysis of all seven factors, utilizing both combined significance tests and effect size analyses.

The findings of the combined significance tests flatly contradicted Hanushek's conclusions:

> [The] data imply that over all the studies, with the few exceptions noted above, there are at least some positive relations between each of the types of educational resources inputs studied and student outcome. . . .
>
> These analyses are persuasive in showing that, with the possible exception of facilities, there is evidence of statistically reliable relations between educational resource inputs and school outcomes, and that there is much more evidence of positive relations than of negative relations between resource inputs and outcomes.[19]

The article then turned to the effect size analysis. Not all of the seven factors were related to a positive effect on pupil achievement, but "taken together the effect size analyses suggest a pattern of substantially positive effects for global resource inputs (PPE) and for teacher experience." The effects of several other factors were usually, though not always, positive; that of class size was mixed; and one factor, teacher education, was mystifyingly correlated with lessened pupil achievement. Combining all the results, however, led to an unequivocal conclusion:

> This [overall effect] coefficient is large enough to be of considerable practical importance. It suggests that an increase of PPE by $500 (approximately 10% of the national average) would be associated with a

0.7 standard deviation increase in student outcome. By the standards of educational treatment interventions, this would be considered a large effect.[20]

In more familiar terms, students in a school that raised per pupil expenditure by $500 would enjoy a nearly 24 percent increase in achievement compared with similar students in a school that pursued no spending increase.[21]

For good measure, the article included the results of "robustness tests," or sensitivity analyses, of their findings. Such tests examine what happens to the results when potentially distorting or deceptive factors such as outliers—rare, extreme cases—are removed. If the results remain substantially the same, the findings are said to be robust or sound. Three such tests showed this to be the case. "No matter how you slice the data," says Hedges, "you get essentially the same answer."

For Hedges, publication of the article, though gratifying, meant only one more item in his long list of writings; for Laine and Greenwald, it was an epochal and thrilling event. Less thrilling, however, was Hanushek's reply in the next issue of *Educational Researcher* (the editors had sent him advance proofs and requested his reply). Hanushek said that Hedges, Laine, and Greenwald claimed their meta-analytic methods were "more sophisticated" than vote-counting but that "more sophisticated is not synonymous with correct." He called their interpretation of the data "absurd," "unwarranted," and "potentially very misleading when it comes to policy matters."[22] After finding fault with a number of their procedures, he summarily rejected their meta-analytic techniques as fancy terms of little substance:

> The couching of their analysis in technical phrases like "combined significance tests," "robustness testing," and "median half-standardized regression coefficients" gives the misleading impression that sophisticated statistical methodology has led to conclusive results, where the previous analysis did not. Such a conclusion is clearly wrong. . . .
>
> [Their] conclusion is, I believe, misleading and potentially damaging. . . . It would be very unfortunate if policy-makers were confused into believing that throwing money at schools is effective. More serious reform is required if we are to realize the full benefits of our schools.[23]

Hedges, Laine, and Greenwald had the last word, however, in the form of a brief "Reply to Hanushek." Rebutting each of his criticisms, they defended meta-analysis against his aspersions:

> Hanushek seems to question the validity of meta-analysis. We, and many other scientists, disagree. For example, a recent report of a com-

mittee of the Mathematical Sciences Board of the National Research Council (1992) concluded that "quantitative research synthesis—meta-analysis—has gained increasing use in recent years and rightly so. Meta-analysis offers a powerful set of tools for extracting information from a body of related research."[24]

Laine and Greenwald were all for thoroughly bashing Hanushek, but Hedges, with long years of academic experience, preferred a more politic approach and the "Reply to Hanushek" ended on a collegial and positive note:

> This interchange has moved the discussion forward. It has evolved from (a) the position that Hanushek's sample of studies show definitively that there is no relation between resources and outputs to (b) a discussion of how large the positive relations might be and of the characteristics of the studies that best reveal this relation. This strikes us as progress.[25]

Privately, they have other thoughts. Laine, at least, says candidly, "We felt that Hanushek knew there was a better method of analyzing the data but ignored it because it detracts from his message, it attacks his bread and butter. Recently, though, he's begun to modify what he says; now it's 'We need to focus on the ways in which money does matter.' But his previous work lives on in a lot of people's minds, and conservatives still say that money doesn't matter." Greenwald's feeling, based on meetings he has attended lately, is that the meta-analytic view is now widely accepted in the field. *Science*, the *New York Times*, *Phi Delta Kappan*, and *Education Week* have all paid major attention to the Hedges, Laine, and Greenwald analysis, and the *Journal of Education and Finance* devoted its entire summer 1994 issue to "Further Evidence on Why and How Money Matters in Education."

Hedges, Laine, and Greenwald, though they remain embroiled in controversy with Hanushek, have moved into a larger sphere of inquiry: They have adopted what Greenwald refers to enthusiastically as "the new universe"—a collection of studies far more extensive than Hanushek's—and have meta-analyzed it for the effects of educational inputs, including money, on pupil achievement. They believe this larger sample is more definitive, wide-ranging, and fine-grained than Hanushek's.[26]

What began as a seminar paper five years ago still has a claim on the time of all three co-authors and promises to for years to come. Most gratifying, perhaps, their work seems likely to play a significant part in the continuing struggle over the funding of public education in America.

IN BRIEF . . .

What Good Is Homework?

Is homework useful or a waste of time, good for students or harmful, an aid or an impediment to the learning process? Educators and the public have swung back and forth in their views of this matter in response to changing fads in education, historic events (the launching of Sputnik, for example), and other factors.

Surely, research can provide an answer. Indeed, it has provided a number of answers—which, however, contradict each other. "Reviews of homework research," writes Harris Cooper, professor of psychology at the University of Missouri, "give appraisals that generally fit the tenor of their times. Through selective attention and imprecise weighting of the evidence, research can be used to muster a case to back up any position."[27]

In 1986 Cooper, whose two young children were then entering school, saw this as a challenge that could be met by meta-analysis, about which he had been an enthusiast for over a decade. For some, meta-analysis is an acquired taste; for others, a case of love at first sight. Cooper, a lean, denim-clad, bearded man in his early forties, was instantly smitten by it when he was a postdoctoral fellow at Harvard. He had meant to become an experimental psychologist, but in 1975 his Harvard mentor, Robert Rosenthal, was writing a book on methodology and let Cooper read a draft copy of a chapter on combining the results of independent studies. Cooper says he was "tickled" by it, though "hooked" would be more accurate. In the two decades since then, although he has done a fair amount of social psychological research, more than half of his time has been devoted to teaching, writing, and editing books about meta-analysis. And of course, practicing it.

The meta-analysis he considers his best concerns the homework issue.[28] When this topic captured his attention, he secured a grant from the National Science Foundation, hired graduate students as assistants, and went at it full throttle. Defining the universe of studies very broadly, Cooper and his assistants did a huge on-line and library search, then slogged through the bibliographies of retrieved articles and books, hunting for other sources. And that was only the beginning. Cooper recalls,

> I had a feeling that in this area there might be a lot of unpublished material, so I wrote to fifty-odd state departments of education and to twenty deans of the most active educational research schools. I also

located an organization of research evaluation specialists in education, got the names of their members in 106 school districts, and wrote to all of them. I asked everyone I wrote to for recent doctoral dissertations or any other forms of research on homework—I requested copies, or abstracts, or mere citations, or whatever they could give me. Most of them helped to some degree, but the state departments were particularly good and sent me a lot of "fugitive literature"—surveys and reports meant for internal use that would never show up on any formal index.

I looked at about a thousand documents, read the 250 or so that were worth reading, and used the 120 that were empirical studies of whether or not homework works. The rest were either advocacy pieces or reviews of someone else's work or other stuff that wasn't useful for a meta-analysis. Many of the 120 were by teachers and some of these were very bad in terms of methodology, but I didn't exclude any on grounds of quality. I did, though, code their methodology carefully so I could find out later whether poor studies gave different effects than good studies and, if so, adjust for it. For the same reason, I used both controlled and uncontrolled studies but coded them so I could see later whether that made a difference in the reported effect size, and, if so, take it into account.

Cooper developed a number of hypotheses to be tested by meta-analytic methods. The most obvious was whether students given homework assignments got higher grades than students given none. Another was whether the amount of time spent on homework made a difference in student achievement. A third was whether there were any differences in the effectiveness of homework for boys and for girls.

Cooper's data analysis relied on two standard methods. He calculated average effect sizes—the difference in achievement between treatment and control groups or between two different treatments—and estimated 95 percent confidence levels for the findings. He also did a homogeneity test to be sure the samples were drawn from the same population.[29]

The meta-analysis decisively settled some long-debated issues. Students given homework assignments did better than those not given homework assignments by about one-fifth of a standard deviation; this signified that the average student doing homework outperformed about 60 percent of those students not doing homework. The amount of time spent on homework was even more important: Long assignments yielded almost four-tenths of a standard deviation of improvement over short assignments. Homework was equally beneficial for both sexes.[30]

All of this answered questions that had simmered in the education field for some time. But one finding that emerged from the meta-analysis was totally unanticipated:

> I had routinely called for cross-tabulations by grade level but never ex-
> pected what I found—that homework is very effective in high school
> but almost totally ineffective in elementary school. High school stu-
> dents doing homework average about one-half of a standard deviation
> higher in achievement than no-homework students, junior high stu-
> dents one-quarter higher, and elementary school students only about
> one-twentieth higher.[31] That was dramatic and absolutely unex-
> pected—a question nobody had ever asked, and a finding I came upon
> never expecting such a difference.

Nothing in Cooper's sources or meta-analysis indicates why such differences exist but, Cooper speculates, "I think it has to do with children's ability to teach themselves. Elementary school children haven't learned how to study, haven't learned how to learn on their own. High school students have. It's the mental capacity we call 'meta-cognition'— the awareness of our own thinking processes."

Cooper's meta-analysis appeared in short form in the journal *Educational Leadership* in November 1989 and in detailed form as a book, *Homework*. The article and book briefly hauled Cooper out of his quiet academic life and into the public arena: He appeared on the Larry King show, was interviewed by a dozen newspaper reporters and radio talk show hosts, and was quoted in various periodicals, including the *Wall Street Journal* and *Reader's Digest*.

Most important to him was the opportunity to recommend to educators a detailed homework policy based on his results; he set forth the specifics in *Homework* (1989) and in *The Battle over Homework* (1994). The most noteworthy concern his unanticipated finding regarding grade differences: He urged that although elementary school students be given homework, it should be short, use materials commonly found in the home, and lead to successful experiences; it should not be expected to improve test scores but merely to help children develop good study habits and positive attitudes toward school, and to acquire the idea that learning takes place at home as well as at school. Not until junior high school should the academic function of homework begin to emerge, and not until high school should homework serve as an extension of the classroom, requiring students independently to integrate skills or different parts of the curriculum.[32]

New Knowledge

As in Cooper's meta-analysis of homework studies, new knowledge, particularly in the form of findings not sought by the original studies, is a frequent product of the meta-analytic process. Sometimes this is due to the greater statistical power of the meta-analysis, as two examples illustrate:

- Meta-analyses of perinatal care have found, contrary to the accepted findings of small clinical studies, that routine episiotomy (surgical incision of the vulva during birth to enlarge the canal) was not generally beneficial, and have led to recommendations against it.[33]
- A number of small clinical trials reported that lidocaine was useful to control arrhythmias (dangerous irregularities in the heartbeat). When the trials were meta-analytically combined, however, it turned out that lidocaine actually increased the risk of mortality, at least in certain groups of patients.[34]

In these two cases, new knowledge came from combining studies, but it also, and perhaps more typically, comes from *comparing* different studies—that is, searching for the moderator and other variables (differences in the circumstances, personnel, methodology, and subjects of the studies) that might account for discrepancies among the findings. Such comparisons sometimes enable the meta-analyst to make inferences that "go well beyond the original results," according to *The Handbook of Research Synthesis*.[35] Harris Cooper and Larry Hedges, the editors of the *Handbook*, amplify the point: "Current methods . . . permit the testing of hypotheses that may never have been tested in primary studies. For yesterday's synthesist, the variation among studies was a nuisance; it clouded interpretation. For today's synthesist, variety is the spice of life."[36]

By comparing results *across* studies that look at the same phenomenon but that involve different methods, researchers, subjects, and other variables, the analyst can test new hypotheses. Betsy Jane Becker, an educational statistician at Michigan State University, sees this as even more exciting than what can be learned by combining studies. "What meta-analysis is really great for," she says, "is what Dick Light has called 'capitalizing on variation.' It's a way of looking at differences in studies and saying, 'Why are these studies different?' And understanding that really does give you the solution to the puzzle."

When studies of any given phenomenon vary considerably or actually contradict each other, meta-analysts will search first for errors and methodological flaws that might be to blame. But if important differences remain after they have been excluded, the meta-analysts try to identify the moderator and mediator variables that might be responsible. Statistical tests of subsamples show whether such a variable, present in some studies and not in others, plays a significant part.

An example of this type of meta-analytic "by-product" was briefly alluded to in the previous chapter. Alice Eagly and Linda Carli meta-analyzed 148 studies of the persuasibility and tendency to conform of men
and women in a variety of group situations. The meta-analysis confirmed the familiar findings of many primary studies that under group
pressure women are more easily influenced and more conformist than
men. Because there were inconsistencies across the three subgroups of
studies—those dealing with persuasion, with conformity under group
pressure, and with conformity not under group pressure—Eagly and
Carli looked for variables that might help explain them. To their surprise, the sex of the researcher turned out to be strikingly influential:
Male authors were much more likely to report that girls and women were
more easily influenced and more conformist under group pressure than
boys and men.[37]

Eagly and another colleague, Wendy Wood, then reanalyzed the
meta-analysis mentioned earlier in which Judith Hall reported that
women were better at decoding nonverbal cues than men. Again they
found that the sex of the researcher was an influential variable: Female
authors reported larger tendencies for women to be accurate at such decoding than did male authors.

In each case, therefore, Eagly and her collaborators made the unexpected finding that researchers tend to report effects that are flattering
to their own sex.[38] The finding does not mean that such studies are
worthless; rather, it provides a basis for adjusting the results to counter-
act gender-associated bias.

A quite different source of new knowledge in meta-analysis comes
from outlier studies—those with outcomes far higher or lower than the
majority. The usual attitude toward outliers is that they are pestiferous;
as an authoritative biostatistics textbook puts it, "Almost any collection
of data will be infested with outliers."[39] Even one or two extreme outliers can considerably affect the average of the sample, and if the unusual
effect sizes of the outliers are due to recording errors or other methodological flaws, they distort the central truth the meta-analysis would otherwise reveal. One way of dealing with them, therefore, is to excise them
from the sample.

But there is another possibility: "Careful examination of outliers,"
writes Frederic Wolf of the University of Michigan, an expert in medical
meta-analysis, "can provide important understandings and generate new
hypotheses that might otherwise be missed."[40] In a meta-analysis of
school data, for instance, one researcher focused on the outliers rather
than the main effect; by looking at the exceptionally successful schools,

he was able to discover certain features special to them.[41] In other cases, an outlier may have an unusual effect size because it combines certain moderator and/or mediator variables that together exert a special "interaction effect." If that combination of variables more often leads to the desired outcome than the individual variables working alone, the meta-analysis has produced new knowledge as to what works best, and why.

Sex and Science Achievement

To hear Becker talk about meta-analysis or to read her abstruse contributions to statistics, you would never suppose that in high school in the 1970s she opted out of chemistry and physics in favor of French and chorus and that she nearly managed to sidestep math—which turned out to be her main interest in life. (Her doctorate is in education, but her specialty is statistical methodology.)

Becker, a slim, pert woman who is forty but looks thirty, has recently spent time exploring those decisions in a meta-analysis of the differences between males and females in scientific achievement. In particular, it is commonly argued that while females have exactly the same cognitive capacities as males but are steered away from science by parents, teachers, and the male power structure of the sciences. Becker, however, suspected that opinion was seriously incomplete; had it been correct, she herself would never have become a statistician and meta-analyst. A more complete and objective view, she felt, should encompass the empirical evidence of the "predictors" of science achievement for both boys and girls. A full explanation of how girls and boys make their choices would take into account whether these predictors have the same influence on each sex. Do science-related aptitudes and attitudes impel girls toward scientific achievement as strongly as they do boys? Does persistence in taking science courses have the same impact on each sex? How important is the influence of socializers (parents, teachers, and others) on the scientific achievement of boys and of girls? And so on.[42]

Becker's opportunity to explore the matter came in 1986, when the Russell Sage Foundation invited her and a handful of other scholars to propose meta-analyses that would provide explanations, rather than just syntheses, of research issues.[43] She responded with a plan for using a path model of sex differences in science achievement. As she later wrote,

> One approach to the synthesis of studies predicting achievement and persistence in science might be to simply amass all available studies with

those variables as outcomes and to synthesize the existing results for each of the predictor-outcome relationships found in the literature. . . .

A second approach, used here, is to guide the synthesis by the use of conceptual and empirical models. The models were drawn from the literature on science achievement and the literature on social and psychological influences on the development of general achievement behaviors.[44]

The purpose of using a path model is to picture the successive stages or links in a complex process. The strength of the connections among the stages is indicated by correlations found by research; the net result is to suggest the causal chain of events leading to the outcome because often it is not possible to know which component in a correlation is cause and which is effect unless one of them clearly occurs first.

Becker used two theoretical models of science achievement that had been proposed by other social scientists, one a simple structure of four components with six interconnections, the other a complex structure of eleven components with eighteen interconnections. Her goal was to find out, by meta-analyzing relevant studies, how many of these suggested linkages were validated by correlations. To the extent that they were, she would have an evidence-based, rather than merely hypothetical, explanation of how boys and girls become scientific achievers.

With her grant, Becker hired a research assistant and collected 522 titles of interest, of which only thirty-two, containing thirty-eight studies, met her requirements. But those thirty-eight presented her with an alarming mass of possibilities: From their data on age, grade levels, achievement scores, aptitudes, self-image, socializing influences, and so on, she and her assistants—she now had four—extracted a daunting total of 446 correlations.

Through statistical legerdemain of various kinds, Becker combined these correlations into a relative handful. She found five that corresponded to and validated five links of the simple model, four that fit four links of the complex model. The simple model, with the correlations, is shown in figure 3-1.

The numbers in parentheses indicate confidence intervals, at the 95 percent confidence level, around the average correlations; those in the upper left corner, for instance, show that for boys the correlation between abilities and interest is fairly strong, lying somewhere between .36 and .42, and for girls somewhat less strong, lying between .24 and .31. For

Figure 3-1 Simple Path Model of Predictors of Male and Female
Scientific Achievement

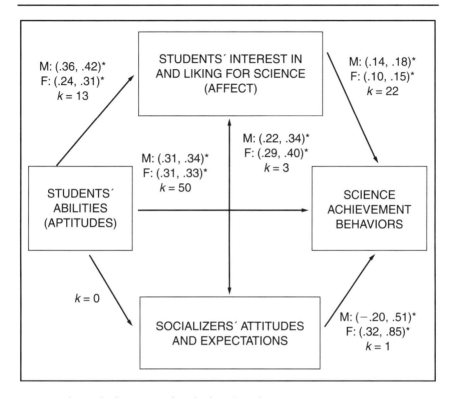

Source: Becker and others, in Cook and others (1992) p. 248.

Note: Asterisks represent sets of heterogeneous correlations. The number of correlations for
each sex is denoted as k. Correlations shown are significant at the 0.05 level.

girls, the correlation between abilities and actual achievement is stronger
(between .31 and .33)—and, intriguingly, virtually the same as that for
boys (between .31 and .34). As for the influence of socializers, the confidence intervals are extremely wide and hence the actual correlations are
hard to estimate, but the midpoints of the two intervals, which are at least
suggestive, are only .15 for boys but .58 for girls. The intricacies of the
complex model are beyond the scope of this book; for the curious, however, figure 3-2 shows it with the confidence intervals, at the 95 percent
confidence level, entered at the four links to which they apply.

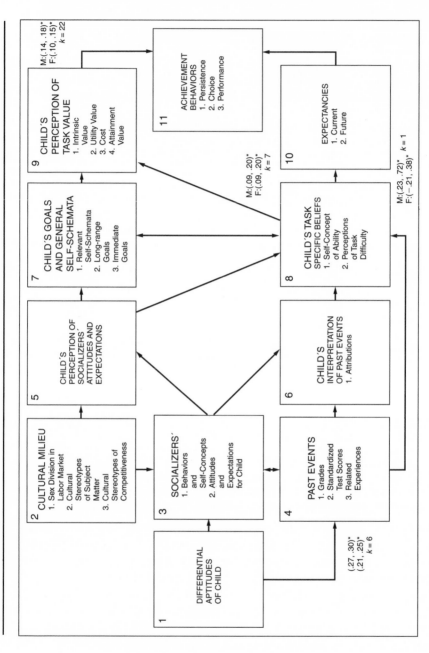

Figure 3-2 Complex Path Model of Predictors of Male and Female Scientific Achievement

Source: Becker and others, in Cook and others (1992) p. 249.

Note: Asterisks represent sets of heterogeneous correlations. The number of correlations for each sex is denoted as *k*. Correlations shown are significant at the 0.05 level.

The two path diagrams look esoteric but their message is actually plain and simple. Becker explains,

> So many people have said, "The real reason girls don't do better is because they don't get encouraged by other people"—or "The real reason is that they just don't like science"—or "The real reason is peer pressure." But all these things aside, it still is the case, and both models show it clearly, that ability is a strong predictor of achievement for both girls and boys.
>
> Interestingly, liking for science is only weakly related to later achievement for both sexes. And it's striking and surprising that, although the levels of importance of the variables differ between boys and girls, the results are really fairly similar.
>
> What's far more surprising is one of the main findings that shows up in part on the complex model, namely, that previous achievements in science are a major predictor of later achievements. Now, that sounds boring, but it is really a strong result, much more so than many others. If kids haven't dropped out of science by high school, then what they did before does predict pretty well what they do later; success in elementary school science projects is as likely to lead to success in science in later grades and in life for girls as for boys.
>
> One "nonfinding" that I consider important is that in the complex model, which has eighteen paths from one component to another, less than half have been studied. Meta-analysis can show what you don't know as well as what you do know. We learned a lot from this study about what we don't know and should be researching in the future.

Despite its limitations, how much does her meta-analysis contribute to a causal explanation of science achievement in boys and girls? Becker's answer:

> I'm much more cautious than many people want me to be. I say things in a very cautious way. Where there's a statistical relationship in the model, I don't say A causes B, I prefer to say that you can make a causal inference with a particular degree of certainty—95 percent confidence for those data shown. And there were a number of other correlations below that level that I didn't put in but that do seem to support the complex model.
>
> I think a correlation analysis is always going to be an approximation of a causal inference. All you'll get out of it will be the probability of a causal connection. Still, if I didn't believe there was some hope of making an inference about A predicting B, I wouldn't be doing it at all.

The Bugaboo of Causality

Becker's wariness about claiming she had established causal connections is not unusual. Only in the physical and biological sciences, where it is often possible to specify the total set of circumstances that inevitably produce a particular event, does the term "cause" have the same meaning for scientists that it does in everyday thought and speech. To quote the advisory committee of *Meta-Analysis for Explanation: A Casebook*,

> Theories of the structure and function of DNA aspire to [causal explanations], as does natural selection theory and quantum mechanics. Such explanations are likely to be reductionistic, to approach full prediction of a particular event or relationship, and they usually provide powerful clues about what to manipulate in order to bring about a particular end. . . .
>
> Few explanatory analyses in the social sciences involve causal forces as generalizable, well-substantiated, predictive in their consequences, and flexible in their cross-situational transfer as some in the physical and natural sciences.[45]

The reason, as mentioned earlier, is that events in the social sciences almost always involve multiple and interacting variables, and the evidence of a connection between any one of them and the effect is usually relatively weak compared to evidence in the hard sciences. Typically, a large change in an independent variable, A, is accompanied by only a small change in the dependent variable, B. That being so, can one hypothesize that A is the cause (or a cause) of B? Not always, not often; A and B might be simultaneous effects of some other cause. Fever and coughing, for example, are highly correlated in influenza cases, but neither causes the other; both are effects of the disease.*

Still, if a B *always* occurs after an A has occurred but *never* occurs without A, we can feel somewhat more certain that A is part of what makes B happen—but, in the social sciences, only part. The behavior of human beings is multiply determined by complex forces; a truly causal explanation of a behavior involves the entire web of influences, past and present, without which B would not follow A.[46]

In consequence, in recent decades many social scientists have avoided "cause" and "causality," preferring to use the mushier but more defensible terms "correlation," "covariation," and the like. Instead of saying "A causes B," they have guardedly said, "A is positively correlated with B," or, if the two are correlated and A always occurs first, "If A occurs, then B is likely to occur." These are far weaker statements than, say, "Raising the temperature of pure water at normal sea-level barometric pressure to 100° C. causes it to boil."

---

*An additional problem in much social science research is that researchers cannot randomly assign subjects to the experimental and control conditions; to be sure, they can do so in laboratory experiments, but in much real world research, such as the education studies summarized by Hanushek and meta-analyzed by Hedges, Laine, and Greenwald, it is possible only to compare apparently similar—but not rigorously controlled—groups that potentially differ in ways other than the treatment variables.

But the semantic pussyfooting of social scientists is on the wane as they become increasingly able to explain events in specific detail. The change is easy to see in psychology: When researchers knew that the administration of a particular psychotropic drug was followed by a change in mood but had no notion of the mechanism involved, it made sense to describe the process in terms of correlation but not causation. Today, they know that the drug plugs up certain receptors in the brain's synaptic gaps, preventing a particular neurotransmitter from being rapidly absorbed and destroyed, and consequently they can give a causal explanation of the change in the individual's mood.

In the social sciences, path models are being used more and more to picture probable causal sequences. In meta-analysis such modeling is assuming a new importance, partly because it is now more widely used in primary research and partly because meta-analysts are becoming more interested in explaining processes rather than merely identifying general patterns and central tendencies.[47]

Still, some meta-analysts think it wise to continue minimizing any unequivocal claim to causality. Thomas Cook, for instance, distinguishes between "descriptive causal models" and "explanatory causal models." He illustrated the distinction for me as follows:

> In a descriptive causal model, I say: "If I turn the light switch, the light goes on." In an explanatory causal model, I talk about the wiring plan, the science of the flow of molecules and electrons, and so on. In many a meta-analysis we have a reliable, useful, causal description but without any causal explanation. I think that path models have a heuristic value but often seduce the reader and scholar into giving them more weight than they deserve.

Not all meta-analysts tiptoe as carefully over this thin ice; William Shadish, for one, tramps across it, boldly asserting that causal explanations are the ultimate and rightful goal of meta-analysis:

> Is it really any secret that we are interested in causal inferences in meta-analysis? After all, we are exploring orientation effects because we want to know if, say, behavior therapy causes better patient outcome than systemic therapy. . . . Multiple-equation models and latent variable models, in principle at least, can increase the explanatory power of meta-analyses by allowing models that more realistically reflect the processes that may have generated study data.[48]

Similarly, Joseph Durlak of Loyola University and Mark Lipsey of Vanderbilt University write in their "Practitioner's Guide to Meta-Analysis" that meta-analysis has been primarily descriptive but can be explanatory:

Meta-analysis becomes explanatory rather than descriptive when it begins to integrate evidence on multiple, interconnected relationships rather than focusing on a single key relationship. . . . [It] can be used effectively to summarize evidence on the effects of a social intervention. But the outcome of such an intervention can be thought of as the end result of a causal chain that involves a series of intermediate interactions among environmental, participant, and change agent variables.[49]

By using such models to identify and measure the parts played by treatment, moderator variables, and mediator variables, meta-analysts not only advance theory but furnish the kind of practical, detailed information that enables the healers of personal and social ills to do their work more knowledgeably and effectively.

Chapter 4

"Who Shall Decide, When Doctors Disagree?"*

Too Many Studies, Too Few Answers

Dr. Thomas Chalmers had a serious problem. As associate director for clinical care at the National Institutes of Health in the early 1970s, it was incumbent on him to stay fully informed of the latest research in medicine, but he could neither keep up with the increasing flood of clinical reports—more than a thousand were being published yearly in English-language journals alone—nor reconcile the dissimilar findings that were emerging on nearly every topic.

Chalmers, in his mid-fifties at that time, was not one to suffer such difficulties passively. Tall, lean, and patrician of feature, he was a restless, tightly strung workaholic (as he still was in his late seventies when I visited him) driven by a need to *know*—to know the realities of medicine—with certainty or near-certainty. (I was able to meet with him before his death in December 1995.) He recalled for me, often pacing around his office like a caged tiger, the roundabout route by which he met this problem and solved it:

> I trained in internal medicine and practiced for about five years in Boston until I felt I was making too many mistakes—all because the information I was looking at in the journals and textbooks was inaccurate. I decided I couldn't be an expert in all fields, so I became one in gastroenterology until I realized I was prescribing therapy without having anything to base it on because there were no good clinical trials. So I quit practice and started devoting myself to doing clinical trials, first at the Shattuck Hospital in Boston, and later at the V. A. and the National Institutes of Health in Washington.

Having worked earlier on a research project with William Reynolds, a biostatistician, Chalmers had been converted to and become a tireless

* By "doctors" Alexander Pope meant scholars, but I borrow his line to express the basic quandry of modern medicine.

proselytizer for the use of controls, randomization, and statistical analysis in the clinical trials of medical procedures. His incisive letters on these issues to journal editors and his pointed questioning of speakers at seminars earned him the reputation of gadfly, which he rather liked. Over the years he conducted or took part in scores of randomized controlled trials on a broad range of important subjects, including liver disease, iron deficiency, lung cancer, and gastric ulcers. His phenomenal production of ten or more research papers a year—"I have no hobbies," he told me, "my work is my hobby"—enabled him, despite his acerbic criticisms of medical education and research methods, to move steadily upward in top medical schools, the Veterans Administration, and the National Institutes of Health, and in 1973 to become president of the Mount Sinai Medical Center in New York and dean of its medical school.

It was during his stint at the National Institutes of Health that Chalmers, striving to stay abreast of the growing torrent of research studies and to make sense of the discrepancies among them, had an idea that changed his life and that would eventually help other physicians to cope with the information explosion. As he described it in a recent minibiography:

> Just as I was beginning to suffer from "input overload," I discovered that the medical literature was full of studies with data crying to be put together to make more sense of an issue than each article could as a stand-alone. This was especially true in the clinical-trials field, where the importance of the type II error (concluding that there is no difference between the effects being studied when there really is, frequently because the study sample is too small) was seldom recognized.[1]

But how to put studies together? Knowing nothing of Tippett's and later statisticians' work in pooling the findings of agricultural and other studies, Chalmers set out to increase his limited knowledge of statistics enough to devise a stratagem for combining clinical trials. Having done so, by 1977 he and several associates completed what one authority calls "the first major meta-analysis in clinical medicine"—a summing up of findings on the clinical use of anticoagulants—and within the next several years several more of other medical issues.[2]

Chalmers remained unaware that a similar methodology was being used in other fields. When the president of the Evaluation Research Society phoned to tell him he had won its 1982 annual research award for his meta-analyses, Chalmers, puzzled, asked, "What are those?" and only then learned that his statistical innovation was part of a notable development taking place in a number of sciences. In 1983, he left Mount Sinai and moved to Boston to work with the renowned statistician Frederick Mosteller of the Harvard School of Public Health and to become a visiting professor there. He thereafter occupied himself full time with medical meta-analyses and, with various co-authors, completed dozens of them on a variety of topics.

One, published in 1992, is of special interest: it led to the writing of what Dr. Iain Chalmers (a friend but no relative), director of the UK Cochrane Centre, an institute that conducts medical meta-analyses, has called "one of the most important papers ever to have been published in a medical journal."[3] The story behind that paper is worth hearing, and we will do so shortly, but first a brief digression.

Second and Other Opinions—and Combined Opinions

In contrast to the complex, fuzzy questions posed to meta-analysis by the social sciences, those put to it by medicine are usually more sharply focused and amenable to precise answers.[4] Does treatment A cure the disease faster than treatment B, and if so, how much faster? Does treatment C have a lower mortality rate than treatment D, and if so, how much lower?

One might suppose that primary clinical trials would answer such specific questions and that meta-analysis adds little value to clinical research. But most trials are small in scale and, as mentioned earlier, the smaller the sample, the greater the likelihood that the result is due to, or distorted by, sampling error. At the $p < .05$ significance level, there is at most a one-in-twenty likelihood that the effect of a treatment is due to chance, but possible sampling error makes the *size* of the effect uncertain; it might lie anywhere within a range of values—the confidence interval— ranging from a clinically important effect to a clinically unimportant one. As a result, in a small trial researchers may be unable to say with certainty, or even to recognize, that a beneficial effect exists.[5] And even if the results are clearly significant, those of small clinical trials often differ so widely— sometimes actually contradicting each other—that physicians are unsure what to believe about a new treatment and, mindful of the Hippocratic maxim "At least, do no harm," are slow to use it.

Between 1969 and 1983, for instance, eleven of fifteen clinical studies of the prophylactic use of antibiotics before colorectal surgery found that it reduced mortality, but one reported that it made no difference and three others that it actually increased the mortality rate.[6] A surgeon or gastroenterologist could hardly be blamed for ordering only the usual bowel-cleansing methods before surgery and not dosing patients in advance with antibiotics.

Again: Between 1981 and 1989, thirty-five studies compared the mortality rate when bleeding peptic ulcers were treated by surgery with that of a newer method, endoscopy, in which the physician treats the bleeding area using a hollow tube passed down the esophagus. Most of the studies reported lower mortality from endoscopy than from conventional treatment, including surgery, but seven studies muddied the waters by finding the very opposite; in any case, only two of the thirty-five studies were statistically significant.[7]

In both instances, the solution, obvious now but not twenty years ago, was to combine the results of such studies. A meta-analysis in which Thomas Chalmers took part showed that when the inconsistent and confusing findings of twenty-six clinical trials of preparation for colorectal surgery were statistically combined, it became quite clear that antibiotic prophylaxis saved lives: the death rate among patients not getting preparatory prophylaxis was 11.2 percent, among those getting it, 4.5 percent. In another meta-analysis conceived by Chalmers, when twenty-five clinical trials comparing endoscopic treatment of bleeding peptic ulcers with conventional treatment, including emergency surgery, were combined, it turned out that the death rate from endoscopy was 30 percent lower than that from conventional treatment.[8]

It is important to note that effect size is often measured differently in medical research than in the social sciences. We have already seen two ways of expressing an effect size. Correlation coefficients can be used when the two variables in a relationship are continuous (each can assume any value within a given range, as in the case, for instance, with class size or with student achievement). The d-index, Glass's effect size, can be used when one variable is dichotomous, consisting of two groups, such as clients receiving two different kinds of psychotherapy, and the other variable is continuous, such as the number of days the client was absent from work.

A third possibility, used most often in medical studies, is one in which both variables are dichotomous, such as a comparison of two different treatments of cancer and two different outcomes—survival after five years and death within five years. For such studies, statisticians have developed a metric known as "odds ratio" (or, in other versions, "risk ratio") to describe the relation between the variables.

Here, for example, are the results of a hypothetical trial comparing surgery and radiation, in cancer patients, in terms of five-year survival data:

	Surgery	Radiation
Alive after five years	75%	60%
Not alive after five years	25%	40%

For surgery, the odds of five-year survival are 75:25, or 3 to 1; for radiation, 60:40, or 1.5 to 1. To compare the effectiveness of the two treatments, we create a single number that compares the odds of one to the odds of the other; we do so by simply forming a ratio of the odds—in this case, surgery, three to one, over radiation, 1.5 to one. The odds ratio is two; the chance of five-year survival is twice as good for surgery as for radiation. Thus, an odds ratio of one would mean that the two treatments being compared are equally effective; an odds ratio greater than one, that the treatment in the numerator is more so; and an odds ratio smaller than one, that the treatment in the denominator is more so. Of course, research results are rarely as simple as in this example. Accordingly, meta-analysts have to adjust odds ratios, weighting them for different sample sizes (so that large trials count for more than small ones) and other factors before combining them. Some meta-analysts also weight the effect sizes according to the quality of the study, but this process is highly controversial and shunned by many. The issue, however, is simple: Should researchers use data only from high-quality studies or include the data of poorly designed studies, and if they include the latter, should the poor ones count for less? The easy answer is to use only high-quality studies, thus protecting one's work from the charge mentioned earlier that meta-analysis is "garbage in, garbage out." The greater challenge is to include poor studies but give them less weight, the rationale being that, although their results are less likely to be accurate, they may add valuable information and any distortions can be statistically corrected. A common way to weight for quality is to give every study points for each of several characteristics: Were the subjects properly assigned to treatment and control by randomization? Were the researchers "blind" (unaware of who was getting treatment and who placebo)? Were they blind as to what any dropouts had been getting? Were the details recorded adequately enough to ensure that the data being combined were truly comparable?[9] And so on.

Meta-analysts take sides on weighting for quality. Gene Glass, in his historic 1976 address introducing the concept of meta-analysis, said he had found no difference between the effect sizes of high-quality and low-quality studies of psychotherapy outcomes, and so included them all.[10] A 1990 study by the Technology Assessment Group of the Harvard School of Public Health examined seven meta-analyses that used quality scoring and concluded, "We found no relation between treatment difference and overall quality score."[11] Frederick Mosteller's tart opinion: "We do not have any theory that justifies weighting studies by their quality score." On the opposite side, there is evidence, according to some meta-analysts, that well-controlled studies have smaller effect sizes than poorly controlled or uncontrolled studies—one authority acidly says that "results can always be improved by omitting controls"—and according to others that randomized experiments have larger effect sizes than nonrandomized experiments.[12]

Recognizing that meta-analysis is still suffering growing pains, most practitioners remain confident that the quality issue will be resolved sooner or later. Let us leave the matter there to continue with Chalmers' story.

The Streptokinase Case

The article so highly praised by Iain Chalmers was based on several previous meta-analyses by Thomas Chalmers and others, particularly the 1992 meta-analysis alluded to above. To appreciate the article's importance, we must first hear the story of that meta-analysis, which combined a group of clinical trials of the treatment of acute myocardial infarction (AMI)—heart attack due to blood clots—by various therapies, including the use of streptokinase, an enzyme that dissolves clots.

In recent decades, medical researchers have conducted clinical trials of at least fifteen different treatments of AMI, one of them being the intravenous administration of streptokinase. Between 1959 and the early 1980s researchers in several countries conducted over two dozen randomized controlled trials of streptokinase treatment, comparing its results with those of placebo or no treatment, and within the next few years several meta-analyses of these trials were performed. Two of the more important meta-analyses were by researchers at the Radcliffe Infirmary, at Oxford University, and another was by Chalmers and others at the Mount Sinai School of Medicine. Although the results of the individual clinical trials had been contradictory and unreliable, all three meta-analyses found that when the trials were combined, they showed that clot-dissolving agents almost certainly reduced the risk of death by a considerable margin (22 percent in one of the meta-analyses, somewhat less in the other two).[13]

The impact of this information on medical practice was, disappointingly, almost nil. To Chalmers it was an old story; for years he had been exasperated at seeing meta-analyses overlooked by the experts in the field whose views shaped the practice of most physicians. The streptokinase case struck him as a particularly deplorable instance of the medical establishment's rigidity when presented with a new and superior, but different, approach to knowledge. "It was discouraging that physicians were not paying attention to meta-analyses as they should," he told me. "Streptokinase was the classic example. The meta-analyses showed clearly that the effect on mortality was statistically significant, but the experts in cardiology and the textbook authors whose opinions dominated the field weren't even beginning to recommend it until the late 1980s, and then only little by little."

Chalmers had known for some time that meta-analysis could show that a new treatment was valuable long before the mounting weight of many clinical trials led experts to recommend it. "At Mount Sinai," he said, "Henry Sacks and I got a couple of medical students to help us do the meta-analysis on the prevention of infection among patients undergoing colorectal surgery. When they got the papers together and we went over them and combined them, we discovered that, my God!, this has been statistically significant for ten years!"

At some point it occurred to Chalmers that if he were to arrange clinical studies in the sequence in which they had been performed and do a meta-analysis of the first two, then of the first three, then of the first four, and so on, he could discover the earliest point at which enough trials had been conducted to yield a statistically significant meta-analytic result. He told me that he thought the idea of this procedure, which he later named "cumulative meta-analysis," might have come up in discussions with Sacks and the medical students at Mount Sinai. He went no further with it for some years, however, because carrying out such a series of meta-analyses, with the technology then available, would have been extremely onerous and time-consuming.

It was therefore a happy accident that in 1988, when Chalmers held the post of Distinguished Physician at the Boston Veterans Administration Hospital, he met Joseph Lau, an internist and researcher on the staff. Lau, then thirty-eight, a scholarly looking man with owlish glasses and a dark forelock flopping over his forehead, had been born in Hong Kong, raised in New York, and had earned a medical degree at Tufts. Since then he had been engaged primarily in research on clinical decision-making and the use of computers in medical research. What he heard from Chalmers about meta-analysis appealed to him and they began to work together, Lau's computer skills being his chief contribution to the partnership. Lau conveyed the nature of his work to me as follows:

> Initially, I didn't know much about meta-analysis, but one of the first things I noticed when I began to work with Tom Chalmers was the lack of computer software to do meta-analysis efficiently. The existing programs for combining clinical trial data were primitive and inadequate. So I set out to write my own meta-analysis computer program.

While I was working on it, the subject of cumulative meta-analysis came up in my discussions with Tom. Traditionally, when you want to perform a meta-analysis, you look for all the studies that have been published and combine the results and get one answer. But with the program I was writing, you could do it in a cumulative way—you could collect all the papers, but begin by looking at the impact of the second trial on the first one and get an answer, then the impact of the third one on those first two and get another answer, and so forth. Each time, you add one more study to those you have already pooled, so you get a kind of running total, a summary of all studies up to any given point in time. This gives you trends as well as the cumulative evidence up to the point at which it becomes strong enough to be statistically significant.

Chalmers, who had not been wholly satisfied with the existing meta-analyses of trials of myocardial infarction treatments (including his own), decided to conduct a new one with Lau's help, using the cumulative method to see how early a meta-analysis could have provided a strongly significant finding of treatment effect.

Lau, working in a tiny office jam-packed with files and materials at the V. A. Hospital, did the search for titles and collected copies of the papers. He gathered 268 randomized clinical trials of treatments of myocardial infarction, each comparing a treated group to a control group, that had been conducted between 1959 and 1988, and most of which had been included in previous meta-analyses.[14] Instead of relying on the data extractions of those meta-analyses, Lau redid the process on all 268 trials, a monumental chore that took him much of the two thousand hours he spent on the project.

Fortunately, the most critical piece of data to be extracted, the measure of outcome, was simple and unambiguous: the mortality rates within specified periods after the heart attack. As Chalmers, Lau, and their four co-authors later forthrightly put it, death is not only a reported datum in almost all studies but a "reliable" one.

The papers that Lau processed all met the guidelines set by Chalmers: All were randomized, had control groups, and compared treated patients both to the controls and to patients getting a placebo. These were the only criteria for inclusion; Lau had excluded no studies on the basis of other issues of quality, for Chalmers was dead-set against using only high-quality trials in meta-analyses. "Anything like screening out on the basis of quality is subject to bias," he told me. "It's all too easy to think that a study that disagrees with your own conclusions is lousy and that one that agrees with your views is good." Chalmers did believe in rating studies for quality in order to weight their data, but he had assistants "blind" the papers before evaluators rated them, deleting all clues to quality—author's name, journal title, date, and the like that might unconsciously influence them. After the studies had been ranked, Chalmers would experimentally lop off the poorest; if this made little or no difference in statistical significance, there was no problem; if it did, he would retain all the studies and undertake more detailed analyses.

By 1990, the data were ready, and so was the software; Lau had completed writing his program, "Meta-Analyst," into which he had built seven ways of combining the data. Entering the data of the 268 trials into the computer was tedious and time-consuming, but performing the meta-analytic computations took about five seconds; Lau's 486 desk-top computer—not at all fast by current standards—could do in that brief time what it had taken the mainframe used by Gene Glass and Mary Lee Smith hours to do.

The results were all Chalmers and Lau could have hoped for, in particular the meta-analysis of a subset of thirty-three trials of intravenous streptokinase. Figure 4-1, adapted from the published report of the meta-analysis, tells the story.

Lau interpreted the graphs for me when I visited him in the spacious office he now occupies as a member of the research staff of the New England Medical Center:

> The graph on the left shows the individual analyses of the trials of intravenous streptokinase, the thirty-three placebo-controlled studies published from 1959 to 1988. The line down the middle, where the odds ratio is one, divides the trials into those favoring treatment and those favoring control. A black dot—the odds ratio—on the left side of the midline means that in that study, fewer people treated with streptokinase died than did in the control group. A black dot on the right side means that in that study, fewer people in the control group died than people treated with streptokinase.
>
> Even though most of the dots are on the left side of the line, most of those results could be due to random variation. The horizontal lines in each case—the confidence intervals—represent the range of possibilities at the 95 percent confidence level. So in the first study in 1959, where you see the line extending to both sides of the odds ratio midline of one, the study is not statistically significant and would be reported as not showing any benefit from streptokinase. The same for the next two. But the fourth one down, "European 2," has a confidence interval entirely to the left of the line, so the finding of that one is statistically significant.
>
> Yet even after that, there are more studies again with results on the other side, favoring control, but not statistically significant. This flip-

Figure 4-1 Conventional and Cumulative Meta-Analyses of Thirty-three Trials of Intravenous Streptokinase for Acute Myocardial Infarction

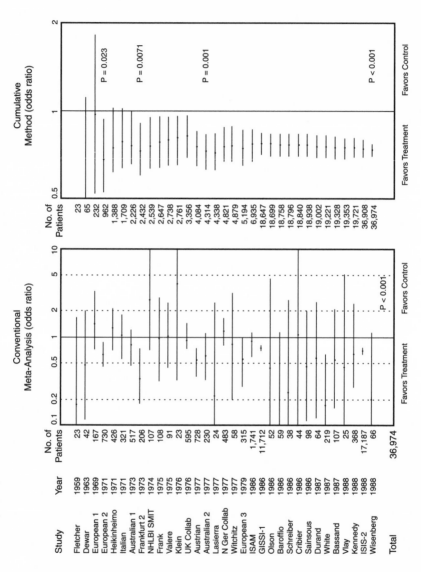

Source: Lau and others (1992).

Note: The odds ratios and 95 percent confidence intervals for an effect of treatment on mortality are shown on a logarithmic scale.

flopping would be confusing to doctors; they'd wonder if the treatment was really effective or not. And this continues, with only three statistically significant studies before the two big ones in 1986 and 1988 that finally convinced the medical world and the FDA [Food and Drug Administration] that this drug is effective.

Our meta-analysis of those thirty-three trials gave us the result you see at the bottom, where it says "total" and shows a result definitely favoring streptokinase—with p smaller than 0.001. But now look at the graph on the right side, which shows what we got when we did cumulative meta-analyses of the same trials one by one. By 1973, the seventh cumulative analysis—with a total of only eight trials and 2,432 patients—finds a statistically significant effect. That early, there was at least a 97.5 percent chance that the treatment reduced mortality, and at least a 50 percent chance that it did so by 20 percent or better.

By 1977, after trials involving 4,084 patients, the results were even more definite: The probability that the treatment was effective was greater than 99.5 percent, and the probability was 97.5 percent that it reduced mortality by about 10 percent.[15] Most important, these early findings were remarkably close to those of the two massive trials of 1986 and 1988, and to the net result of all thirty-three trials.

Would it be fair to say, I asked, that even on the basis of a handful of relatively small studies meta-analysis can come out with an answer almost as good as a massive study?

"That's the conclusion," Lau said, beaming. "There are still some disbelievers, but they're dwindling in number."

Measures of Outcome

Meta-analysts must decide early in a project what outcome measure to use when combining the effects of research studies. The term "measure" does not mean an instrument or scale but some characteristic resulting from the treatment that can be measured and statistically cumulated. Examples include the per acre yield of a fruit or vegetable in studies of pest control, the survival rate of cancer patients getting a particular form of chemotherapy, the change in IQ scores of students receiving special training, the recidivism rate of alcoholics in a treatment program, and the level of self-esteem of psychotherapy clients before and after treatment.

In the primary studies that the meta-analyst plans to combine, there may be anywhere from one to a great many outcome measures; Smith and Glass, as we saw, found a wide array in the 375 studies in their psychotherapy meta-analysis. Deciding which measures are the most valid and which lend themselves best to combination is no easy matter; Nan Laird and Frederick Mosteller have written that "in combining information from several sources, the variety of measures that might sensibly be combined can paralyze our thinking and actions."[16]

Some fortunate meta-analysts face no such problem. Chalmers and Lau, in assaying the efficacy of streptokinase treatment, had available to them data on deaths within three months of heart attack (and in some cases, other time periods), an outcome measure of unsurpassable simplicity and distinctness. Another outcome measure used in many medical meta-analyses, one that is nearly as simple and unambiguous, is the proportion of patients receiving a treatment who show "significant improvement" minus the proportion receiving a placebo who show similar improvement; if the treatment has any real effect, significantly more treated patients than placebo patients improve.

Another relatively simple and clear measure is the time needed to recover from an illness or procedure or time spent in the hospital. In 1981, Elizabeth Devine, a doctoral student in nursing science at the University of Illinois at Chicago, undertook as her dissertation a meta-analysis of studies of "psychoeducational interventions" with surgical patients. Such interventions, carried out by nurses and sometimes other hospital staff, include providing patients with information about the procedures, events, and discomforts they are likely to experience, training them in recovery skills, and giving them psychosocial support. Devine meta-analyzed 105 studies with a variety of outcome measures, including pain, anxiety, and complications, but the most unequivocal and impressive measure, reported by forty-nine of the studies, was the length of hospital stay. When Devine combined the data and compared the results to comparable control cases, she found that patients receiving such treatment, which in most case lasted less than an hour, spent 1.31 fewer days—12.4 percent less time—in the hospital than control patients.[17]

Frequently, however, outcome measures are complex, diverse, and equivocal. The authors of a recent meta-analysis of the treatment of aphasia (loss of speech) following stroke write,

> How should we define outcome? Some of the 114 studies used standardized tests of aphasia, of which there are over a dozen; some reported overall scores as well as subtest scores; some reported only subtest scores. Some studies selected certain subtests from standardized tests, while other used rating scales, homemade tasks, and all possible combinations thereof.[18]

They decided that the most workable scheme would be to limit their universe—a body of studies forming a representative sample—to those studies that provided a single overall outcome, measured by formal tests or rating scales, both before and after treatment. Only thirteen of the 114 studies they collected met these criteria, but this restricted set yielded data they could combine. The result: The average aphasia patient who received treatment (speech therapy) for about three months following the stroke showed more improvement than 78.8 percent of the patients who did not receive treatment.

Even when diverse outcome measures are statistically combinable, meta-analysts must consider how to pool them. The gains indicated by one measure may be more important in some sense than those indicated by another. For instance, a 20 percent reduction in ventricular fibrillation following an acute heart attack might be of less significance as an effect than a 20 percent reduction in mortality. The answer is to weight the measures by importance, but unless there is some sound empirical basis on which to do so, most meta-analysts will either combine the different measures separately or will consider the measure a moderating variable and statistically test to see if results of the variables differ.

Many studies of psychosocial phenomena use unreliable outcome measures with a large built-in sampling error. For example, in a meta-analysis of the effectiveness of juvenile delinquency treatments (skills training, supervised early release, counseling, and so on), the most readily available outcome measures are officially recorded arrest, probation violation, and reconviction data, but these represent only a small fraction of delinquent acts—those that result in official contact with the justice system. That being so, Mark Lipsey of Vanderbilt University, who conducted the meta-analysis, estimates the reliability of these outcome measures at only about .20 to .30, meaning that they account for only about 20 to 30 percent of the variance (dispersion of these data from the mean); this suggests that for the most part the dispersion reflects random error. When measures are so "noisy," effect sizes based on them can seriously underestimate the strength of the relation between variables; correcting the data for low reliability—in effect, correcting for random error—causes the data to lie closer to the mean, making the connection between treatment and effect stronger and, thus, the measured effectiveness of the treatment greater. Lipsey has performed such a correction of the data and reported that the real effect size of juvenile delinquency treatment is probably twice as large as it appears when based on the uncorrected data.[19]

Time and Lives Lost That Could Have Been Saved

The 1992 meta-analysis by Lau, Chalmers, and four colleagues of trials of streptokinase and other treatments of myocardial infarction appeared in the July 23 issue of the prestigious *New England Journal of Medicine*. Two weeks earlier, in the equally prestigious *Journal of the American Medical Association*, there appeared the article based on that meta-analysis that Iain Chalmers called one of the most important ever published in a medical journal; it demonstrated that cumulative meta-analysis could have demonstrated the efficacy of particular treatments of heart attack long before medical experts were able to recommend them. The very title of the article signaled a challenge of a major tradition of the medical establishment: "A Comparison of Results of Meta-Analyses of Randomized Control Trials and Recommendations of Clinical Experts."[20]

Thomas Chalmers said to me about the latter article, which was written by him, the eminent cardiologist Elliott Antman, and three other members of the meta-analysis team,

> Our goal was to find out in as many areas as possible whether doctors were paying any attention to randomized control trials. We used our own cumulative meta-analysis of streptokinase, and fourteen meta-analyses of other treatments of AMI that we reworked by the cumulative method, as a basis for finding out how long it took clinical experts to recommend these treatments after meta-analysis had already shown, or could have shown, that they were effective.

To create a data base of experts' recommendations, the team conducted a search that netted them forty-three review articles and one hundred textbook chapters on treatments of AMI; such sources play a major part in physicians' choices of treatments and how they perform them. Then Chalmers and Antman read each article or chapter and classified its recommendations concerning each treatment, the categories being that the treatment should be used routinely, used only in selected patients, used rarely or never, or used only experimentally (or, as was true in some sources, not even mentioned). Chalmers read the papers unblinded, Antman with all references to the author, source, and date whited out; then they sat together and, leafing through a heap of blinded copies on the table before them, thrashed out differences in their ratings.

They and their three co-authors then compared the experts' recommendations with the results of the cumulative meta-analyses of the eight treatments. Their arresting findings:

In five of the six instances in which the published RCTs [randomized controlled trials] and the cumulative meta-analyses revealed the treatment effect to be statistically significant in reducing hospital mortality, it was several years before the experts recommended the therapy with any consistency. An important example was the thrombolytic [clot-dissolving] drugs that did not begin to be recommended even for specific indications until 13 years after they could have been shown to be effective. Six years elapsed between the time the first meta-analysis showing an impressive reduction in mortality by thrombolytic therapy was published in a commonly read journal and the time when the majority of reviewers recommended it for routine or specific use. Since 1985, when an approximately 20% reduction in the risk of death was established at the $P < .001$ level . . . 14 reviews did not mention the treatment or felt it was still experimental.[21]

The team also faulted the experts for their recommendations for secondary prevention of heart attack:

The most striking example was the antiplatelet drugs . . . that did not begin to be recommended for routine use by more than half of the reviewers until 1986, 10 years after they could have been shown to be effective by cumulative meta-analyses, and 6 years after the first published meta-analysis.[22]

The message of the article was thus two-fold. First, experts' recommendations for treatment lagged far behind the available evidence of clinical trials. Second, cumulative meta-analysis could have established the effectiveness of the thrombolytic treatments even earlier—perhaps many years before the experts began to recommend them.

The number of trials needed to yield such strong and decisive findings through cumulative meta-analysis varies with the size of the trials and their odds ratios, but one principle prevails: Lacking any completed massive trial, a cumulative meta-analysis of small trials can yield the earliest possible significant finding of the effects and value of a treatment.

In later articles, Chalmers and Lau continued to criticize experts and researchers who overlook the meta-analyses of small trials and questioned the ethics of launching more controlled studies after a meta-analysis has already demonstrated a treatment's effectiveness (or lack of it). Notably, the two massive trials of streptokinase completed in 1986 and 1988 included control groups that received no streptokinase, even though both trials began long after the treatment had been validated by meta-analysis. Lives that could have been saved were lost because researchers unconvinced by the meta-analyses of small trials withheld the treatment from control patients in order to gather evidence on a scale they preferred.[23] Chalmers and Lau commented wryly,

> If all investigators performed a meta-analysis before undertaking a randomized control trial, they would see what data they needed to produce to settle the important questions. . . . They might even find that their proposed study is unnecessary because the question has already been answered. It is appreciated that these ideas are very upsetting to the majority of members of the clinical trial community.[24]

Are Big Trials Necessary?

Despite the foregoing evidence, the charge that a meta-analysis of small clinical trials can make subsequent large controlled trials unnecessary and unethical remains highly controversial. On the pro side are the arguments made by Chalmers, Lau, and a number of other meta-analysts. As Chalmers and Lau wrote in 1993, "A very important lesson [can] be learned from the meta-analysis of RCTs of the same treatment carried out over time. Cumulative meta-analyses . . . can demonstrate the effectiveness or lack thereof of a new treatment long before an RCT with sufficient power to do so can be undertaken."[25]

In addition to the streptokinase case, at least two other instances in which meta-analyses arrived at the same answer as a later massive trial lend some credence to this view: one dealt with the treatment of AMI by beta-blockers, the other with the use of phototherapy in the prevention and treatment in newborns of an excess of bilirubin, a liver product that can cause jaundice.[26]

On the opposite side, however, a small meta-analysis (seven trials, 1,301 patients) of intravenous magnesium in acute heart attack found it useful, but a later huge clinical trial (ISIS-4, 58,050 patients) found no benefit; the consensus was that the meta-analysis had been biased by the nonpublication of studies that found no newsworthy effects (a problem discussed in the next chapter).[27]

The American Statistical Association, weighing into the debate in a 1992 report for the National Research Council on methods of combining information, said that the meta-analysis of a series of small studies not only can reach strong conclusions but, thanks to variations among the small studies, "may suggest superior ways to implement the treatment and may identify the subpopulations of subjects on whom the treatment is most effective."[28]

None of this is to say that large trials are never necessary, only that they *may* not be necessary if a small-scale meta-analysis has yielded a strongly significant odds ratio or risk ratio. Nonetheless, much of the medical community both in this country and others continues to think of large RCTs as desirable and necessary.[29] Salim Yusuf, an eminent cardiologist formerly at Oxford University and now at McMaster University in Hamilton, Ontario, is an advocate and practitioner of meta-analysis, yet he and two co-authors of a chapter in a recent textbook on treatment of acute myocardial infarction take issue with Chalmers's and Lau's claims for it, specifically in the streptokinase case. Yusuf himself had taken part in a meta-analysis of streptokinase in the mid-1980s; he and his textbook co-authors say that in 1973 not enough was known about thrombolytic therapy to make large-scale RCTs unnecessary, and specified the lack of details about side-effects, allergic reactions, the incidence of hemorrhages, and so on:

> The argument that a technique such as cumulative meta-analysis would have facilitated the earlier use of thrombolytic therapy in AMI is not substantiated by historical facts; clinicians were not prepared to change practice on the strength of the evidence provided *before* the publication of the ISIS-2 study in 1988 (well after the first major meta-analysis and GISSI-1). Cumulative meta-analysis is likely to be a useful method for synthesizing and updating information from RCTs. However, at the present time there is no evidence that it is a substitute for well-designed, well-powered large RCTs.[30]

A similar view is taken by two respected medical researchers who specialize in collecting and combining data from clinical trials, Richard Peto and Rory Collins, co-directors of the Clinical Trial Service Unit of the Radcliffe Infirmary, Oxford University. In a chapter they wrote for the *Oxford Textbook of Medicine*, they acknowledge that small-scale meta-analyses can be useful but take a strong stand on the need for large-scale randomized evidence:

> Small-scale evidence, whether from an overview [a meta-analysis] or from one trial, is often unreliable and will often be found in retrospect to have yielded wrong answers. What is needed is large-scale randomized evidence; it does not matter much whether that evidence comes from a properly conducted overview or a properly conducted trial. . . . It is only when really large groups of patients are compared that the proportion of patients with truly good and bad prognosis in each can be relied on to be reasonably similar.[31]

Collins, whom I visited, told me that the Clinical Trial Service Unit is working on overviews of anticlotting and fibrinolytic therapy of AMF and treatments for colorectal cancer, breast cancer, leukemia, and lymphoma, but that he is not convinced by overviews of small trials:

What's needed is much better evidence than is customarily accepted as good evidence. In Bayesian statistics, which we use, new information is added to the "prior" belief—the total previous information about any phenomenon. What Tom Chalmers might describe as good evidence of benefit, I wouldn't, because that approach takes a p value of .01 or even .05 to be good evidence without adding that evidence to a reasonable prior belief that the effects are probably near null—which is reasonable because, in fact, most treatments don't have big effects, if any. The key thing one needs to change such a prior belief is a sufficiently large amount of randomized evidence, whether from a meta-analysis or a single trial.*

What is "sufficiently large"? It depends on the question. In the *Oxford Textbook of Medicine*, Collins and Peto write that mid-1980s' overviews of clot-dissolving treatments involved a total of "only about 6,000 patients"—not enough to convince cardiologists—but that "the situation has been saved by two large randomized trials, ISIS-2 and GISSI-1, both of which involved more than 10,000 patients." In general, they write, "20,000 patients may be required for reliable assessment of the effects of treatment on mortality and major morbidity" but a few hundred may suffice for assessment of quality-of-life measures.

Seeking a resolution of the conflicting opinions as to the worth of meta-analysis with a relatively small pool of patients versus very large single trials or a meta-analysis with a large pool, I visited Iain Chalmers at the UK Cochrane Centre in Oxford. The center, one of nine sibling Cochrane centers, coordinates the work of the Cochrane Collaboration, an international network of individuals and institutions that prepare, update, and disseminate reviews of research on the effects of a wide range of health care procedures. Meta-analysis is the method used in much, though not all, of its output.

"We do what we call 'systematic reviews,'" Iain Chalmers told me. "That term implies the analysis of information using some kind of systematic approach that minimizes biases and random errors. Most of our systematic reviews—perhaps as many as 90 percent—do use meta-analytic statistical techniques to combine data, but in some cases such synthesis is not advisable or even possible."

---

* Bayesian statistics use many of the same procedures as standard statistics but start from a different point—the best estimate, based on previous experiences, of the size of a phenomenon—and add the new data of a study to it rather than deal only with new data.

Chalmers, prior to his death, had been working with a Bayesian statistician but had seen no reason to change his views on the needed size of meta-analytic samples. See Lau, Schmid, and Chalmers (1995).

What is the position of the Cochrane Collaboration, I asked, as to the meta-analysis of small trials versus single massive trials?

"There is no Cochrane position on that," Chalmers said. "There can never be a position on what represents truth. One must make a leap of faith to arrive at such a judgment, and some people make that leap earlier in the accumulation of evidence than others. Rory Collins needs either a mega-trial or a mega-synthesis before he's prepared to believe. I'm prepared to believe sooner." How much sooner? I asked. He said, chuckling, "I've been accused of having so open a mind that my brains are falling out." Then, seriously, he added, "The tradition in medical research is to use the 95 percent confidence level. The tradition in the Clinical Trial Service Unit is probably 99 percent." It seemed fairly clear that his stance is closer to that of his nonrelative, Thomas Chalmers, than that of Rory Collins and his colleagues at the Radcliffe Infirmary.

IN BRIEF . . .

The Surprising Finding of a Large Breast Cancer Meta-Analysis

Collins told me that for findings to be reliable, they must be based on an appropriately large amount of randomized evidence, whether from a meta-analysis or a single trial. But he added that a meta-analysis of large trials can provide more information than any of the component trials contributing to it, as strikingly evidenced by a massive meta-analysis of breast cancer studies in which Collins himself had a hand.

Performing very large meta-analyses is one of the two main functions of the Clinical Trial Service Unit of the Radcliffe Infirmary, the other being the conducting of clinical trials. The unit is housed in a plain modern building in the infirmary complex, which is about a mile north of Oxford and totally alien to the ancient town's quaint, half-timbered houses and the Gothic halls of the colleges. In the unit's three-story building some eighty people, a third of them scientists and the rest support staff, housed in offices cluttered with computers, printers, and copiers, continually collect and meta-analyze data on medical trials from around the world and supervise their own clinical trials.

Collins, trained in cardiology and statistics, is a tall, lean man of forty who works and talks in high gear, as if there were never enough time to do what must be done. It is an attitude befitting him as co-director of the Clinical Trial Service Unit, which, in addition to conducting its own trials, is the headquarters of a number of international networks of "trialists" (the British term for researchers conducting medical trials). From them, the unit receives not only their published results but a torrent of data about thousands of individual patients whose cases the unit staff analyze individually.

One of the networks is the Early Breast Cancer Trialists' Collaborative Group (EBCTCG), comprising some two hundred medical researchers or research teams in England, Germany, Russia, Japan, New Zealand, the United States, and dozens of other nations. On behalf of the EBCTCG, and with the support of the Imperial Cancer Research Fund, Collins, co-director Peto, and several other colleagues have been collecting data on breast cancer treatments since the EBCTCG came into existence in 1985 and have issued three meta-analyses on different forms of treatment. The latest, published in *Lancet* in January 1992, presented the results of the treatment of early breast cancer by hormonal, cytotoxic (chemotherapeutic), and immune therapies, and combined the data of 133 trials and 75,000 cases.[32]

The hormonal section of the meta-analysis highlighted a surprising and important conclusion about the drug tamoxifen, an estrogen antagonist. Like other findings in the meta-analysis, it was arrived at by pooling the samples of the studies and adding their effect sizes, thus getting a mega-sample and an overall effect. Collins spoke about the tamoxifen conclusion with fervor:

> No single trial had provided clear evidence of the benefits of tamoxifen for breast cancer patients, but the overview did. Before the overview, the general opinion among oncologists was that tamoxifen didn't save lives. The overview made it absolutely clear that it did, and many doctors were convinced by the evidence. After the overview, there really wasn't a need to do a large trial to demonstrate the overall effect of tamoxifen on mortality, because the overview finding was so incontrovertible.
>
> The fifty or so trials, with a total of some thirty thousand women, gave follow-up data for various periods of time, but no single trial had been large enough to provide reliable data for five-year and ten-year survival though they tended to point in that direction. But the overview established the size of the benefits over time so conclusively that there was only a one-in-a-hundred-thousand probability that the results were due to sampling error or other chance errors.
>
> What was most surprising was that five-year follow-up showed a saving of about three to four lives per hundred, but ten-year follow-up showed that by that time the benefit *doubled*, with about six lives saved per hundred. That's for all women; the benefits are even larger for node-positive women, those in whom cancer had spread to the lymph

nodes; for them the benefit was five lives per hundred at five years and eight to nine lives at ten years. You can see it here—

At this point, he handed me a copy of the *Lancet* report opened to a figure, adapted here as figure 4-2. In the graph, he explained, the lines for tamoxifen and controls continue to diverge and are roughly twice as far apart, for both node-negative and node-positive women, after ten years as after five. The data for cytotoxic chemotherapy similarly showed about twice as much benefit at ten years as at five years. Collins added,

> Before we presented the ten-year results at a meeting here five years ago, we asked the hundred or so collaborators to predict the ten-year results. Their predictions, both for tamoxifen and for chemotherapy, were that the two curves would run parallel after five years. Then we put up the overview results, and the very people who had conducted the trials were astonished. It's the only time I've ever presented a result where there was an audible *gasp* from the audience.

Figure 4-2   Mortality in Meta-Analysis of Tamoxifen Trials

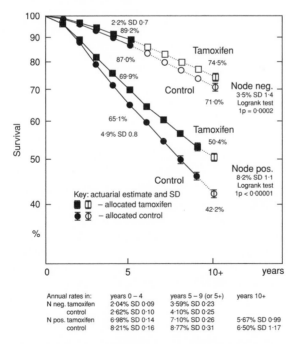

Source: Early Breast Cancer Trialists' Collaborative Group (1992).

Meta-Analytic Epiphanies

The benefits of tamoxifen over time, not apparent in any single trial, were disclosed by meta-analysis because the combining of the studies created a large enough sample to generate statistically significant time-line data. This is one reason, familiar to the reader by now, why meta-analysis can reveal a truth not visible in single studies. Sometimes, however, combining studies over a period of time manifests a hitherto unseen truth for a different reason, as pointed out by Richard Light and David Pillemer in *Summing Up*:

> As more and more data accumulate under improved conditions, knowledge converges upon underlying truths. For example, as we design stronger and stronger evaluations of Head Start, we are better able to close in on its "true" effect. If this idea is correct, estimates of the effect of a program, or relationship, should have *less variation over time.*[33]

The meta-analytic finding of less variation in later studies can thus indicate to researchers that the effects observed in those studies are a more accurate representation of reality than those in earlier studies.

Actually, change over time can be due to any of three causes. In addition to the one pointed out by Light and Pillemer, improvements in methodology can affect the magnitude of the effect size estimate. There may also be an actual change in the relation of the variables, quite apart from the methodology or number of studies available. One goal of meta-analysis is to identify such a shift, or rule it out, as the source of change over time. For instance, a number of studies have found that men outperform women in certain mental functions, among them quantitative and visual-spatial thinking; these differences have been thought by many to be genetically determined, but when Robert Rosenthal and Donald Rubin arranged the findings chronologically and noted the sizes of the reported differences, they discovered that later studies reported smaller differences than earlier ones. Whatever the causes of the trend—Rosenthal and Rubin did not try to identify them—they ruled out at least one possibility: It had taken place too fast to have a purely genetic explanation.[34]

Change over time is only one type of meta-analytic finding that can yield a scientific epiphany. Another is the discovery of substantial heterogeneity—a wide range of effect sizes—among a group of related studies. This, as already mentioned, is a signal to search for moderator variables responsible for the differences in effect sizes; the result is a more complicated but better explanation of the phenomenon. In chapter 1 we heard that ten large studies measuring how much the risk of ischemic heart disease (blockage of heart arteries) is reduced by lowering serum cholesterol arrived at widely differing conclusions. But when the findings in each study were subdivided according to the ages of the subjects and then these age groupings were combined across studies, the discrepancies were explained. The benefits of lower cholesterol levels diminish with age: A decrease large enough to lower the risk of heart disease by 54 percent in forty-year-old men lowers it by only 20 percent in seventy-year-olds.[35]

Any marked incongruity among a set of studies can, in the course of a meta-analysis, lead to some unsuspected truth. A leading statistics textbook gives this example of a phenomenon often called "spurious correlation": A group of studies of the survival of patients after surgery finds that more patients die in better hospitals than in poorer ones. The finding, contrary to common sense, is mystifying. But meta-analytic analysis dispels the mystery: Higher-risk patients—those in poorer condition or in need of more dangerous surgery—more frequently go to the better hospitals.[36]

Sometimes meta-analysis will come up with a finding directly contradicting those of single studies. In 1982 a Senate committee asked the General Accounting Office for a study summing up the effects on medical costs of providing home health care for elderly citizens. The committee's expectation was, as single case studies seemed to show, that home health care would cut costs because the chronically ill, cared for at home, would make less use of hospitals. A meta-analysis of small programs of the proposed type found the opposite to be true: Total costs would not decline but might even increase because the new availability of home health care would considerably increase the total number of people asking for such care.[37]

Similarly, an unexpected, even startling, truth may sometimes appear when meta-analysts look at the effects of a medical treatment at a later point in time than the one chosen for the measure of effect in the primary studies. Nan Laird collaborated with L. K. Hine, Thomas Chalmers, and others in a meta-analysis of the use of lidocaine to prevent arrhythmias following AMI. A number of studies had shown that lidocaine reduced ventricular fibrillation after AMI, but none had shown a statistically significant effect on mortality, and this was thought to be due to small sample sizes. When the studies were combined and endpoint measures meta-analyzed, Laird wrote, "To our surprise, we did demonstrate a treatment effect on early mortality, but in the opposite direction: the combined evidence suggests that lidocaine therapy may actually increase the death rate!"[38]

The Case of the Does-and-Doesn't-Work Vaccine

One of the most extreme instances of disparate results of a medical procedure is that of Bacille Calmette-Guérin (BCG), a vaccine to prevent tuberculosis; over the past half century, the findings of clinical trials and other studies have put its protective benefit as high as 80 percent and as low as zero—or worse, two studies actually reporting a *higher* rate of TB among the vaccinated than the unvaccinated.[39]

Early in the century, Léon Calmette and Camille Guérin of the Pasteur Institute in Paris discovered that virulent bovine tubercle bacilli lost their malign power when cultured on a medium containing bile and that that weakened bacillus could confer a degree of immunity against either bovine or human tubercle bacilli. The use of BCG began in France in 1921 and gradually spread throughout the world; to date, over three billion doses have been given.

But its use has been controversial from the start. Some doctors immediately called it unsafe and their views seemed borne out by an early tragedy: In 1930, in Lübeck in northern Germany, sixty-seven of 249 babies vaccinated with BCG died of acute tuberculosis within months. Investigation revealed that a live culture of virulent bacilli, stored in the same incubator as the BCG, had contaminated it, but the doubt and fear endured. From the 1940s on, medical researchers in a number of countries conducted studies of BCG to settle the question of its effectiveness, but the extraordinary diversity of their findings left the question unanswered; the truth about BCG remained a mystery.

The need to clear up that mystery recently became urgent for U.S. Public Health Service officials. The incidence of tuberculosis has been rising in this country since the mid-1980s, largely among AIDS victims but also spreading from them to others, especially minority poor people; there has also been an alarming rise in cases of drug-resistant TB. In 1992, the federal Centers for Disease Control and Prevention (CDC), seeking information on which studies to base a program of control of TB, awarded a $99,000 grant to a research team at the Harvard School of Public Health to meta-analyze the existing studies of BCG's efficacy against TB and arrive at an overall estimate.

The head of the project was Graham Colditz, an Australian by birth. In his upper thirties, Colditz is good-looking enough to be a model, fast-talking as a carny pitchman, and enthusiastic as a football coach. For all that, he is a man of serious purpose: After only two years practicing internal medicine, he realized that research in disease prevention was his calling and took up the study of public health. In 1981 he met Frederick Mosteller, whose grandfatherly looks and gentle manner give no hint of his international eminence as a statistician, though Colditz was well aware of it. When Mosteller invited Colditz to work with him on a grant, Colditz gladly seized the opportunity and under Mosteller's avuncular influence became an aficionado and practitioner of meta-analysis. The BCG study, on which Colditz worked with six colleagues, including Mosteller and Dean Harvey Fineberg of the School of Public Health, has been his most ambitious meta-analysis to date.

Ambitious is certainly the word for the literature search the team conducted. Colditz, whom I visited in his little office, perilously overloaded with piles of books and papers, at the Channing Laboratory of Brigham and Women's Hospital in Boston, told me about it:

> We started with MEDLINE, of course, but its files go back only to 1966 or thereabouts and many of the studies we wanted to look at were published in the forties and fifties. So three of us plowed through *Index Medicus* in the library and copied out hundreds of entries by hand. We also wrote to specialists in many countries, had people translate papers for us from the Russian, talked on the phone to people working in China, and so on and on—we tried to make sure we didn't miss *anything*. Over three months, we collected 1,264 articles or abstracts, and spent another three months going through them, paper by paper by paper.
>
> And discarding most of them—all but 2 percent—because we wanted only studies that measured the efficacy of BCG in preventing TB cases or deaths, used established comparison groups of people not receiving BCG, and involved diagnosed cases of TB, not just reports of skin reactivity. These and other criteria ruled out all but twenty-six studies—fourteen clinical trials and twelve case-control studies, which are not trials but compilations of case records of people who had tuberculosis and of others, like them in important respects, who did not have it.

Even within this relatively small collection, the findings ranged from the 80 percent effectiveness reported by a 1985 Colombian case-control study of fewer than two hundred people to the total absence of benefit in a seven-year clinical trial in Madras of nearly 177,000 vaccinated and nonvaccinated people.[40] To make sense of these extremely diverse findings, the team sought to link the variant results of the studies to different environmental and other moderator variables rather than merely calculate the overall average. Their statistical analysis, which took another three months and involved special regression methods, solved the mystery of BCG by showing that a number of special factors, rather than unreliability on the part of BCG itself, accounted for most of the variation.

Of the seven factors the team investigated, the most interesting, and one of the most influential, was the distance of the study site from the equator. That fact was mentioned in the published meta-analysis but not really analyzed, and I asked Colditz why they offered no explanation of it. He said that the facts were undeniable but that the explanations were suppositious:

> The most plausible was that atypical bacteria from the family that TB is in seem to vary with latitude. Maybe if you're near the equator you get more exposure to these, and so get some natural protection from the organisms in the environment, so adding BCG doesn't help as much—that might partly explain the Madras case, although there are other serious flaws in that trial. But farther from the equator there are fewer atypical bacteria and you get less natural protection, so BCG is of greater benefit. It's a possible explanation. But a speculative one.

The other of the two factors most responsible for variation among the studies was the "data validity score"—a rating the team gave each of the twenty-six trials and studies based on the quality of its experimental design, its criteria of diagnosis, the availability of follow-up, and so on. This method of scoring the studies—in essence, a rating of quality—was valid and not at all speculative, since each of its components has been thoroughly studied and tested by many meta-analysts.

Having explained much of the variation among the studies, the team, toward the end of a year of work on the project, had produced what the CDC needed: an estimate of the overall efficacy of BCG in preventing TB. Combining the odds ratios and risk ratios of the twenty-six trials and studies, they reported that BCG has a substantial preventive effect. As they wrote in the conclusion of an article in the March 2, 1994, *Journal of the American Medical Association* that summarized their 188-page report to the CDC:

> Based on a meta-analysis of data from 14 prospective trials and separately from 12 case-control studies of BCG efficacy, we conclude that BCG vaccination significantly reduces the risk of active TB cases and deaths. The overall protective effect was 50% against TB infections. The BCG vaccine protected against pulmonary TB as well as disseminated TB (78% protective effect), tuberculous meningitis (64% protective effect), and death (71% protective effect).[41]

What the CDC and the medical establishment will do with this information is uncertain as of this writing. "Some people in the medical community think that 50 percent protection isn't enough to warrant mass immunization, others think it is," Colditz told me. He continued:

Who you are and where you live has a lot to do with your judgment as to the value of BCG vaccination. If you were an intern in New York City exposed to drug-resistant TB and you had the choice of having 50 percent protection or none, I think you might well choose the 50 percent protection.

But of course a meta-analysis such as ours doesn't resolve everything. It *does* raise questions, however, and it certainly has stimulated debate within the medical community about whether and how to use BCG in a strategy to control TB.

Central Question

A central question in meta-analysis, to which we come back again and again, is what accounts for variations in effect sizes across the studies in a sample. In the BCG case, the variations were so wide, Colditz told me, that the team based its statistical analysis on a "random effects model" rather than a "fixed effects model" of the universe of which their twenty-six trials and studies were a sample. These terms refer to an important issue raised only some years after meta-analysis was born, namely, whether the studies gathered for a meta-analysis are a representative sample of a known universe with known characteristics (the fixed effects model) or an unrepresentative sample of several different universes which are represented in the sample in an unknown and imperfect fashion (the random effects model).[42] (The appendix elaborates on this complex subject.)

An example may clarify this murky verbiage. It is known that the outcomes of a treatment on patients within one hospital are often more alike than those on patients drawn from different hospitals.[43] Suppose, now, that you are seeking to estimate the average effect of a new treatment from a stack of case records from which identification of the treating hospitals has been removed. If you assume the patients were all treated in one hospital, and indeed they were, you would find the degree of variation in effect sizes relatively small and have no cause to look for unknown variables; this resembles using the fixed effects model correctly. If you assume they were treated in one hospital but they were actually treated in several different ones, you would find a disturbingly large variation in effect sizes and hunt fruitlessly for an explanation; this is like using the fixed effects model when the random effects model is a better representation of the reality. But if you suspect that the patients were treated in several hospitals, you would conclude rightly that the large variation in effect sizes was due to differences in the hospitals and would statistically take that into account; this is like correctly applying the random effects model.

Each study in a meta-analysis is analogous to the individual patient in this example; researchers will arrive at one conclusion as to the confidence interval around the combined effect size estimate of a treatment if the studies in their collection are thought to come from a specified universe, and a different conclusion if the studies are thought to come from an unknown number of universes of whose characteristics one has no definite knowledge. Gene Glass, in the first meta-analysis, assumed that his collection of 375 studies was a very good sampling of the universe of psychotherapy outcome studies; he therefore attributed all the variation in effect sizes, except for the result of sampling error, to differences in the treatments. In the BCG case, in contrast, Colditz and his colleagues assumed that the extraordinary variation in effect sizes in their sample meant that the data had come from several universes that differed in unknown ways and that the variation in effect sizes was due in large part to that circumstance; accordingly, the confidence interval within which their effect size estimate lay was far wider than if they had based their calculations on the fixed effects model.

A finding within a narrow confidence interval is, of course, more rewarding and newsworthy than a finding within a wide one, which may or may not be significant. This may well be why, according to Larry Hedges, "Fixed effects models have passionate defenders and far more users than random or mixed models." Most meta-analyses of clinical trials are based on fixed effects models and, Hedges adds, "Fixed effects models sometimes provide an excellent fit to the data, suggesting that essentially no additional variation is present."[44]

Since the clue as to whether a group of studies represents a single universe or several universes is the variability in the effect sizes, meta-analysts often use a statistical test of homogeneity—a measure of the degree to which effect sizes agree—as a guide to deciding whether to make a fixed effects or random effects analysis.[45] If the test indicates that the studies come from the same universe, meta-analysts are justified in using fixed effects calculations; if not, they have to use random effects calculations, even though this means the results will look less impressive.

The issues involved in a meta-analyst's choice of either a fixed effects model or a random effects model are difficult for nonstatisticians to understand and nearly impossible to translate into everyday language. But the expertise and skills of those who have recently analyzed the issues and developed techniques for applying each model have led most meta-analysts to regard these considerations and techniques as rational, reliable, and vital tools of scientific inquiry.

Chapter 5

Firming Up the Shaky Social Sciences

Judging a Stranger in Thirty Seconds

Is it possible to accurately size up a stranger in half a minute? Surely not: We have all been told not to judge a book by its cover, and that haste makes waste; moreover, any suggestion that we ourselves could be so quickly appraised by others would strike us as demeaning and unbelievable. Yet the ability to gauge swiftly and correctly the character of strangers is manifestly so advantageous that evolution presumably should have favored it.

A recent prize-winning meta-analysis would seem to support this deduction, furnishing evidence that human beings are able to make reasonably accurate judgments about people they have seen only very briefly.[1]

As, indeed, one might do when meeting the principal author of the meta-analysis, Nalini Ambady, a native of India and an assistant professor of psychology at Harvard. Petite, young, with a bright, agreeable, pale café-au-lait face, she comes across, even after only a half-minute's observation, as a friendly, cheerful, self-possessed, intelligent, communicative woman, and, since she laughs self-deprecatingly when talking about her accomplishments, modest.

How valid such quick appraisals are has preoccupied Ambady much of the past half dozen years. As often happens to scientists, this question unexpectedly preempted her interest when she was planning to investigate something else:

> In 1987, when I was in graduate school at Harvard, I was looking for a dissertation project and discussing possibilities with Bob Rosenthal, my adviser. Like all graduate students, I was doing a lot of teaching and I got interested in what makes for good teaching. Somehow we started talking about the Danforth Center—it's now called the Bok Center—a teaching facility affiliated with Harvard. They have a library of one-hour videotapes of Harvard faculty members teaching undergraduates that they use as instruction material. I got the idea of having volunteers look at the teachers' behavior in these tapes and rate it; then I'd find some way to judge how accurate their ratings were.

(Later, she found the way: She compared the volunteers' ratings with the evaluations students made of the same teachers at the end of a semester's course with them.)

Rosenthal countered with a sharper focus for her project. Years earlier, he told her, he had used brief film clips of researchers and their volunteers in a study designed to see if the researchers had unconsciously behaved in any way that tipped off the volunteers as to what they hoped to find. He suggested that she investigate volunteers' impressions of teachers based not on the one-hour tapes she had in mind but on very brief samples of them. Ambady continued,

> I liked the idea, so I asked the Danforth Center to select a broad range of videotapes for me that included good teachers and not-so-good teachers but not to tell me their evaluations. They lent me thirteen one-hour videotapes, and I went through them one by one, searching for three ten-second segments in each one—one from the beginning of the hour, one from the middle, and one from the end—that showed the teacher alone, because showing students' reactions might be a giveaway. It took a lot of looking, but finally I had three such segments totaling thirty seconds for each of the thirteen teachers.
>
> Then I pinned up a call for volunteers on the bulletin board downstairs [the lobby of William James Hall, the high rise housing Harvard's psychologists] and got nine undergraduate women to sign on for five dollars an hour to view and rate the teachers based on the brief videotape segments. The money for this and other expenses came from a research grant of Bob's; he would be the co-author of the study. Because we were interested in nonverbal behavior, which can be more revealing than speech, over which people have a lot of control, I ran the tapes without sound. That's also why I chose women volunteers; there's both research evidence and meta-analytic evidence that they're better than men at decoding nonverbal behavior.
>
> I had them come in one at a time to view the videotapes on a monitor. After each ten-second segment, they rated the teacher on a scale of one to nine on each of fifteen dimensions—how accepting he or she was, how confident, empathic, warm, supportive, and so on. They didn't find it easy and complained a lot, saying things like, "I can't really do this, there's so little to go on," but they did it anyway.
>
> Then, to compare their ratings with students' actual experiences of those teachers, I turned to the *CUE Guide*. That's a book published each year by an undergraduate panel that compiles students' ratings of each instructor's proficiency and of the course they took with him or her. I didn't look at the *CUE Guide* data until all the videotape ratings were done; I wanted to be blind to who the good teachers were so I wouldn't unconsciously give away anything to my volunteers. Even

when I did finally look at the *CUE Guide* ratings, I couldn't tell from inspection what kind of correlation there was between them and the videotape ratings. When I got the answers from the computer, I was just *amazed*—there was an overall correlation of .76!

Her amazement is understandable. In social psychology, a correlation of .30 is considered good evidence of a connection between two variables and a correlation greater than .50 remarkable. "I took the printout to Bob," she went on, "and he too was astonished. We were both just blown away!"

Later she repeated the study in a high school, using videotapes she herself made of the teachers and, as the criterion of their performance in class, the principal's confidential evaluation of each one. The correlation was a trifle lower than the study using Harvard undergraduates but still an extraordinary .68.

Last, she ran a third experiment using five-second and two-second segments excerpted from the videotape samples of the first two experiments. The correlations based on these extremely brief specimens were somewhat lower but still high for a psychosocial study.

The combined correlation (overall effect size) for all three experiments was .59, a highly significant result: p was less than .001, signifying that there was a less than one-in–one thousand chance that the finding was a statistical fluke. Translated into everyday terms, it meant that the volunteers' impressions of teachers' traits, based on very brief observations without sound, were predictive of the *CUE Guide* ratings about 80 percent of the time.

Many dissertations, although supposed contributions to knowledge, are never read by anyone other than the members of the dissertation committee and have no impact on their field or the author's further research. Just the opposite was true of Ambady's study. Accepted by Ambady's dissertation committee in 1991, it won the 1993 Dissertation Award of Division 5 (Evaluation, Measurement, and Statistics) of the American Psychological Association, and an article she and Rosenthal wrote based on it was published in *Journal of Personality and Social Psychology*, both events calling it to the attention of many psychologists.

More important, the results led Ambady and Rosenthal to think in larger terms—whether their remarkable finding might hold in other areas of human behavior, and if so, how widely. The question could have struck any young social psychologist as worthwhile, but perhaps it had special interest for Ambady, who says that growing up as an "Army brat," shuttling from post to post in India, may have made her more highly attuned to the power of first impressions.

"Bob knew of a number of other studies of judgments made from very brief observations," she went on. "We thought it would be interesting to look at all their data and find out how generalizable our finding was. It might not only be a valuable addition to our knowledge of human psychology but have important practical applications." As a result, they decided to do a meta-analysis of what she and Rosenthal called "thin slices of behavior" in other areas of human behavior, in the hope it would bear important fruit and win greater recognition for their ideas.

How Widely Is It True?

Ambady and Rosenthal had good reason to be surprised and delighted at the magnitude of the correlations in her experiments; only in the physical and biological sciences do typical correlations run to .75 or .80 or higher.[2] The reason is that while physical and microbiological events have highly predictable consequences, psychological and social events do not. The addition of an acid to a solution of sodium bicarbonate will produce a salt and carbon dioxide bubbles not 20 or 30 percent of the time but 100 percent of the time. In contrast, psychosocial interventions such as programs to rehabilitate drug users or provide job training to the unskilled and unemployed are considered successful if they have a measurable effect in as few as one-fifth of the cases.[3]

The behavior of human beings, unlike that of molecules, is the result of a large number of weakly determining causes. On a personal level, how I react to slow service in a restaurant, the disappointing sales of my latest book, or a minor contretemps with my wife is the result of how much sleep I got last night, how hectic my day has been, who else is present and watching, myriad formative events in my past, my genome (my total complement of genes), and other forces, all interacting in ways too complex to fathom. No one of them, alone, accounts for my behavior, though it may seem to me that it does; many or all are responsible to varying degrees. No wonder psychologists, when testing a hypothesized connection between some stimulus and a specific kind of response, are satisfied and pleased if they find a correlation of .30.

Yet evidence from one study does not mean that the same result will be found in other studies or real-life situations involving the same phenomenon. In a famous experiment, social psychologists Bibb Latané and John Darley demonstrated nearly thirty years ago that an individual is less likely to respond to a cry for help if others are present than if he or she is alone. They hypothesized that this "bystander effect," as they called it, was the result of several psychological processes, among them a fear of being seen to behave inappropriately (in the experiment, the others present, who were accomplices of the experimenters, did nothing), and the "diffusion of responsibility" (the feeling that if others also know of the emergency, one's obligation to help is lessened.)[4] But Latané and Darley's findings were based on the behavior of their volunteers, all young undergraduates at a major New York university and all tested in a college setting. Who could say whether noncollege people, older people, small-town residents, drug users, Azerbaijanis, Zulus, or people of another kind in another place would behave the same way?

The great challenge for experimenters who have made an interesting observation is to show that the effect is not an oddity but is generalizable—the expression of a basic human trait which, when acted upon by certain stimuli, will manifest itself in a wide range of circumstances. One way to investigate that possibility is to conduct many additional experiments or make nonexperimental observations of real-life situations differing in sundry particulars from the first one. In the years following the Latané and Darley study, scores of other studies showed that the bystander effect did indeed operate in a wide range of experimental and real-life situations with bystanders of all kinds, although to varying degrees.[5]

Another way to test for generalizability is to collect already existing studies and meta-analytically combine their findings. This is feasible only if the studies measured the same or relatively equivalent phenomena. As Mosteller explained to me,

> What we like to see in a meta-analysis is that everybody measured the same thing—death or survival, or stroke, or cure of a cold, or the value of the dollar, and so on. But in a lot of social science, the measures are different, and in order to get something like a common measure out of them, meta-analysts use Glass's method of turning them all into effect size terms—standard deviation units—and putting those together. That's a good solution—but it isn't equivalence in the same sense that death or the value of the dollar are.

Thus, both the multicausal nature of social science phenomena and the imperfect comparability of the measures of effect limit what social science meta-analyses can yield. In general, they can show that certain variables tend to elicit particular kinds of human behavior under certain circumstances but not that the relationship will exist in all or even most cases. A meta-analysis of, say, the relationship between a form of psychotherapy and the relief of symptoms in clients might find that the treatment is likely to produce relief but not that it will do so under all conditions.

On the positive side, a meta-analysis can provide preliminary tests of generalizability not derivable from any one of the individual studies it merges. Suppose, for instance, a researcher finds evidence that men and women respond differently to a minor wrong, such as a small over-charge on a dinner check. Investigating whether the effect is generaliz-able to other social situations, the researcher attempts a meta-analysis but can locate no relevant studies of the behavior of both men and women experiencing the same minor wrong. He or she does, however, come across some studies conducted solely with men and others solely with women, some of them having to do with being cut off in a grocery line and others with being placed on hold for an inordinate amount of time. Examining the data in these studies, the meta-analyst discovers that 60 percent of the males in studies at groceries objected out loud when being cut off in line while 40 percent of females in other, similar studies did so. In male-only studies of being put on hold, men remained holding for an average of ten minutes before hanging up; in female-only studies, females held for fifteen minutes. Now the meta-analyst has some tentative evidence that the sex difference found in the primary study of overcharges is generalizable, even though no other single study tested it.

But the finding is only as valid as the comparability of the people and circumstances in the studies. The men may have been older than the women, or more affluent, or may have been tested at a different time of day with more or fewer people present, and so on. If so, meta-analysis offers no way to rule out these confounding variables, and whatever cor-relation it finds may either exaggerate or understate the reality.[6] Still, when this is the case, the meta-analyst has come across interesting pos-sibilities for future research.

Despite these limitations, meta-analysis, if interpreted cautiously, can go farther than any individual study or traditional literature review to establish the generalizability of social science phenomena. As Harris Cooper and Kevin Lemke say about its value in personality and social psychology:

> Meta-analysis allows reviewers to formally test the generalizability of findings across people, places, times, and procedures . . . [and to] gen-erate estimates of the direction and magnitude of effects under differ-ent research conditions. The reviewer can then formally test whether research samples, settings, and procedures in fact relate to outcomes. Thus, the meta-analyst, certainly more than the individual primary re-searcher, is in a position to test notions about external validity.[7]

Thin Slices, Fat Findings

Ambady began the thin-slices meta-analysis with the usual computer search: Via the keyboard and an on-line service, she made her way into *Psychological Abstracts* and asked for articles indexed under "accuracy," "deception," and "nonverbal behavior." "But the search bombed," she told me. "My interest was in how long the slices of behavior were and that wasn't coded as a descriptor [index term]. So I got only a few little studies, and I had to do a manual search of twelve social psychology and clinical psychology journals published over the twenty-year span of 1970 to 1990."

That must have been very tedious, I said. "No, it was fun!" she said, laughing:

> I kept getting side-tracked by articles on other subjects that I wanted to read. But whenever I found an entry that looked possible, I wrote it down, looked up the article, and if it was useful, Xeroxed it. I also got some other titles by going through the reference lists of the articles. And Bob, who had done a lot of related work with his students on the detection of lying, pulled a number of useful things off his shelf for me.

Ambady discarded all those articles that gave only ratings based on brief observations; she needed studies in which such ratings were correlated with objective criteria. Also, the correlations had to be based on no more than a total of five minutes of observations. Out of nearly one hundred studies that she collected, forty-four met these criteria; several, however, had used the same subjects, so she combined them in order to prevent their carrying undue weight in the calculations. In the end, she had thirty-eight viable sets of results.

These made up an omnium-gatherum of human contacts in which people judged others' feelings or traits from thin slices of nonverbal and often unintentional behavior. Several studies dealt with the detection of lying or deception from facial expressions and body language; others with the effects on patients of doctors' and therapists' facial expressions and body language; two with nonverbal signs of depression and anxiety; one with the overt behaviors of biased and unbiased teachers; one with men's and women's nonverbal communication with bosses, peers, and subordinates; and one with the effect of newscasters' facial expressions on the voting behavior of their viewers.

After consulting Rosenthal about what kinds of data she would need to analyze, Ambady coded the studies; although she had no assistance with the task, she did not find it a heavy burden, since the number of studies was manageable and she had a limited set of data to extract.

It helped that she worked in an office adjoining Rosenthal's and that she could pop in now and again to ask what kind of statistic to use in extracting a particular piece of information. Rosenthal, in fact, liked to have her bring in sticky data extraction problems:

> Nalini was pretty good at data analysis, but she often needed help in figuring out an effect size when it wasn't given in the original studies. Lots of them didn't include an effect size or even a significance figure because the results hadn't reached significance. But they did give other data from which, one way or another, I could derive an effect size and a significance figure. If they gave the means and standard deviations, it was easy; I could get everything I needed out of those. If they didn't, but compared two groups and said how many subjects there were in each and that there was an F of less than two—that's a measure of how different the groups' results were—I could get an effect size by a roundabout method. I like having to figure out an effect size from clues in a study even though its authors never thought in those terms, I really enjoy that kind of thing.

Unlike most meta-analysts, who use computers and meta-analysis software to process their data, Ambady and Rosenthal did most of their data analysis on hand-held Hewlett-Packard Stat/Math 21S calculators. Rosenthal likes to say, possibly stretching things a bit, that he would not know how to do a complicated analysis on a computer and does not need to because he is surrounded by graduate students who can do it for him. In any case, for a small-scale analysis such as the thin-slices study, the Hewlett-Packard was quite adequate. "It's wonderful," he told me, shoving one across the desk for me to see. "It's got all the statistical distributions built in. If I've got a p value or I've worked one out, I can punch that in and a few punches later I've got my effect size estimate, faster than you can get it on a computer."

Ambady, who did the bulk of the calculations, admitted that despite Rosenthal's enthusiasm about the Hewlett-Packard, "the data calculations were quite a lot to do. I worked from formulas I had in front of me and I had to enter about thirteen or fourteen data items in them from each of the thirty-eight sets of results—about five hundred items all told." Unlike meta-analysts who use computers and see all of their results on screen or on a printout, Ambady saw hers piecemeal as she worked them out on the calculator. "Sometimes I was disappointed when an effect size was quite low," she said, "and sometimes I was concerned when one seemed too high." In the end, however, the combined results were credible and intriguing: They showed that human beings have a considerable ability to correctly read the traits and feelings of relative strangers from very small samples of their nonverbal behavior.

Interpreting the statistical jargon of her work for me, Ambady said,

The effect size was .39 for overall accuracy of predictions from observations of less than five minutes. This suggests that 70 percent of the teachers who, on the basis of the thin slices, were predicted to score high in effectiveness did in fact do so, while 70 percent of those predicted to score low in effectiveness did in fact do so. So the students were able to make fairly accurate judgments using thin slices of nonverbal behavior. We also looked at the effect size of thicker slices of behavior and found, surprisingly, that the results were very little higher. Even more surprisingly, still thinner slices were almost as useful; judgments from less than thirty seconds of observation were just about as accurate as those made from five minutes of observation.

Ambady and Rosenthal explicated the significance of these findings in an article that appeared in 1992 in *Psychological Bulletin*, a flagship journal of the American Psychological Association:

Although specific behaviors exhibited within a situation might vary considerably, it appears that some stable underlying essence is picked up by judges. . . . Our findings indicate clearly that certain affective, interpersonally oriented dimensions of personality can be judged quite rapidly, efficiently, and accurately. It is certainly possible that judgments of these dimensions that are based on thin slices of behavior are accurate because recognition of these dimensions may be more important for survival and adaptation to the environment. . . . [The results] provide additional support for the accuracy of the layperson's intuitive judgments.[8]

The results also had practical implications. Among those Ambady and Rosenthal named: Researchers could save time and money by using thin slices of behavior to predict important emotional variables in their work; thin-slices ratings might be useful in identifying biased teachers and gauging the impact of newscasters and others who reach a broad public; and they might be useful in selecting, training, and evaluating people who need strong interpersonal skills, such as managers, salespersons, teachers, and therapists. Finally, and perhaps most theoretically valuable, the results, they wrote, "provide additional support for the accuracy of the layperson's intuitive judgments."

These were important and strong conclusions to draw from only thirty-eight sets of data. Could it be that other studies of thin slices of behavior had failed to yield significant results and simply not been published? If such studies could have been taken into account, would they have weakened or even totally wiped out the correlation and effect size Ambady and Rosenthal had found?

Rosenthal had explored this issue years earlier and devised a formula for calculating how many unretrieved studies with nonsignificant findings it would take to invalidate the significant findings of a meta-analysis of a given size. Applying his formula to the thin-slices meta-analysis, Ambady and Rosenthal dismissed the matter in a brief paragraph: to negate their findings, there would have to be 7,110 such studies. Since that was highly improbable, Ambady and Rosenthal's results stood as a valid and credible summation of what was known about thin slices of nonverbal behavior.

The scientific establishment's appraisal of the meta-analysis came fairly soon. Ambady had submitted the paper to the American Association for the Advancement of Science (AAAS), which annually awards its Behavioral Science Research Prize for the year's best piece of work in that field. Nine months later, by which time she had forgotten about having submitted it, she got a phone call telling her that she and Rosenthal had won the award for 1993; she was so exhilarated that she could do little useful work for a week. The award made her known throughout the psychological community and highly regarded by her colleagues at Harvard.

Although Rosenthal had won a dozen major awards over the years, he was as thrilled by the AAAS award as Ambady. In 1960, when he was young and unknown, he had won that same award, a high point in his professional life—"but to win it a second time, so many years later," he says, "was just *wonderful*, because you expect that as you get older you may become more appreciated for your cumulative impact on the field but you don't think you'll still be doing anything of prize-winning quality. It made me feel good, very good."

The File-Drawer Problem

Rosenthal's calculation that it would take more than seven thousand nonsignificant studies to wipe out Ambady's and his thin-slices results was based on his solution of what he called "the file-drawer problem." This term, which has become part of the language of meta-analysis, refers to the possibility that there may exist, buried in file drawers, a number of unpublished studies that could nullify the findings of the meta-analysis.

The nonscientist might suppose that file-drawer studies, because they failed to be published, were poor in design or execution, and so could safely be ignored. But in fact what dooms many such studies is "publication bias"—the preference of journal editors for studies that report strongly significant results.

Sherlock Holmes once referred to "the curious incident of the dog in the nighttime." "The dog did nothing in the nighttime," Watson replied. "That was the curious incident," said Holmes. It takes one with a penetrating mind to know when a non-event is significant, and editors of scientific journals often miss the significance of a nonsignificant finding. The more prestigious the journal and the more stringent its review procedures, the stronger the publication bias. One survey of psychological research articles found that a statistically significant finding is nearly ten times more likely to appear in a refereed journal than a nonsignificant finding. A series of six studies in medicine and psychology found that two-thirds of significant results got published as against only one-third of nonsignificant results. A study of randomized clinical medical trials found that 55 percent of those strongly favoring a new therapy over an old one got published, as compared with only 22 percent of those showing no difference. Still other studies show that the larger the effect size reported, the greater the likelihood that a study will be published.[9]

So well known is this editorial bias that researchers themselves exacerbate it by not bothering to submit nonsignificant findings, especially to the more prestigious journals. The survey of psychological research articles just mentioned found that researchers were eight times more likely to submit their results to a journal if they were statistically significant than if they were not.

The preference of journal editors for dramatic results is understandable; as a note in the *British Medical Journal* dryly puts it, "Negative results have never made riveting reading."[10] But using this criterion to select what is to be published distorts what is known about a subject and leads their readers and researchers to overestimate the statistical significance of a treatment.[11] Similarly, the tendency of published studies to have larger effect sizes than unpublished ones creates a warped view of reality.[12]

The file-drawer problem poses a particular threat to a small meta-analysis; the smaller it is, the greater the chance that its conclusions, even if very strong, could be weakened or voided if a body of nonsignificant results were to come to light. As Salim Yusuf writes, "Even if extreme results such as a 3 standard deviation difference is observed on a small amount of data, one should be wary. . . . Even a small study with unpromising results that remains unpublished could wholly negate or considerably dilute the results."[13]

This is not to say that nonsignificant results necessarily portray the truth. They may be the result of methodological problems that suppress real differences, errors due to unreliable measures, or sampling error due to small sample sizes. But if none of these is the case, a nonsignificant result may have a real bearing on the phenomenon being studied, and null or nearly null results may legitimately contribute to a more accurate picture of the true state of affairs.[14]

Meta-analysts tackle the problem of publication bias primarily by using every possible method of unearthing unpublished studies, such as writing or phoning department heads and knowledgeable investigators in the field, and asking them for leads on studies known to have been conducted but not published. Whenever a search cannot be this thorough, the favored way to handle publication bias is Rosenthal's file-drawer test. Rosenthal assumes that unpublished studies have an average significance of zero (their findings may be to either side of zero within the nonsignificant range but balance out). The question then becomes, how many studies of this kind are needed to negate the results of the meta-analysis? The answer depends on the size of the data base of the meta-analysis and the strength of its findings; Rosenthal's formula takes all this into account.[15]

The file-drawer test may cast doubt on a small meta-analysis with weakly significant findings, but a large meta-analysis with strongly significant findings is unlikely to be shaken. A meta-analysis by Rosenthal and statistician Donald Rubin—the story of which we will hear next—combined the results of 345 studies and yielded a large overall effect size with a high degree of statistical significance; when Rosenthal and Rubin applied the file-drawer test, they found that it would take 65,122 unknown nonsignificant studies to overturn their findings, a circumstance they characterized, with masterful understatement, as "unlikely."[16]

Some statisticians and meta-analysts have criticized the file-drawer test because it is based on the null hypothesis and assumes an average zero significance for the unknown studies.[17] To estimate possible publication bias more precisely, they have developed another and far more complex method, which relies on the effect sizes of the meta-analytic sample and estimates those of the unpublished studies. The *unpublished* studies?—how could anyone estimate their effect sizes? Answer: By means of "weighted distribution theory." The analyst, relying on how the meta-analyzed studies were gathered, calculates the probable total weight of the effect sizes of all the studies that were missed, and this enables him or her to judge whether or not they nullify the meta-analytic findings. But the theory behind the method is abstruse, the techniques of applying it mathematically advanced, and experts say that it is not yet recommended for widespread use.[18]

IN BRIEF . . .
The Great Expectancy Effect Controversy

Robert Rosenthal hardly seems the type to be involved in a long-running, brass-knuckles, intellectual brawl. Short and comfortably made, easily moved to smiles and laughter, and effervescent in his responses to others' comments or questions, he is, despite his position as Edgar Pierce Professor of psychology at Harvard and his distinction in the field, so unassuming and easy-going that even first-year graduate students call him Bob. Nonetheless, one of his research contributions provoked such heated, intemperate, and continuing controversy that even a massive meta-analysis by him and Rubin failed to stamp it out; only with the passage of nearly two decades have the flames more or less died down.

The issue is Rosenthal's doctrine that research psychologists, teachers, and therapists often unwittingly evoke from their subjects, pupils, and patients the responses they are hoping or looking for by unconsciously acting in ways that cause their expectations to be self-fulfilling prophecies. Not surprisingly, Rosenthal's "expectancy effect" theory has been about as welcome to researchers, teachers, and therapists as the Copernican heliocentric doctrine was to seventeenth-century Inquisitors.

Rosenthal stumbled upon the expectancy effect in the mid-1950s when he was carrying out an experiment for his doctoral dissertation at UCLA. He planned to have some subjects succeed at a task (fitting oddly shaped blocks together in a limited amount of time) and others fail (he would call time on them before they could finish). His research goal was to find out whether the moods engendered by success or failure at the task would affect the behavior of subjects in his experiment, which involved the defense mechanism of projection.

As part of the design of the experiment, he gave his subjects a projective test before giving them the block-fitting task; afterward, he gave them the test again to see how greatly success or failure at the block-fitting task had altered their general outlook. He expected that those who succeeded at block-fitting would show the greatest positive change, those who failed would show the least. There was no reason to suppose that they would differ on the pretest, but, to his astonishment, they did: Those whom he had scheduled for success (by random selection) at the block test scored low in the pretest, and those whom he had scheduled for failure scored high. In both cases, therefore, their pretest scores favored his hypothesis. "Without my awareness," he says, "I was somehow influencing them so that they were behaving as I wanted them to behave *before* the task that was supposed to affect their behavior. I didn't know what it was that I had done, and today, four decades later, I'm still working on that general problem."

Fascinated by the thought that experimenters' expectations can cause them to unconsciously influence their results, over the next two decades Rosenthal conducted dozens of experiments on this phenomenon, published a hundred or so articles and seven books about it, and conducted a related experiment on the influence of teachers' expectancies on their pupils' development. In the experiment, he and Lenore Jacobson, an elementary school principal, told teachers falsely that tests had indicated that certain of their pupils would make surprising gains in IQ in the next eight months of school. At the end of eight months, the designated children had, indeed, done so, although the only difference between them and other pupils was in the teachers' minds.[19] That research, expanded, was the subject of a 1968 book by Rosenthal and Jacobson that gave the phenomenon the name, "the Pygmalion effect," by which it has been known ever since.[20]

Like hornets whose nest has been attacked, researchers and educational psychologists swarmed to the attack, not only of the Pygmalion effect but of the whole idea of expectancy effects. (Many others, to be sure, rallied to Rosenthal's defense.) The harshest and most persistent attacker of the expectancy effect hypothesis was Theodore Xenophon Barber, a psychologist on the staff of a Massachusetts state mental hospital. Before savaging Rosenthal's findings in print, Barber visited him and said, ruefully and pleasantly, "Bob, it isn't there, it just isn't there." Rosenthal recalls,

> His argument was that p wasn't less than .05 in a lot of the studies. He said I had done thirty-eight studies and only twelve of them had a significant result, and the expectancy effect must not be a real phenomenon or they would all be significant. Well, even though I was much less sophisticated about data analysis in those days than I am now, I knew that that wasn't right, I knew that you had to take all the data into account, and I said so. That's when I began trying to combine the significance levels of a bunch of studies and gradually got into meta-analysis.

By the mid-1970s, even as Gene Glass was developing his own pioneering meta-analytic methods, Rosenthal was familiarizing himself with methods of combining p values and effect sizes. After nearly twenty years of experiments on and controversy about the expectancy effect, he decided that the way to settle the dispute was to do an all-embracing meta-analysis of the many studies that had sought to confirm or disconfirm its existence.

He began with a search for relevant studies. His own files were a mother lode of ore: "I'd been accumulating stuff on this since the early 1960s," he says. "I was so identified with this area that people had been sending me manuscripts for many years." Next, he copied out other titles and essential information by hand from *Psychological Abstracts* and other indexes (on-line data bases and computerized searching did not yet exist), filling several fat loose-leaf binders with hundreds of pages, one per study. Collecting copies of the actual papers, largely by photocopying them in the library, took many months, although he had student assistance with this wearisome chore. After winnowing out unusable items, he had accumulated 345 studies containing 350 sets of results and decided to proceed.

Although meta-analysis was new at that time, Rosenthal anticipated the later interest in moderator variables; he planned to calculate significance data and effect sizes for a number of subsets of his studies to see under what conditions the expectancy effect was strongest. Having spent many years studying the phenomenon, he knew of eight major areas in which researchers had either reported or denied the existence of expectancy effects. These ranged from inkblot tests to judgments of the expressions on pictured faces, and from studies of teacher expectations to research on animal learning. (Even researchers who were misled into thinking they were working with bright and dull rats found the supposedly bright rats quicker at learning mazes than the supposedly dull ones.)

Combining significance figures of the studies in each area posed no great problem; the data were either reported or calculable from other data contained in the studies. Combining effect sizes was another matter; many of the studies gave none and to derive them from the reported results would be laborious or impossible. Fortunately for Rosenthal, he was friendly with Donald Rubin, a young statistician (today a professor of statistics at Harvard), whom he asked to help meta-analyze the material. Rubin recollected,

> I wasn't in on it from the beginning, only later. Bob had analyzed the results of all the studies but hadn't yet combined them, and he would come to me and say that he wanted to do *t* tests here and correlations there and that sort of thing, and what did I think? And I'd try to for-

mulate the problem in a way that made mathematical sense, and see if it satisfied his concerns about his goal and his audience. He did 95 percent of the work; he was the instigator, I was the technician.

One of Rubin's major contributions was a solution to the effect size difficulty: He suggested a way in which they could take the most significant studies in each of the eight areas, derive effect sizes for them from the significance data, means, and sample sizes, and then extrapolate the effect sizes to get figures representing the whole set of 345 studies. Rosenthal, using these instructions, worked out the results one by one on his hand-held calculator. To his gratification, in every one of the eight areas a considerable proportion of the studies showed the expectancy effect to be statistically significant; the proportions ranged from 22 percent for reaction time studies ($p < .02$) to 73 percent for animal learning studies ($p < .005$). Even more gratifyingly, effect sizes ranged from 0.17 for reaction time studies to an astonishing 1.73 for animal learning studies, with a median effect size of 0.70 for all eight areas taken together.

Aware that these findings would probably encounter resistance, even hostility, Rosenthal and Rubin defended their findings against expected major objections to their meta-analytic methods. They ruled out the influence of poor quality studies on their findings; they showed that small sample size rather than negative evidence explained most of the failures to reach significance; they offered proof that their findings were valid both externally (beyond the bounds of the studies in the meta-analysis) and internally (resulting from the expectancy effect and not other variables in the sample).

They then concluded, firmly and confidently:

> We have examined the results of 345 studies of interpersonal self-ful-filling prophecies and some clear conclusions have emerged. The reality of the phenomenon is beyond doubt and the mean size of the effect is clearly not trivial. Depending on the area of research considered, the mean size of the effect varies from small effects for studies of reaction time and laboratory interviews . . . to very large effects for studies of psychophysical judgments and animal learning. The estimated grand mean effect size over eight different areas of research was .70.[21]

It was this result that Rosenthal and Rubin calculated could be overturned by file-drawer studies only if more than 65,000 of them existed.

The meta-analysis appeared in the journal *The Brain and Behavioral Sciences* in 1978. It would be pleasant to report that this ended the controversy, but it did not. Many researchers and educational psychologists were too threatened by the idea of expectancy effects to accept the evidence; *The Brain and Behavioral Sciences* published an outpouring of peer comments, many of them assailing the meta-analysis.

To be sure, more than half of the commentators agreed, at least in part, with Rosenthal and Rubin. The doyen of experimental psychology Ernest Hilgard wrote that their "heroic summarization of 345 studies leaves little doubt that the effects are genuine," and the eminent social psychologist Jerome Singer commented that the meta-analysis "should serve as a valedictory for the area at issue."

But nearly half of the comments attacked the report. Howard Gadlin of the University of Massachusetts asserted that the meta-analysis was itself a prime example of researchers' expectations producing the conclusions they expected. Theodore Barber charged that the research "is pervaded with (sic) deficiencies and biases in data analysis." Wallace Wilkins of the University of Maine, using a vote-counting approach—obsolescent even then—said that since two-thirds of the 345 studies did not reach the level of significance, Rosenthal and Rubin's own evidence refuted their finding.

The debate continued for many years but at a gradually diminishing level, although interest in expectancy effects has remained substantial; since 1978 Rosenthal has added nearly 150 studies to his collection. Today, few research or theoretical psychologists dispute the existence of the effect, even if they take issue with some of the technical aspects of the Rosenthal and Rubin meta-analysis. The slow victory of Rosenthal's view may be due less to changes of mind brought about by the evidence than to attrition; as Max Planck once commented, "A new scientific truth does not triumph by convincing its opponents and making them see the light, but rather because its opponents eventually die, and a new generation grows up that is familiar with it."

Checking for Leaks

In testing their meta-analysis for validity, Rosenthal and Rubin were making sure that their findings would not seep away under close scrutiny. The validity of a meta-analysis refers to the soundness of the original studies and the procedures used to combine their data, and at least three dozen potential validity leaks have been identified in those procedures.[22] Reading about all the possible weaknesses, one may feel that the whole enterprise is hopeless, but the situation is no worse, to change metaphors, than that of an aircraft pilot reading a preflight checklist. Before take-off in even a simple single-engine plane, the pilot must check against at least a score of possibly disastrous conditions, and in a multi-engine commercial jet many more. But the checking and testing makes it possible for planes to fly with only minimal risk of equipment failure. Meta-analyses, similarly, succeed when researchers use a validity checklist.

The threats to meta-analysis can be grouped into four general classes: those relating to external validity, internal validity, construct validity, and statistical validity. (Some threats, however, arise from weaknesses not in meta-analytic procedures but in the primary studies fed into a meta-analysis; sometimes the meta-analyst can correct for them, sometimes must exclude the faulty studies, and sometimes fails to recognize their flaws and produces a flawed meta-analysis. We have already heard a fair amount about external validity: the extent to which the findings of a meta-analysis hold true across a wide range of circumstances. For example, a primary study might find that homework had considerable benefit for twelve-to-sixteen-year-olds in private schools in the 1980s, but extending that finding to all private schools in the 1980s would be of doubtful validity if the meta-analysis did not include studies of schools differing in size, location, teaching practices, ethnicity of the students, and other potentially influential variables. Generalizing the finding to public schools and to other periods of time would obviously involve an even larger leap of faith. But if no primary studies exist that encompass the needed conditions, the meta-analyst cannot safely extend the findings.[23]

The threat to external validity from the limitations of sampling of the primary studies is not something meta-analysts can overcome; they cannot alter how the primary studies were run. They can, however, guard against overgeneralizing their findings through the use of the homogeneity tests discussed earlier. If a test of homogeneity shows that a set of effect sizes is not drawn from the same population, a general statement about the effect under study is probably inaccurate.

Suppose a meta-analysis on the effect of homework finds that the achievement of students who do homework is .20 standard deviations above students who do not. Making a general claim about the effect of homework is warranted only if the set of effect sizes in the primary studies is homogeneous. If not, the meta-analyst must look for moderators of the differing effect sizes that will separate them into homogeneous groups. If it turns out that homework has a larger effect for older than younger students, this caveat must be applied to the findings.

A different question underlies threats to internal validity: Does the implementation of the primary studies and the meta-analysis justify the claims the researchers are making—that is, do the primary studies and meta-analysis actually test what the researchers say is being tested? Over a dozen threats to internal validity have been identified.[24] In primary studies, most can be avoided by the use of proper methods, with random assignment of subjects to treatment and control conditions being the most obvious. In meta-analyses, researchers can guard against most of the major threats to internal validity by using only primary studies that employ randomization or by making statistical adjustments that compensate for its lack.

Two other important threats to the internal validity of meta-analyses include incomplete literature searches, which yield biased samples of studies, and unreliable coding of information from studies. These threats can be guarded against by more complete methods of collecting studies and by checks on coding discussed earlier.

Construct validity has to do with whether the measure used to appraise the outcome is a trustworthy indicator of effect or if it distorts the true intervention-outcome connection.[25] One meta-analysis, for example, examined how well a mental test of job abilities correlated with individuals' actual job performance. Of the measures used in the primary studies, the mental test was known to be fairly reliable, while the job performance rating, based on a single supervisor's opinion in each case, was generally unreliable. Statistically adjusting for this weakness, John Hunter and Frank Schmidt found the "true" correlation to be .57, or twice that reported when the correlations were unadjusted for reliability.[26] By such methods, meta-analysts are able to plug up the leaks in construct validity that occur in primary studies.

The fourth and final category concerns threats to statistical validity. These involve errors in how the data are analyzed. At the primary-study level, such errors include using statistical tests that are inappropriate for the type of data, capitalizing on chance, and not reporting statistical tests that were performed. At the meta-analytic level, statistical threats include inappropriate assumptions when effect sizes must be estimated, bias in transforming effect sizes, and failure to weight the studies' results by sample size, among others.

Although the list of threats to validity may seem overwhelming, there is good reason to take heart. Unlike the pilot's checklist, on which any item overlooked could spell disaster, it is generally agreed by even the most finicky statisticians that a meta-analysis is not an automatic failure if it has a shortcoming or two in validity; to fail, its validity problems must be serious or multiple.[27] Nevertheless, after looking at the validity threats to meta-analysis, one can only agree with Ingram Olkin that doing a meta-analysis may be easy but doing one well is hard.[28]

Rehabilitating Juvenile Delinquents: Is It True That Nothing Works?

For the past two decades many criminologists and legislators have despaired of doing anything constructive about juvenile delinquency. A 1975 survey of 231 studies of correctional treatments reported that with few exceptions rehabilitative efforts had no appreciable effect on recidivism, and a 1977 update of the survey concluded, "The blanket assertion that 'nothing works' is an exaggeration, but not by very much."[29] Since then, the same view has been reiterated in a number of other surveys and reviews.

The negative findings of the 1975 and 1977 surveys perplexed Mark Lipsey, a young professor of psychology at Claremont Graduate School in California. In the late 1970s he and one of his graduate students, David Cordray, were evaluating correctional programs for Los Angeles and Orange Counties and finding lower recidivism rates among delinquents and predelinquents who had received rehabilitative treatment than among those who had not.

"All the respectable researchers concluded that nothing works," Lipsey, now a professor at Vanderbilt University, told me. "There was this huge literature, using vote-counting methods, that said so, yet our studies seemed to be showing positive effects. Either we were nuts or we had done something wrong." He began studying the techniques of meta-analysis, which, he soon recognized, offered a far better way to judge the effects than vote-counting surveys. As he did so, says Lipsey, "I began to think that we were basically right and that in those other studies a lot of statistical noise was concealing the statistically modest signal."

Lipsey proposed a meta-analysis of juvenile delinquency treatment research to the National Institute of Mental Health and in 1985 was awarded a substantial grant. He expected to complete the project in three years; today, middle-aged, grizzle-bearded, bespectacled, and with a high, retreating hairline, he is still working on it. He has published some interim papers on his findings but does not expect to complete the meta-analysis for several years and says, with a wry chuckle, "I didn't know when I started it that it was going to be my life's work."[30]

When the grant came through, Lipsey assembled a staff of student assistants and directed them in a heroically dogged search for relevant studies. They probed twenty-three on-line data bases, compiled additional citations from the studies they retrieved, and sought still others in the bibliographies of literature reviews and in meta-analyses of studies of juvenile delinquency treatment, five of which had been completed by then but none of which was extensive or decisive.

By 1987, with a cadre of twenty part-time graduate students working for him, Lipsey had amassed more than eight thousand citations. One student team looked at the cited sources in the library, rejected those that were obviously unsuitable, and photocopied the rest. Another team, working in Lipsey's three-room suite at Claremont, more closely evaluated the retrieved documents while coding them; the coding manual, an agonizing 154 items long, ruled out all but well-designed studies with good data, thereby weeding out the great majority. In the end, Lipsey's sample included only 5 percent of the eight thousand citations; even that fraction was a substantial set of 443 studies.

The majority of studies included data on several delinquency outcomes; in each case, Lipsey and the students selected for primary analysis whatever measure was most widely used in other studies, usually some aspect of recidivism. The team weighted each measure according to the size of the sample in the study, used Hedges' method of calculating effect sizes, and drew on later statistical procedures to correct for sampling and other errors.

When the overall results emerged from the computer, they answered the question, "Is it true that nothing works?" with a whispered "No"—whispered, because the average effect, although positive and statistically significant, was only about one-tenth of a standard deviation (in the social sciences, as noted earlier, one-fifth of a standard deviation is considered meaningful but small). Lipsey, however, said in an interim account of the work that the reported effect size is more important than it appears to be:

> At first impression, this sounds quite trivial. [But the] figure is more meaningful if we translate it into something more directly relevant than standard deviation units. Since the modal measure represented in these data is a rearrest recidivism rate, one alternative is to express the mean effect in those terms. . . . This procedure shows that .10 standard deviation units is equivalent to a decrease of 5 percentage points from a 50 percent baseline . . . a 10 percent decrease in recidivism (5/50).[31]

In a later article, Lipsey stressed the significance of the finding:

> While not an overwhelming effect that can be announced as a "cure" for delinquency, a net 10% average reduction cannot be called trivial— it is, for example, within the range of effects viewed as significant in medical treatment and other such domains.[32]

Moreover, the true effect was almost certainly larger than this, Lipsey added, since unreliable outcome measures (such as rearrest rates) make effect sizes appear smaller than they really are. As mentioned in the previous chapter, Lipsey used a widely accepted statistical method to correct the weighted mean effect size for low reliability; this doubled the estimated decrease in recidivism, making it 20 percent, or "quite large enough to have practical significance."[33]

A clue of great importance showed up in the course of the data analysis: The effect sizes reported by the studies varied widely—indeed, three or four times as much as would be expected if they all measured the same basic treatment effect. "We had calculated mean effects and found that everything works," Lipsey says:

> That issue is boring. What's *not* boring is the considerable variance around the means. In any significant kind of intervention, you rarely find homogeneity around the mean; there's more variation than you'd expect from sampling error. That means some studies are producing much bigger effects than expected and some much smaller. I wanted to know which ones are up at the top and which at the bottom, and why. Those would be findings of real value.

First, he had to exclude whatever variability was due to other causes. Standard statistical theory enabled him to determine that a quarter of it was due to sampling error, and further analysis showed that about half of it resulted from differences in research methods, such as how long after treatment the researchers measured the effects.

The remaining unexplained variability had to be due to differences in the treatments used; statistical analysis of these differences yielded the most valuable findings of Lipsey's long years of work. The effect sizes of specific treatments, such as those focused on skills training, behavior management, and employability, ranged from .20 to .37; the effect sizes of more general treatments, such as counseling, probation and parole, and community residential programs, ranged from .02 to .16; and deterrence (fear-based programs such as brief "shock incarceration" or tours of prison facilities) actually had a *negative* effect size (−.24). Lipsey's summation:

At the high end . . . are treatments that have a more concrete, behavioral, or skills-oriented character. At the lower end of the continuum are treatments that are more oriented to psychological processes, e.g., the several forms of counseling. The middle ground is held by various enhancements to juvenile justice supervision (e.g., early release, reduced caseloads, restitution) and general casework or advocacy approaches. . . .

Some particular attention should be given to the few treatment categories associated with negative effects. Most notable are the deterrence approaches such as shock incarceration and boot camps. Despite their popularity, the available studies indicate that they actually result in delinquency increases rather than decreases.[34]

Such intriguing results from so thorough a meta-analysis should influence correctional policy, and although no data have yet been gathered on this point, Lipsey says that the professional community has shown enormous interest and that he has had a great many calls on the boot-camp question. At present, however, the prevailing attitude of Congress, many state legislatures, and much of the public favors punishment rather than rehabilitation, which is associated with liberal social policies.

Undaunted by the current mood of legislators and the public, Lipsey urges that juvenile delinquency treatment and research be conducted along the lines indicated by his decade-long meta-analysis:

It is no longer constructive for researchers, practitioners, and policymakers to argue about whether delinquency treatment and related rehabilitative approaches "work" as if that were a question that could be answered with a simple "yes" or "no." As a generality, treatment clearly works. We must get on with the business of developing and identifying the treatment models that will be most effective and providing them to the juveniles they will benefit.[35]

Lipsey's final report will appear in a few years; whether it will fall on fertile or barren soil is anyone's guess.

The Noise-to-Signal Ratio

The metaphor that statistical noise can drown out a statistical signal is a useful way to conceive of the flaws and distortions afflicting social science studies. As Lipsey puts it, "In a stereo system, you want no distortion of the music introduced by any component of the system from beginning to end. In meta-analyzing social science research, similarly, we want the phenomenon being studied to come through our methods without distortions. But half of what we get out of the far end is distortion." The distortions introduced by research methods are often called "artifacts" or "artifactual errors." When that part of the effect size estimate due to artifacts is corrected for—similar to filtering out noise in a stereo system—what remains can be attributed to the real differences between treatment and control groups.

Perhaps the simplest kind of artifactual error is a mistake made by the primary researchers when recording data—the simplest, but probably the least likely to be noticed and corrected. Fortunately, according to a study by Rosenthal, the typical rate of recording error in social science meta-analyses is about 1 percent, which would not greatly affect the conclusions of a meta-analysis.

Many potentially more serious artifactual errors have already been discussed. Publication bias, for one, can be a significant source of artifactual error in a meta-analysis, inflating the size of an estimated effect by neglecting unpublished nonsignificant findings; it can be likened to the distortion of a radio signal by technical flaws that exaggerate some frequencies, underrepresent others, and thus transmit a warped version of the original signal. But as we have seen, this artifact can be minimized by thorough search procedures or can be statistically corrected for by means of Rosenthal's file-drawer formula.

Another source of noise is random error in measurement; such error affects every measurement and, therefore, every effect size in a meta-analysis. Such errors do not cancel one another out when combined, their net result being to diminish the effect size estimate, analogous to the masking of a sound signal by hiss or other noise; however, this problem can also be statistically corrected.

A third serious artifact is coder unreliability, which adds to the general variability of results and so distorts average findings. An 80 percent agreement rate between coders is considered acceptable, and 90 percent is considered good[36]—but even a 10 or 20 percent disagreement among coders means that some error is being introduced into the meta-analytic data before it is statistically combined. That error cannot be corrected later; it can be avoided only by more thorough training of coders and by comparing and reconciling their work before combining the data. Still other variables that make noise include differences in the locales of studies, the ages and other characteristics of the subjects treated, and the particular treatment employed.

Lipsey illustrates the noise-to-signal problem by means of a pair of graphs—reproduced here as figure 5-1—in which each point represents the effect size found in a study. In the top panel of the figure, the results

Figure 5-1　Noise-to-Signal Problem in Meta-Analysis of Juvenile Delinquency Treatment

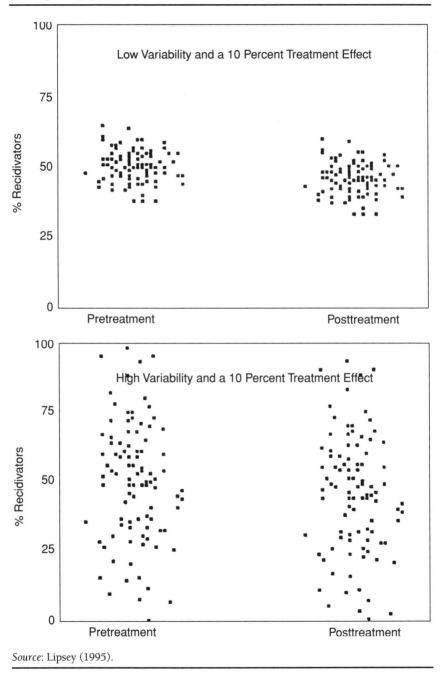

Source: Lipsey (1995).

of the juvenile delinquency studies are closely clustered both before and after treatment; this makes it easy to see—analogous to a clear, sharp signal that is easy to hear—the 10 percent improvement. In the bottom panel, the results are widely dispersed; this makes it difficult to see— "hear"—the 10 percent improvement.

Still, the dispersion in the bottom panel is useful in one sense: It suggests that factors other than chance, probably moderator variables of some importance, are affecting the results. To fail to identify them is to incorporate methodological noise into one's findings; to ferret out those variables and measure their effects can be the most valuable part of a meta-analysis. As Lipsey puts it,

> The main purpose and value of meta-analysis is to explain the differences among studies, not just report central tendencies. When you ask how much difference the methodology makes, you're left with variability that is worth exploring. What's so powerful about meta-analysis is that you can combine studies that used different methods, examine the patterns of variation, and tease out how much of the variation is noise coming from the equipment and how much is the signal coming from the material you're studying.

Chapter 6

Lighting the Way for Makers of Social Policy

A Tough Customer Makes a Tough Request

The letter on U. S. Senate stationery that arrived on Eleanor Chelimsky's desk one July day in 1983 bore good news and bad news. Good news, because it offered an excellent opportunity for her fledgling Program Evaluation and Methodology Division (PEMD) of the U.S. General Accounting Office (GAO) to show what it could do; bad news, because it dealt with a politically touchy issue and came from a powerful and notoriously aggressive senator. The letter, addressed to Charles Bowsher, the head of GAO, read in part:

> Dear Mr. Bowsher:
>
> As you know the Senate Committee on Agriculture, Nutrition, and Forestry has jurisdiction over the Special Supplemental Food Program for Women, Infants, and Children, often referred to as the WIC program. . . . Increasingly, there appears to be conflicting testimony about what is actually known about the program's effectiveness from evaluations which have been conducted for this purpose. . . .
>
> The current authorization for WIC expires at the end of fiscal year 1984. Next year, the Committee will have among its highest priorities consideration on [sic] reauthorizing the WIC program. . . . I would request that the General Accounting Office undertake an objective analysis of the evaluations which have attempted to assess the WIC program . . . that this request be given high priority by GAO, and that the written analysis be completed by the week of January 9, 1984. . . .
>
> Specifically with regard to maternal health, the analysis should focus on the impact of WIC on miscarriages and still births, [etc.]. In relation to infant and child outcomes, the analysis should examine the evaluations which purport to find that WIC has a positive effect on increasing the birth weights of infants [etc.].
>
> I want to emphasize that I am not requesting a new study but rather a careful examination of existing research to determine the technical and methodological soundness of these evaluations and the credibility of the claims based on them.

> Members of the Committee staff have been in touch for several weeks with GAO staff. . . . I understand that GAO has developed a process of review called evaluation synthesis . . . which sounds as if it would meet our need to learn what is really known from the evaluations about the impact of WIC program participation.
>
> > Sincerely,
> >
> > Jesse Helms, Chairman[1]

WIC, which had gone into effect in 1972, provided nutrition education, food supplements, and health care to low-income pregnant and postpartum women and to children up to age five with health and nutrition risks. The program's budget, $20 million in fiscal 1974, had ballooned to nearly $1.2 billion in fiscal 1983, by which time WIC was serving some three million women and children.

In asking for an "evaluation synthesis" of WIC, Senator Helms was using GAO's preferred term for meta-analysis. Eleanor Chelimsky, a petite, auburn-haired, effervescent woman in her middle years, had introduced meta-analysis to GAO when Elmer Staats, the head of GAO, created a new division, PEMD, in 1980 and appointed her its director. Chelimsky, a political scientist with many years of experience in program evaluation, had read and been impressed by Gene Glass's 1976 AERA address, and over the next half-dozen years had read up on meta-analytic methodology. PEMD, a tiny specialized division of GAO—its staff totals under one hundred, that of GAO about 4,500—stays abreast of new research methods and uses them in carrying out certain technical studies. It also informs the other five divisions of GAO how the new methods can be used in the 1,300-odd audits and evaluations of federal programs and activities they complete every year.

Part of the immense output issuing from GAO's vast, drab, brick building in a seedy quarter of Washington is generated by congressional committee members who ask GAO for reports on how well programs up for reauthorization have been working and how well proposed new programs are likely to work. Often, GAO will answer such a request by doing a new study, which takes up to two to three years. Sometimes, however, if the information is needed in a hurry, the request will go to PEMD, some of whose staff members are versed in meta-analytic methods of locating existing studies and synthesizing the data. They can turn out a meta-analysis in half a year or so. Since 1980, PEMD has produced more than thirty ambitious meta-analyses. (This is only a fraction, however, of its total output, which numbers well over three hundred surveys and evaluation studies.[2])

Congressional requests for meta-analyses most often concern controversial programs that some studies have found successful but others unsuccessful. That was very much the case with WIC. "There was a special interest group of people who *loved* this program and claimed it worked," Chelimsky told me, "and other people who just wanted to *destroy* it because they said it was a failure and, besides, they didn't believe government should be helping disadvantaged people. I don't think Senator Helms' position was that we shouldn't help disadvantaged people but that we shouldn't spend money in this way because it wasn't doing any good."

Clearly, whatever PEMD reported about WIC, it was likely to draw fire from one side or the other. There was no help for that; the only political guidance Chelimsky could have given to the half-dozen staffers she assigned to the project would have been to impartially report what the meta-analysis revealed, but since they were meta-analysts—and civil service employees—such advice was unnecessary.

Doing Meta-Analyses for Congress: A Challenging Task

Almost all of the meta-analyses discussed earlier in this book were initiated by the researchers themselves, who, even if funded by a government agency, took up issues that they wanted to examine and that they thought would interest their academic peers. The situation of PEMD meta-analysts is quite different: Their topics are dictated by the members of the U.S. Congress who are their "customers"—PEMD staffers actually call them that—and satisfying this audience entails special difficulties.

An obvious one is that Congress is made up of hundreds of persons with diverse and often conflicting interests; accordingly, a meta-analytic finding that pleases one member or group of members is likely to displease or even anger others. A study may seem totally impartial to those whose position it supports but is almost sure to seem biased to those whose position it undermines. The latter may, in self-defense and retaliation, publicly attack the PEMD's work. But unlike embattled academics, PEMD's meta-analysts are employees of Congress and cannot counterattack.

Another source of difficulty for PEMD meta-analysts is the difference between the backgrounds and goals of the legislators and those of the researchers. As Chelimsky said in her keynote address to the 1994

National Conference on Research Synthesis sponsored by the Russell
Sage Foundation:

> Legislators and researchers are, after all, separated by different goals,
> different standards of evidence, different tolerances of uncertainty. The
> researcher's first goal—knowledge—is far down on the legislator's pri-
> orities, and evidence, for that legislator, is merely instrumental to a ne-
> gotiation or a decision. For the researcher . . . evidence is an end in it-
> self, and a researcher invokes certainty only when the evidence
> provides such certainty. . . . But in public policy-making, positive value
> is placed on "making a decision," regardless of whether there's suffi-
> cient objective evidence to support that decision.[3]

The meta-analyst wants to find out what all the evidence shows; the
legislator more often wants the evidence that bolster's his or her stance
on an issue. Robert York, recently retired as director of program evaluation in the Human Services Areas of PEMD, says, a trifle glumly, "By the
time you get to be a representative or senator, you have positions on
things and you're not too likely to be easily swayed by a study, not even
an evaluation synthesis."

Legislators, furthermore, are performers and often argue in terms of
anecdotes or specific cases rather than scientifically gathered samples
and averages. They may counter a meta-analytic conclusion with a
single contrary case—"Your report is very impressive, but I was in such-
and-such a place and saw that approach tried, and it simply didn't
work"—as if that one instance outweighed the hundreds of cases combined in the meta-analysis. Or they may say, as one congressman did at
a hearing where the pooled results of scores of high-quality investigations had just been presented, "How is it that your report fails to include the study by the world-famous scientist Dr. So-and-so—who happens to be from my home state—in which he says just the opposite of
what you're saying?" Whoever is testifying for PEMD—until she retired
in 1994, it was usually Chelimsky—has the ticklish job of explaining
the technical grounds on which Dr. So-and-so's work was excluded
from the meta-analysis.

PEMD meta-analysts are, furthermore, subject to a constraint absent
from academic meta-analysis, namely, the policy-oriented limitations of
the customer's questions. Academic meta-analysts answer any interesting questions that occur to them or that are generated by their search
and data extraction; government meta-analysts answer only those asked
by the representative or senator and hence must often explore questions
not couched in terms amenable to scientific testing while ignoring others that might lend themselves to it.[4]

The same factor is at work even in the meta-analyses that PEMD itself initiates (about a quarter of its meta-analytic work). PEMD does so when its staff members see an issue that they think will interest some congressional committee; after such a meta-analysis has gotten under way, a GAO liaison person talks to staff on various congressional committees in an effort to "sell" the study and get a formal request for it, lacking which it would be quietly interred in a PEMD file drawer. Generally, such efforts succeed, but at some risk: PEMD's self-generation of studies seems to some members of Congress, if the conclusions of a study displease them, to imply advocacy of policy, which they consider their prerogative and out of bounds for GAO.[5]

A frustrating aspect of doing meta-analyses for congressional customers is that for political reasons the study's findings may have little or no impact on the programs in question. In July 1995, PEMD submitted a meta-analysis of "welfare-to-work" experiments that had been conducted in a number of states and reported that the most successful of them offered a broad package of employment-related services, such as education, training, and support services, especially child care.[6] The report had been requested by Senator Daniel Patrick Moynihan, the ranking minority member of the Senate Committee on Finance, whose influence on the committee's final welfare reform bill was limited by his minority status; as a result, only some of the services found valuable by the meta-analysis were included in the bill approved by the committee.

One other exasperating aspect of doing meta-analysis for legislators, according to David Cordray of Vanderbilt University who spent some years working for PEMD, is that "congresspeople who favor a proposed piece of legislation use the positive outliers in the study as evidence supporting their position, and those who don't favor it use the negative outliers. All we can do is stress the distribution and main effect as against the outliers, and try to educate policy people to the ways in which the political process can distort social science information. It's a real problem."

A Meta-Analysis Changes a Senator's Mind

Because Senator Helms wanted the meta-analysis of WIC outcomes within six months, Chelimsky hastily got a team of five PEMD staffers—two men and three women, all of whom had some experience with meta-analysis—started on it. She also arranged to have two academic meta-analysts, Cordray, then at Northwestern University, and Richard Light of Harvard, act as consultants.

When the PEMD team first met, they were somewhat daunted by Helms' request. He had asked for a report covering five topics, each substantial enough to warrant a meta-analysis of its own: the effects of WIC on maternal health and nutritional status, on infants' birth weights, on the incidence of miscarriages, still births, and neonatal deaths, on the incidence of anemia in infants and children, and on the incidence of mental retardation. His letter alluded to the conflicting evaluations of WIC programs—a number of states had ordered reports on their programs, all of which differed slightly—but the PEMD team had no idea how many dealt with all or any of these topics and how many were rigorously controlled studies and not just impressionistic observations.

The first step was to locate and collect the evaluations, many of which were unpublished in-house reports. The team went directly to the two government sources that were likely to have copies of WIC reports or know their whereabouts: the Food and Nutrition Service of the Department of Agriculture (which administers WIC) and the Congressional Research Service. From each they got a bibliography of the WIC reports in its files or those others they knew about. They then collected copies of the reports, combed their bibliographies for useful-looking titles, and hunted for other unpublished reports by writing or phoning eighty-eight nutritionists, health professionals, and others with a special interest in WIC.

Within weeks, the team had gathered over a hundred documents and divided them up for a first reading. During this first pass, nearly a score were discarded because they dealt with special topics, such as the availability of transportation to WIC clinics, that were unrelated to the issues Helms had asked about. Another nineteen dealt with relevant matters but contained no data, and thirteen others summarized or critiqued WIC evaluations but were not themselves primary sources of data. The remaining fifty-four documents, containing sixty-one studies, were the raw material of the PEMD meta-analysis.[7]

Few of these, however, dealt with all the questions at issue. As Chris Fossett, a small, intense, hard-working woman who was on the team, told me,

> One study might have impact data on pregnant mothers and birth weight of their babies, another something on nutrition of one-year-olds, another of five-year-olds, and so on. It was all very complicated and confusing, and hard for us to know how to organize the materials. But finally Dr. Richard Barnes, the senior member of the team, drew up a huge chart showing exactly which of the various topics was covered in each document and how fully, and we constantly consulted it.

The staff also appraised the quality of each study's research methods, assigning a rating to each study. Because the studies ranged from the highly professional to the downright amateurish, Cordray and Light had recommended that the team rank every study in this fashion as a basis for drawing conclusions from the evidence. The team, using a scale of one to nine, rated nine aspects of every study, among them research design, reliability and validity of the measures of effect, and the appropriateness of the statistical methods.

To maximize interrater reliability, they compared notes constantly: Fossett recalls,

> We were forever popping into each other's cubicles to discuss what we'd just read, and to complain about how one thing or another was difficult to rate. An evaluation might, for instance, have a very good research design, but the evaluators couldn't get some of the data they wanted to collect—but went ahead and published their findings anyway. How were we to rate such a study? Even our outside consultants didn't always agree. One of them—I won't say which one—scored many aspects of the studies higher than the other one or than us. But this had its good side; his reasoning helped us sharpen up our rating process.

Of the 178 different topics or variations of topics covered in the sixty-one studies, the team gave scores of four or higher, meaning "relatively credible," to only thirty-seven of them.[8] They meta-analyzed only these findings because, Fossett explains,

> Members of the Senate committee staff, with whom we met from time to time to report on our progress, had heard conflicting reports about how good the evidence was and were very concerned about it. So we felt it was important to use only the better quality data. We knew that other meta-analysts might say that wasn't the right approach and that they would have based their findings on the total aggregate of data, but we felt we couldn't do that.

Before synthesizing the data, the team weighted the outcome measures according to the credibility rating of each study and the size of its sample.[9] Then, by means of standard meta-analytic formulas and procedures, they combined the data, using hand-held calculators. They compared WIC recipients with nonrecipient comparison groups on nine issues ranging from a single outcome measure, such as mean birth weight, to a combined outcome measure, lumped together maternal nutrition, fetal and neonatal mortality, anemia in infants and children, and the length of time the mother or child had been a WIC participant.

The team recognized, as the analysis proceeded, that on most issues the evidence was not strong enough to justify any overall conclusion. WIC was successful, however, on one or two measures, and when the analysis was nearing completion, Chelimsky thought it wise to forewarn Helms, and phoned him. She recalled the conversation for me:

> I said, "Senator, we've found something I don't think you were expecting—we've found fairly unambiguous evidence of improvement in birth weight." He said, "Is that so? . . . Would you like to come in and have a cup of coffee, dear lady? Let's sit down and talk about this." So I went over there in fear and trembling, thinking this man is going to take my head off. On the contrary, he listened to me carefully and asked questions—just a few, but very probing ones—about the credibility of the evidence. It was a great experience, because I had the answers and I convinced him—let's say, the *study* convinced him—that this was the case. And he said he'd hold hearings on it. Now, you don't know how unusual that is. When we did a study for another senator and found something he didn't want to hear, there was no hearing and nobody ever knew about our findings. Whereas Senator Helms, who fully expected us to find that WIC was a failure, and who, so many people say is a terrible man, was so gracious about it you can't imagine.

The team then collectively drafted, and Chelimsky edited, the report, which was issued on January 30, 1984, six weeks in advance of the first scheduled hearing. The report, more than eighty pages long, included thirteen complex multipage tables and a 104-item bibliography and set forth in great detail and in dense, often technical, language the team's appraisal of the raw materials and the procedures they had used to evaluate and combine their data. But, as in most research reports written for Congress, the crucial findings were summed up in a simple and almost jargon-free digest only eight pages long. As Chelimsky says, "People in Congress won't read the actual report. You're lucky to get fifteen minutes of their time at the end of a long hard day."

Since Helms had asked not for a new study of WIC's effectiveness but for an evaluation of the existing evidence, the digest of the PEMD report (somewhat abridged below) offered the team's evaluation of WIC indirectly and circumspectly:

> GAO's critical review of the evaluation designs and their execution leads to the finding that the information is insufficient for making any general or conclusive judgments about whether the WIC program is effective or ineffective overall. However, in a limited way, the information indicates the likelihood that WIC has modestly positive effects in some areas.

> Six of the WIC studies containing information about infant birth-weights are of high or medium quality. . . . [According to these] studies, about 7.9 percent of the mothers in WIC had infants who were less than 2,500 grams at birth, compared to about 9.5 percent of the mothers who were not in WIC. This translates into the positive finding that the proportion of infants who are "at risk" at birth because of low weight decreased as much as 20 percent.[10]

This was followed by brief discussions of seven other issues mentioned in the committee's five questions, among them WIC's effects on fetal and neonatal mortality, maternal nutrition, and so on. The team found some evidence that WIC was of benefit in six of the seven, but said that the quality and quantity of the evidence were not sufficient to be conclusive; as to the seventh—the combined effects of three aspects of WIC and the length of time in the program—they reported that almost no information was available.

The digest of the report concluded, again in a guardedly neutral tone:

> The shortage of credible evaluative information does not mean that WIC is ineffective; rather, it means that there is not enough clear and indisputable evidence to draw a firm conclusion about it. . . . GAO finds some sound, but not conclusive, evaluative evidence of favorable program effects on birthweights and little credible evidence on several other measures of effectiveness.[11]

What may have conveyed a sharper sense of the findings was a graph created by Fossett (reproduced here as figure 6-1). When the report was being drafted, she had compiled two tables of results, one showing the quantity and the other the credibility of the statistical evidence on each of the issues. Fossett fretted for days about the fact that GAO's congressional customers might not have the patience or skill to integrate the two in the mind's eye; then she thought of a way to combine them in a self-explanatory chart. The *quantity* of statistical evidence would be the vertical dimension, the *credibility* the horizontal one. The report's evaluation of the evidence would then be represented by dots located in a field ranging from bright knowledge, in the upper right-hand corner, to dark ignorance, in the lower left-hand corner. This is the report's prudent exegesis of the chart:

> The absence of topics in the unshaded area of the chart indicates that GAO finds no conclusive evidence of any kind about WIC's success or failure. Data on the birthweight question are substantial, but GAO finds that their quality is moderate. Findings relevant to the remaining

Figure 6-1   Meta-Analytic Findings by GAO of the Effects of WIC Programs

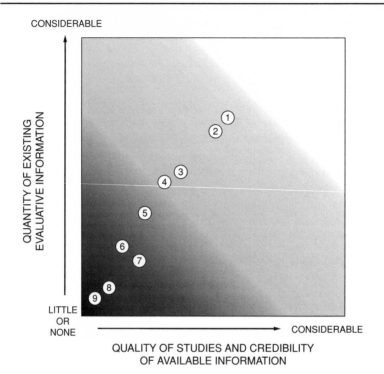

CONSIDERABLE

QUANTITY OF EXISTING
EVALUATIVE INFORMATION

LITTLE
OR
NONE

CONSIDERABLE

QUALITY OF STUDIES AND CREDIBILITY
OF AVAILABLE INFORMATION

LEGEND:
☐ CONCLUSIVE EVIDENCE
▨ SOME OR MODERATE EVIDENCE
■ GAPS IN KNOWLEDGE

KEY: 1. INCREASE IN MEAN BIRTHWEIGHTS
2. DECREASE IN PERCENTAGE OF LOW-BIRTHWEIGHT INFANTS
3. EFFECTS, FOR HIGH-RISK GROUPS AND FOR THOSE
   PARTICIPATING LONGER THAN 6 MONTHS, ON BIRTHWEIGHTS
4. IMPROVEMENT IN MATERNAL NUTRITION
5. DECREASE IN INCIDENCE OF ANEMIA IN INFANTS AND CHILDREN
6. DECREASE IN INCIDENCE OF FETAL AND NEONATAL MORTALITY
7. EFFECTS, BY LENGTH OF PARTICIPATION AND FOR HIGH-RISK
   GROUPS, ON MATERNAL NUTRITION, FETAL AND
   NEONATAL MORTATLITY, AND ANEMIA IN INFANTS AND CHILDREN
8. DECREASE IN INCIDENCE OF MENTAL RETARDATION IN
   INFANTS AND CHILDREN
9. EFFECTS OF THE THREE SEPARATE WIC COMPONENTS

Source: U.S. General Accounting Office (1984) p. iii.

questions are pushed toward the "gaps in knowledge" corner of the chart, indicated by the darker shading. . . . In sum, the information is insufficient for making any general or conclusive judgments about whether the WIC program is effective or ineffective overall. However, in a limited way, the information indicates the likelihood that WIC has modestly positive effects in some areas.[12]

In a press release issued by Helms' committee a few weeks later, Helms was quoted as saying, "GAO has produced a balanced and objective analysis of WIC program studies. Based on the actual evidence, it seems that some past witnesses clearly have exaggerated the effectiveness of the program." The press release, citing the report's qualified conclusions, added, a touch sourly, "It would be much more reassuring to the taxpayers to be more confident that the money spent is actually improving the health of poor women, infants, and children—its intended and worthwhile purpose."

Although this seemed to forecast trouble for WIC, the general tenor of both sessions of the hearing—March 15th and April 9th—was amiable and distinctly positive. Senators Helms and Thad Cochran were present at the first hearing, Senator Rudy Boschwitz at the second. The senators, their aides, and the witnesses sat around a conference table in a room of the Russell Senate Office Building, a milieu Senator Helms preferred to the formal courtlike setting so familiar to television viewers in recent years.

The first witness was Chelimsky, who briefly gave the main findings of the report. Although only two of the eighteen senators on the committee were present that day and only one at the second session, what may have impressed the others when they read the transcript was that many other witnesses echoed what Chelimsky reported about WIC's influence on birth weights and stressed its importance. Dr. David Rush of Albert Einstein College of Medicine, who was heading a nearly completed five-million-dollar study of WIC for the Department of Agriculture, said he had to apologize because his remarks would be so much like Chelimsky's. Dr. David Paige, professor of maternal and child health at the Johns Hopkins University, said that the effects on birth weights that the PEMD reported had "a major public health implication." Robert Greenstein, director of the Center on Budget and Policy Priorities, a liberal think-tank, said that the PEMD's finding of a decrease in low birthweight infants by close to 20 percent was of "striking significance."[13] In addition to the PEMD appraisal of the existing evidence, the committee heard the pro-WIC testimony of twelve other witnesses and received pro-WIC statements from a number of other experts, plus a report by the Congressional Research Service that judged WIC to be cost effective.

Of all this input, the PEMD meta-analysis carried the most weight with Helms, according to Chelimsky, who told the 1994 National Conference on Research Synthesis, "Our finding that the program was responsible for a 3.9 percent increase in infant birthweight convinced Senator Jesse Helms not to go ahead with plans to reduce or zero the program's funding."[14] Undoubtedly, the other testimony played some part in the outcome, but the committee's decision to endorse continued funding for WIC and Congress's vote to follow suit are clearly an instance, and probably the first on record, of meta-analysis having a direct influence on congressional policy-making.

Meta-Analyses and Congressional Policy-Making

There are good reasons why policy-makers are likely to find a meta-analysis, particularly in the social sciences, more persuasive than primary research. One is its political impartiality. As Kenneth Wachter, professor of demography and statistics at the University of California–Berkeley, says,

> A lot of social science research, even though it's an attempt to do good science, comes looking tainted by a certain set of political values—liberal or conservative—held by the people doing research in the field. But meta-analysis has the ability to bring studies from all sides together and review them in a quantitative way. That convergence of views gives them some protection from the charge of politicization.

Another reason meta-analyses carry special weight with legislators and agency staffers is that meta-analysts, in looking at the impact of a program, often dig deeper than main effects and ferret out the special effects of moderator and mediator variables. Policy-makers, as a result, hear not only whether it works but an answer to the question, "What works best?"[15] Meta-analysts can even build what Mark Lipsey calls "policy models" for difficult social problems, such as drug abuse. A policy model, he explains, is "an interconnected set of statements of relationships that embrace the key variables in the problem" and that enable the analyst and policy-maker to carry out "what if" simulations of the probable results of specific changes in the treatment, the kinds of people administering it, and other projections of the future.[16]

A noteworthy example of meta-analysis effectively bringing nonpartisan findings to bear on a fiercely debated issue is a series of PEMD reports in the 1980s of studies of the "Bigeye bomb." This was a chemical weapon being developed by the Department of Defense (DOD) that would produce a lethal agent by combining two nonlethal substances. DOD claimed that its studies demonstrated the potential effectiveness of the new weapon, but Representative Dante Fascell, chairman of the House Committee on Foreign Affairs, wanted a more impartial appraisal and asked PEMD for a meta-analysis of those studies. PEMD's analysis found that the DOD studies cited expert opinions as if they were objective evidence but that they often lacked experimental data. Moreover, the meta-analysis of such objective evidence as existed found serious technical uncertainties as to the reliability and effectiveness of the proposed weapon. PEMD's initial report—it conducted several—startled, alarmed, and enlightened many members of Congress. Representative Fascell later wrote to Chelimsky that PEMD's work "proved to be a crucial factor in the formulation of U.S. policy," leading to high-level negotiations and agreements with the Soviet Union about chemical weapons, the elimination by Congress of all funds for such weapons, and the eventual cancellation of the Bigeye bomb program by the DOD.[17]

The breadth of vision a meta-analysis can offer policy-makers is exemplified by the impact of a PEMD report on a bill affecting the nation's supply of low-cost rental housing. In December 1989, Representative Henry Gonzalez, chairman of a subcommittee of the House Committee on Banking, Finance, and Urban Affairs, asked for a PEMD meta-analysis of the probable effects of a proposed change in the National Housing Act. The change would have enabled owners of more than a third of a million housing units to prepay their federally insured mortgages; if enough chose to do so, and then opted to sell their houses at a profit, the national supply of low-rental properties would undergo considerable shrinkage. A "windfall profits test" was supposed to control the shrinkage, but existing studies, made in different regions of the country, differed widely as to the likely effect of the proposed change.

The meta-analysis portrayed the probable impact of the proposed change as no single study had done and as no mere review of the studies could do. PEMD concluded that it was very uncertain whether the "windfall profits test" could control the loss of rental housing and that the potential loss was serious enough to warrant revising the windfall profits test guidelines. These findings, presented at a hearing on the new housing bill, impressed Representative Gonzalez enough that he changed the bill then and there along the lines of PEMD's recommendations.[18]

Meta-analytic evidence has also played an important role in passing new legislation aimed at the public's general well-being, even when it conflicts with partisan and commercial interests. A particularly striking instance is PEMD's study of the effects of drinking-age laws. Legislation enacted in 1984 required that a portion of federal highway funds be withheld from states that did not raise the minimum drinking age to twenty-one. Most states complied, but some state legislatures, pressured by beer lobbyists, resisted, maintaining that raising the drinking age did little to reduce driving accidents. Some other states, that had passed such laws, were considering repealing them, and South Dakota sued to overturn the federal requirement, claiming that it was unconstitutional.[19]

In late 1985, Representative James Oberstar, chairman of a subcommittee of the House Committee on Public Works and Transportation, asked PEMD for a meta-analysis of the effects of drinking-age laws on traffic accident rates. PEMD collected more than four hundred relevant documents and selected fourteen that met all its criteria for inclusion, among them five kinds of outcome measure, such as driver death, driver injury, and total fatalities.

The meta-analysis, released in March 1987, found that raising the drinking age to twenty-one unquestionably and significantly reduced alcohol-related accidents among youths.[20] The U.S. Supreme Court used the meta-analysis in 1987 to dismiss questions as to the effectiveness of such laws; then, reviewing South Dakota's case, it ruled that the federal law was constitutional. The remaining noncomplying states thereupon enacted drinking-age laws and those considering whether to repeal theirs abandoned those plans. The National Highway Traffic Safety Administration publicly credited PEMD with convincing the states and the Supreme Court of the effectiveness of drinking-age laws.[21]

These odds and ends of evidence certainly suggest, though they do not prove, that PEMD meta-analyses influence the decisions of policymakers. Since no rigorous study of the matter exists, we have only the subjective impressions of those involved to bolster that view, though admittedly these are skewed by temperament and general outlook. For example, York (the codirector of PEMD when I visited him), elegantly tall, slim, white-haired, and low-keyed, said,

> Staff people read our reports first, and it's their job to pass on the gist of the reports to their bosses. But I don't really think they pay more attention to an evaluation synthesis than to other kinds of studies. And very few congressmen and congresswomen actually read more than the executive summary. We try to convince ourselves that the person who reads our evaluation synthesis will be overwhelmed by the power and majesty of our presentation, but that happens in our dreams, not in reality. To be realistic, I'd say that the policy impact of our evaluation syntheses is modest.

Chelimsky, spirited and chronically cheerful, was considerably more upbeat:

> Congressmen and congresswomen are political people, and their understanding of your work has to do with how relevant it is to their constituencies, how much money it involves, and other power-type questions. But we *have* had a major effect in a number of cases—the Bigeye bomb case, the drinking-age-law case, WIC, and others. From a policy point of view, meta-analysis is the answer to all those policy-makers who say, "I saw this tried in Podunk and therefore I think it won't work" or "It worked in Podunk, so I think it would be good for the United States as a whole." And it's also very useful for informing policy before it's started; we've had that kind of impact a number of times—the low-cost housing bill is a good case in point.

She summed up the policy influence of meta-analysis in her keynote address to the 1994 National Conference on Research Synthesis in these words:

> The use of [our] findings has been appropriate and considerable; new agency research has been commissioned or mandated when information was missing; sound studies have been used and reused; and finally, the synthesis has not—as we had feared—driven out congressional requests for studies requiring original data collection: on the contrary, I'd say it has actually sharpened the congressional appetite for impact evaluation.[22]

A postscript: In mid-1996 PEMD was disbanded and its staff redistributed throughout the GAO as a result of a tightened budget made necessary by an economy-minded Republican-dominated Congress. Wherever they are now located, however, GAO staffers who have worked on meta-analyses will still be able to conduct others when requested to do so by Congress.

IN BRIEF . . .
Lumpectomy Versus Mastectomy

Early in 1993, Judith Droitcour, a PEMD staff member, was discussing breast cancer research with George Silberman, a senior staffer with whom she had often worked. Both were interested in the subject, Droitcour because her sister-in-law had recently been diagnosed with it, Silberman because, having done a number of cancer studies, he was in the habit of keeping up with new developments in the field. Droitcour, an attractive, birdlike, little woman, recalled for me how their conversation led to a PEMD meta-analysis:

> We talked about the fact that large numbers of women are diagnosed with breast cancer every year and that many of them have to make a decision between lumpectomy and mastectomy but that it's difficult to do so because there's some controversy about the matter. We knew that there had been randomized clinical trials and that experts had said in 1990 that patient survival rates following lumpectomy and mastectomy were equivalent, but the trials had been conducted in cancer centers and it wasn't at all certain that the results of the treatments were the same in day-to-day general medical practice.
>
> That seemed an important question and one that could best be answered by a "cross-design synthesis"—a combination of a meta-analysis of clinical studies and data from case records of medical practice in the community.

(The previous year, Droitcour and Silberman had worked out the methodology of cross-design synthesis, and GAO had published a 121-page report on it written by them.[23])

With Chelimsky's approval, Droitcour took on a cross-design synthesis of breast conservation versus mastectomy. She worked mostly alone, though she got some help from another staffer, Eric Larson, and from half a dozen other PEMD staffers and eighteen outside oncologists, meta-analysts, and statisticians. When the study was nearing completion, a member of GAO's Office of Congressional Relations described the project to staff members of the Subcommittee on Human Resources of the House Committee on Government Operations. Because that committee oversees the activities of, and grants made by, the National Cancer Institute, the subcommittee chairman formally requested the report.

To gather her data, Droitcour, aided by a librarian, did an on-line data base search for randomized studies conducted in major cancer centers. She looked for studies that compared the five-year results of the two treatments on node-negative patients (patients showing no evidence of metastases to the lymph nodes) and that included radiation as part of the treatment. Droitcour also wrote to a number of breast cancer researchers to make sure there were no other studies she might have missed.

Only six studies met all the criteria—three in single centers, three in multiple associated centers—but all were of high quality and taken together had a total of nearly 2,500 patients. In each of the six, lumpectomy and mastectomy patients had similar survival rates, and in all six the odds ratios of both treatments were close to one, suggesting equal effectiveness of the two. The patients in the studies were all seventy or younger and, for the most part, had tumors measuring four centimeters or less in size.

Droitcour, with the guidance of several of her expert advisers and the help of an advanced software program, synthesized the data to get precise, statistic estimates of the treatment effects. The combined odds ratio for patients treated in cancer centers was 1.05, which indicated a minuscule advantage for lumpectomy; actually, there was no difference in five-year survival rates for the two kinds of treatment.[24]

Then, for data on patients in day-to-day general medical practice in the United States, Droitcour turned to SEER (an acronym for Surveillance, Epidemiology, and End Results), a data base maintained by the National Cancer Institute. SEER is an up-to-date compilation of almost all cancer cases in five states (Connecticut, Hawaii, Iowa, New Mexico, and Utah) and four metropolitan areas (Atlanta, Detroit, San Francisco–Oakland, and Seattle–Puget Sound); these nine areas are varied enough in population to effectively represent the nation.

From SEER's huge data base, Droitcour was able to extract cases that matched those in her combined set of randomized clinical trials: The computer came up with 5,326 women aged seventy or younger who had had node-negative breast cancer with tumors four centimeters or smaller in size. About one-fifth had had lumpectomy plus radiation and nodal dissection; the rest had had mastectomy. All of them had been followed for five years, or until death if it occurred sooner.

Some of these patients, however, were more likely to have been offered lumpectomy by their doctors than others and to have selected it— younger women, women living in sophisticated areas, and so on—so it was not appropriate simply to calculate the survival rate for all lumpectomy cases and compare it with the survival rate for all mastectomy cases. Droitcour had to sort the women into five groups according to how *likely* they were to have received lumpectomy, whether or not they actually got it. In the least likely fifth were women close to seventy, those diagnosed as early as 1983, those living in Iowa, and those with tumors close to four centimeters in size; in the most likely fifth were younger women, those more recently diagnosed, those living in San Francisco–Oakland, and so on.

At that point Droitcour could make a valid comparison of the outcomes of lumpectomy and mastectomy, since her survival rates were now free of the selection bias arising from group differences in lumpectomy rates. She then combined the lumpectomy rates and the mastectomy rates she had calculated for each category within each sample; the combined rates for the two forms of treatment turned out to be very similar, there being only six-tenths of 1 percent better survival rate for mastectomy, a nonsignificant difference.[25]

The crucial next step was to compare these SEER cases with those of the randomized clinical trials. Since the clinical trials had been conducted in cancer centers and the SEER cases came from general medical practices, one might suppose that the results of lumpectomies in clinical trials would be superior to those found in general practice. But the comparison offered genuine hope to *all* women diagnosed early with breast cancer. As Droitcour summed up the findings in her report,

> Our three-step analysis indicated that . . . the effectiveness of breast-conservation therapy has, on average, been similar to that of mastectomy in community medical practice as well as in randomized studies. Specifically, for medical practice cases, the adjusted 5-year survival rates . . . were 86.3 percent for breast-conservation patients and 86.9 percent for mastectomy patients. These results clearly correspond to the results of multicenter randomized studies (88 percent 5-year survival for breast conservation and 88 percent for mastectomy). Single-center studies reported somewhat higher survival for both treatment groups. Thus, on average, for breast cancer patients of physicians in regular medical practice who are similar to patients in randomized studies, there appears to be no appreciable risk associated with selecting breast-conservation therapy rather than mastectomy.[26]

Into the Black Hole

The breast conservation report was issued on November 15, 1995, but as of late 1996 the Subcommittee on Human Resources of the House Committee on Government Operations, to which the report was submitted, had made no recommendations to Congress or congressional agencies based on it. From that standpoint, the PEMD report, like a small star sucked into the unappeasable maw of a black hole, had disappeared without a trace. To be sure, PEMD had included no policy recommendations in its report, but the lack of response may also have been due to the fact that the report was delivered less than two weeks after the national election that resulted in republican domination of both houses of Congress, which brought about the reshuffling of committee chairmanships and staffing; a number of the staffers who knew most about the breast conservation report had gone and the new chairman's staffers knew nothing about it and had many other things on their mind.

From another standpoint, however, the report had not vanished but been noticed by and had an impact on several nonfederal audiences: physicians treating early breast cancer, breast cancer patients, and health researchers concerned with ways of assessing the outcomes of alternate medical treatments. The National Cancer Institute invited Droitcour to present her findings at a national cancer conference and sent out copies of the report to cancer organizations around the country. The knowledge yielded by her study has been seeping down through the oncological community to general medical practitioners and, to some extent, to the newspaper-reading and television-watching public. It has therefore probably had some influence—albeit unmeasurable—on the National Cancer Institute's official position on lumpectomy and on the policies of cancer centers and oncologists throughout the country. But it has had no impact on congressionally established policy to date, and may never have.

That is the fate of a fair number of PEMD meta-analyses for various reasons. One is, as with the breast conservation report, that a requested meta-analysis may be completed just when compelling political circumstances preempt the attention of potentially interested legislators, the result being that the pertinent legislation is mothballed. By the time the legislation is again discussed, the report either has been forgotten or appears dated.

Another reason a requested meta-analysis may have little or no impact on policy-making is that representatives and senators are rarely moved to action solely by scientific evidence; loyalty to their constituencies is often a stronger influence. As Chelimsky wrote in *Science* a few years ago: "The relation between researchers and decision-makers remains one of inherently imperfect understanding, based as it is on the uneasy juxtaposition of different kinds of rationality and the dominance of politics over scientific logic in democratic societies."[27]

Congressional committee members may choose to ignore a report whose conclusions run counter to their stance or belittle it by invoking moral values, the basic principles of their party, or the views of one of the Founding Fathers. Or they may play the bumpkin role, jesting that the statistical analysis in the report is beyond their comprehension. Or with a fine disregard for the methodology of the study, they may base their proposals and proffered amendments on the few items in the report that support their position, carefully ignoring those that do not.[28] Moreover, legislators, often under pressure to reach decisions and set policies, may be impatient with an exhaustive but still inconclusive meta-analysis; little wonder if they ignore a study that says no good evidence yet exists and offers no policy guidance.[29]

Worse still for the meta-analyst: If a report says what a legislator in a powerful position—a committee chairperson, for instance—does not want to hear, he or she may, rather than blast away at it, simply bury it without obituary or funeral. Several years ago, a meta-analysis that found the opposite of what a senator chairing a committee advocated vanished after delivery. It was never mentioned in the committee's deliberations, let alone at its hearings, and has never been heard of elsewhere.

Smoke Gets in Your Eyes—and Lungs, and That's Nothing to Sing About

In 1964 Surgeon General Luther L. Terry issued an impressive report marshaling evidence that cigarette smoking is a cause of lung cancer and chronic bronchitis; the tobacco industry's Tobacco Research Council counterattacked by funding a number of studies that, not surprisingly, discounted the risks of smoking. Congress, faced with conflicting evidence and, more important, immobilized by the tobacco industry's contributions to political campaigns and the quid pro quo relationships between tobacco-state congressmen and their colleagues, did nothing to limit smoking for many years. Not until the 1970s did the antismoking forces win a victory, and then only a minor one, a law requiring warning labels on cigarette packs.

With Congress so reluctant to act against smoking—the cause of an estimated 434,000 deaths each year, 40 percent of all cancer deaths[30]— it is not surprising that it was even less inclined to act against "passive smoking" (breathing air contaminated by the smoke of others). It was not for lack of evidence, however: In 1986 the National Research Council and the Surgeon General independently issued reports that found "environmental tobacco smoke" (ETS)—passive smoking—to be a cause of lung cancer in adult nonsmokers and of respiratory ailments in children.[31] The tobacco industry again responded by citing other studies—in this round, not funded by it—which contradicted those findings; as mentioned in chapter 1, two studies published in 1984 actually found *less* lung cancer among people exposed to ETS than those not exposed. But in 1988 a meta-analysis by an independent risk-assessment organization combined the hard-to-believe 1984 studies with fifteen others and concluded that ETS increased the risk of lung cancer by fifty percent in women and more than doubled it in men.[32] Still Congress took no action.

But another avenue exists via which evidence obtained by meta-analytic techniques can affect policy, namely, regulatory agencies to which Congress has delegated power, in this case, the U.S. Environmental Protection Agency (EPA). In 1986 Congress passed the Superfund amendment to the Radon Gas and Indoor Air Quality Research Act, authorizing EPA to provide "information and guidance" on the potential hazards of indoor air pollution. On those grounds, James Repace, a senior policy analyst in the Indoor Air Division of EPA, suggested to his superiors that if EPA conducted its own scientific study of the risks of ETS, it could legitimately put forth a policy on passive smoking. Robert Axelrad, director of the Indoor Air Division, welcomed the suggestion, provided the major funding for such a study in 1988, and named Steven Bayard, a biostatistician in the EPA's Office of Research and Development, its technical director.

Bayard, unfamiliar with the scientific literature on ETS, at first doubted that there could be a link between second-hand smoke and cancer.[33] Because he thought that lung cancer studies, taken individually, had very little power to detect the effects of ETS, since virtually everyone is exposed to at least some second-hand smoke, he was more inclined to believe that the combined data of a number of studies would yield a believable conclusion. Bayard assembled a staff of seven highly qualified people: two EPA staffers, an epidemiologist at Yale, a medical researcher at the University of Arizona, and three staff members of his prime contractor, an engineering and risk-assessment research firm in Chapel Hill, North Carolina. He also lined up eighteen specialists at universities and health agencies to serve as reviewers and consultants. The team then exhaustively searched the scientific literature for research on the effects of ETS, ending up with thirty studies of ETS and lung cancer in adults plus more than fifty other recent studies of ETS and respiratory disorders in children.

Because the thirty lung cancer studies, despite having been conducted in eight different countries, used similar methodologies and measures of effect, the team's statisticians were able to meta-analyze them. They also separately analyzed a subset of the higher-quality studies and another of the eleven studies conducted in the United States. For all these poolings, they compared the estimates of the risk for death from lung cancer among nonsmoking wives exposed to their husbands' smoke with that of nonsmoking wives not so exposed. These and other comparisons filled seventy-eight tables of data in the five-hundred-plus page report. Three of the studies showed, contrary to common sense, that passive smokers had less chance of getting lung cancer than other nonsmokers, but when all the studies were meta-analytically combined, the results were quite clear—and totally overcame Bayard's doubts.

After extensive public and expert review, the report was released in January 1993. Some of its most striking conclusions:

- Based on the pooled data of the eleven studies conducted in the United States, the risk of lung cancer death in women nonsmokers exposed to their husbands' smoke was 19 percent greater than the risk for women nonsmokers with nonsmoking husbands. When the eight higher-quality studies were used, the risk was 22 percent greater. The differences were statistically significant.[34]
- Based on the seven U.S. studies that had data on men, the risks for male nonsmokers exposed to their wives smoke was 40 percent higher than for male nonsmokers not so exposed; based on eleven studies from various countries, it was 60 percent higher. Because far fewer men than women had been studied, the results were statistically less certain; even so, the team concluded, the relative risks for men were at least as great as, and probably greater than, those for women.[35]
- While not all studies showed a statistically significant association between ETS and lung cancer, the pooled results of all of the studies did. The risks in other countries and places, among them Greece, Japan, and Hong Kong, were much greater than those in the United States. The four studies from Western Europe, when combined, also showed a positive correlation, but not at a statistically significant level. Only the four studies from China showed no such connection when combined, but many of the Chinese homes were so polluted by heating with smoky coal and by smoky indoor cooking that any ETS effect would be masked.[36]

The report's summary presented these important estimates of the effects of ETS:[37]

- ETS is responsible for about three thousand lung cancer deaths annually in U.S. nonsmokers.
- ETS annually causes an estimated 150,000 to 300,000 cases of lower respiratory tract infections, such as bronchitis and pneumonia, among American infants and young children up to eighteen months of age.
- ETS exposure causes upper respiratory tract irritation and a small but significant reduction in lung function.
- In anywhere from 200,000 to 1,000,000 U.S. children with asthma, ETS causes additional episodes and more severe symptoms. In children who have not yet shown symptoms of asthma, ETS increases the risk of developing it.

In a foreword to the EPA report, Louis W. Sullivan, secretary of the U.S. Department of Health and Human Services, and William K. Reilly, administrator of EPA, wrote,

> [This report] provides important new documentation of the emerging scientific consensus that tobacco smoke is not just a health risk for smokers. It is, in fact, also a significant risk for nonsmokers, particularly for children.
>
> This report demonstrates conclusively that environmental tobacco smoke increases the risk of lung cancer in healthy nonsmokers. The report estimates that roughly 30 percent of all lung cancers caused by factors other than smoking are attributable to exposure to environmental tobacco smoke. Put another way, a nonsmoker exposed to environmental tobacco smoke during everyday activities faces an increased lifetime risk of lung cancer of roughly 1-in-500 to 1-in-1,000. By comparison, EPA generally sets its standards or regulations so that increased cancer risks are below 1-in-10,000 to 1-in-a-million. In other words, estimated lung cancer risks associated with environmental tobacco smoke are more than ten times greater than the cancer risks which would normally elicit an action by EPA.[38]

EPA did, in fact, take action half a year later. In July 1993, it announced guidelines on smoking in public buildings. All companies and agencies operating public buildings were asked to either ban smoking or use ventilation to assure that people are protected from other people's smoke.[39]

By then, EPA's determination that ETS was a cancer hazard was having multiple policy effects: A number of states and cities had enacted or were considering controls over smoking in public places; the Occupational Safety and Health Administration (OSHA) had proposed banning smoking in six million workplaces nationwide; DOD had prohibited smoking in its workplaces worldwide; and hundreds of private real estate companies, restaurateurs, operators of fast-food eateries, and other entrepreneurs were making efforts to control ETS in order to avoid lawsuits based on EPA's finding.[40]

The tobacco industry, accustomed to fighting, struck back: In a June 1993 hometown filing in Winston-Salem, North Carolina, R. J. Reynolds sued the EPA in an effort to overturn EPA's designation of ETS as a known human carcinogen, claiming that EPA had manipulated its scientific studies and ignored accepted statistical practices in order to arrive at its risk assessment.[41] Reynolds and Phillip Morris conducted massive advertising campaigns in newspapers, attacking both EPA's science and motives and depicting smokers as victims of government oppression.

Another attack on the EPA's findings came from a different quarter. The Congressional Research Service, in response to a congressional request, prepared an economic analysis of the Clinton administration's proposal to fund health care reform using new cigarette taxes; the authors of the study, two economists, concluded that the tax would be relatively ineffective, and then, curiously, went beyond the bounds of their assignment to attack the EPA study of passive smoking, citing primarily studies funded by the tobacco industry.[42]

It is worth noting that one of those studies found the levels of ETS in a number of public places to be relatively low—and that Representative Henry Waxman, chairman of the House Health and Environment subcommittee at that time, revealed that three workers on the study told people on his staff that their superiors had altered their data and consistently underreported the measurements of cigarette smoke.[43] But the tobacco industry's attacks and the Congressional Research Service report did not reverse or stay the course of events. The National Research Council's findings, supported by the EPA's meta-analysis, has been the propelling force behind a steady series of legislative and nonlegislative moves to control and eliminate ETS in public places. Angry smokers have put on a few half-hearted demonstrations, and a few hotheads have defied the ban on smoking in airplanes or restaurants (and gotten themselves arrested for their pains). The resistance has come to little; meta-analytic knowledge has prevailed.

"More Ways than One to Skin a Cat"—Mark Twain

As the case of passive smoking shows, meta-analysis can exert an important influence on social policies by means other than legislative acts. The chief such mechanisms are the establishing of policies and practices by agencies to which Congress, state legislatures, and city governments have assigned the authority to do so.

An impressive example is the publication of medical guidelines by the Agency for Health Care Policy and Research (AHCPR). This agency, a branch of the Public Health Service, was established in December 1989 by Public Law 101-239 to "conduct and support general health services research." As part of its broad mandate, AHCPR publishes reports, for the benefit of health care providers, policy-makers, and the public, of the best and latest research on various medical problems and treatments. The reports come in two forms: *Clinical Practice Guidelines*, which are substantial volumes on a number of subjects, including management of cancer pain, diagnosis and treatment of benign prostatic enlargement, and the treatment of major depression; and *Quick Reference Guides for*

Clinicians, which are slim brochures presenting the same material in abbreviated form.

Each *Guideline* is the work of a panel of independent experts commissioned by AHCPR; the panelists gather information in a number of ways, the major one being a literature review that results in a meta-analysis if enough experimental studies are found. A typical example is the panel that produced *Management of Cancer Pain* (*Guideline* Number 9); it searched nineteen data bases, screened 9,600 citations, and, in a meta-analysis of 550 of them, appraised the effectiveness of a number of interventions.[44] (The *Guidelines* run anywhere from about 100 to 260 pages, the *Quick Reference Guides* from twelve to forty pages. The seventeen *Guidelines* and seventeen *Quick Reference Guides* published thus far are available free to practitioners, scientists, educators, and "consumers" [patients]; they can also be downloaded free from the National Library of Medicine's data base, Health Services Technology Assessment Text.) A similar program exists in the United Kingdom: Teams at two centers established by the National Health Service, one in Oxford and one in York, prepare "systematic reviews"—their term for meta-analyses—of existing information on medical subjects and make their findings available to physicians and other interested parties.[45]

In addition to the AHCPR, various institutes within the National Institutes of Health are beginning to base their advisory notices to the medical and scientific communities on meta-analyses. The National Heart, Lung, and Blood Institute, for one, recently issued a warning that the short-acting form of nifedipine, a calcium channel blocker employed to control high blood pressure and heart disease, should be used "with great caution, if at all." Although the Heart Institute's warning was not binding on doctors, it undoubtedly carried considerable weight with them. It was based on a meta-analysis conducted for the institute by a team at the Bowman Gray School of Medicine in Winston-Salem headed by Dr. Curt D. Furberg, chairman of the department of health sciences. The team meta-analyzed sixteen clinical trials involving 8,350 heart attack patients given nifedipine. The meta-analysis showed that during the period covered, patients on high doses of the drug had an average risk of death at least twice that of similar patients receiving either a placebo or no drug.[46]

The meta-analytic findings about nifedipine are exerting an influence on policy in a second way: Dr. Robert Temple, a top official at the Food and Drug Administration (FDA), said that the study provided credible data and that the FDA would be looking at it closely and considering a change in labeling for nifedipine.[47] The FDA itself has recently begun to use meta-analytic findings in some of its reviews of new drug applications. Normally, the FDA reviews randomized controlled clinical studies submitted by the drug companies wishing to market a new drug; when the findings of the studies are inconsistent, the FDA has begun using meta-analysis to resolve the uncertainties and reach decisions about the safety of the new drugs and establish labeling requirements.[48]

A number of the meta-analyses presented in this book appear to be having some influence—"appear," because no measurements of it exist—on policies and practices of America's schools, hospitals, state welfare programs, mental health clinics, courts, prisons, and other institutions. The influence of meta-analytic findings has been exerted through legislative measures, through regulatory policies, and through voluntary changes in behavior, the moral equivalent of policy. That, at least, is the impression of knowledgeable people interested in meta-analysis and policy-making. There is also psychological reason to believe it correct: Information is known to change attitudes, and attitude change is known to be the precursor of behavior change.

With that, let us rest the case for the influence of meta-analysis on policy and conclude with a few speculations about the future of this powerful new method of extracting the truth from the thorny and resistant fruits of research.

Chapter 7

Epilogue:
The Future of Meta-Analysis

Elixir of Forecast: Take Minimal Dose

How will meta-analysis develop from this point on? It is a question one may well be wary of answering, for predictors of the future, particularly of social phenomena, often turn out to be embarrassingly wrong. Herbert Hoover assured Americans in 1932 that "prosperity is just around the corner"; it turned that corner fifteen years later. Hitler said that his Third Reich would last a thousand years; it lasted a dozen. As Francis Bacon tartly commented, predictions are good only for winter talk by the fireside.

Well, yes and no. Actually, anyone can quite accurately predict the weather five minutes hence, but even the highly computerized National Weather Service does poorly when forecasting a week ahead. To say how meta-analysis will develop and what role it will play in science a generation from now would be mere guesswork, but one can be fairly certain how it is likely to develop in the next several years.

There are good grounds on which to base these short-range extrapolations. The best evidence is the remarkable growth of meta-analyses in scientific journals (none in 1977, nearly 400 in 1994) and in data banks (none in 1977, nearly 3,500 in 1994). The leveling off of that growth in the last several years suggests that meta-analysis has found and is filling its proper niche in contemporary science.

The foregoing chapters have tried to highlight its achievements in fields ranging from biology and medicine to education and social psychology. What meta-analysis will be able to accomplish in the near future follows logically from them; it is almost certain that meta-analysts will continue to improve the precision and certainty of their findings and be increasingly capable of determining causal connections. The American Statistical Association, hardly a hotbed of enthusiasts and radicals, sees the methodology as having the potential to revolutionize how research, particularly in medicine, is done,[1] and in an article about meta-analysis in *Science*, the statistician and meta-analyst Frank Schmidt of the University of Iowa is cited as predicting that meta-analysis could transform research in the behavioral sciences.[2]

Another indicator of the short-term future of meta-analysis is the waning of disbelief in and opposition to it. No longer do journal editors reject a meta-analysis on the grounds that it is "not original research," and no longer are speakers who present meta-analytic findings at scientific symposia scoffed at. Even the usually arthritic and rule-bound agencies of the federal government are beginning to recognize the value of meta-analysis, and some even to practice it; that growing acceptance is likely to continue over the next several years.

To be sure, there still are some nonbelievers and critics. H. J. Eysenck is doing business at the same old stand and repeating all his well-worn castigations—"garbage in, garbage out," "apples and oranges," and so on. When I recently visited him in London, he even upgraded his old epithet for meta-analysis, "mega-silliness," to "mega-imbecility." In fairness to him, however, it should be said that he does not initiate these attacks on meta-analysis. "It's a sideline, as far as I'm concerned," he said. "I get invited by various journals to write on meta-analysis because everybody seems to be for it and they're looking for somebody who's against it. So they come to me."

A few American critics of meta-analysis are as dead-set against it as Eysenck. In an article in the *American Journal of Epidemiology*, Samuel Shapiro of the Slone Epidemiology Unit, Brookline, Massachusetts, sneeringly characterizes it as follows: "Meta-analysis begins with scientific studies, usually performed by academics or government agencies, and sometimes incomplete or disputed. The data from the studies are then run through computer models of bewildering complexity, which produce results of implausible precision."[3] In *American Psychologist*, David Sohn, a psychologist at the University of North Carolina, is even more caustic and rejecting. As quoted earlier, he argues that primary research is the only valid way to make discoveries, rates the claim that meta-analysis is a superior mechanism of discovery simply farcical, and scorns the notion that "the process of arriving at truth is mediated by a literature review."[4] But his identification of meta-analysis with literature reviews is itself farcical; anyone who has even a nodding acquaintance with the subject knows that meta-analysis is a far different, more rigorous, and statistically objective procedure for extracting truths from a mass of diverse reports.

But not many such voices are raised against meta-analysis today. Sounder and more useful criticisms of, and predictions about, meta-analysis come from those who support and use it while pointing out its pitfalls and shortcomings. They do not scoff at the "apples and oranges" criticism, for instance, but specify how and when it applies, and how and when it does not. They recognize the risk of publication bias but go to great pains to minimize it and to test for it. They admit the multiple threats to validity in meta-analysis but lay out the procedures by which those threats can be circumvented. They freely acknowledge the many kinds of error or distortion possible in meta-analysis and prescribe remedies for each.

Robert Rosenthal spends an entire chapter of his *Meta-Analytic Procedures for Social Research* on the principal weaknesses of meta-analysis and ways to deal with them. Harris Cooper and Larry Hedges, editors of the ponderous and authoritative *Handbook of Research Synthesis*, allocate half a dozen of its thirty-two chapters to the hazards of meta-analytic methodology and how to avoid them, and in their concluding remarks they foresee meta-analysis, incorporating all these precautionary procedures, as becoming part of the standard armamentarium of scientific research:

> There is no reason to believe that carrying out a sound research synthesis is any more complex than carrying out sound primary research. . . . When research synthesis procedures have become as familiar as primary research procedures much of what now seems overwhelming will come to be viewed as difficult, but manageable.[5]

A Few Specific Prophecies

The future is bound to bring numerous minor refinements and innovations in meta-analytic procedures, particularly the statistical ones. Many have been suggested in this book, but some larger and perhaps more important trends are also clear enough to permit credible short-term predictions. Four are worth noting:

Finer slices of the information pie: Founding Father Gene Glass, whose original emphasis was on the main effect, now says,

> What I've come to think meta-analysis really is—or, rather, what it ought to be—is not little single-number summaries such as "This is what psychotherapy's effect is" but a whole array of study results that show how relationships between treatment and outcome change as a function of all sorts of other conditions—the age of the people in treatment, what kinds of problems they had, the training of the therapist, how long after therapy you're measuring change, and so on. That's what we really want to get—a total portrait of all those changes and shifts, a complicated landscape rather than a single central point. That would be the best contribution we could make.

We have, in fact, already seen plentiful evidence in previous chapters of a trend in that direction—the increasing emphasis on seeking out not only main effects but the special relationships between moderator variables, mediator variables, and outcomes that account for the differing results of studies of the same subject. This kind of fine-toothed analysis yields findings as important as the central effect, namely, causal explanations and findings as to what variants of the treatment work best and why.

Continuously updated meta-analytic findings: Joseph Lau and Thomas Chalmers, as we have seen, have campaigned for the more rapid adoption by physicians of meta-analyses of clinical trials and, to make that more feasible, developed the technique of cumulative meta-analysis. Taking that concept a giant step further, in 1992 Lau, Chalmers, and four colleagues proposed to the AHCPR that it fund their research in developing a "Real-Time Meta-Analysis System" (RTMAS) and were awarded a $1.2 million, three-year grant.

By "real-time" Lau and his colleagues mean that their system will provide medical leaders and practicing physicians with updated meta-analyses of drug trials as fast as new studies are completed. In contrast, the present dissemination of meta-analytic data on new treatment outcomes is slow and tortuous; years can elapse between the completion of an important clinical trial and its incorporation and publication in a meta-analysis. The RTMAS, when fully developed, will solve this problem: It will be a methodology, fully translated into a systematic software program, for promptly evaluating and processing the data of new clinical controlled trials and then incorporating those data into one or many ongoing and always up-to-date cumulative meta-analyses. It will be, Lau says, "a research tool to do meta-analyses more efficiently and reproducibly via standardization of data extraction and analytic methods, while maintaining flexibility and the 'recycling' of previous research efforts."[6]

The Cochrane Collaboration: A different and even more ambitious use of meta-analysis is already being made by the Cochrane Collaboration. This organization, as mentioned in chapter 4, is an international network of two dozen "collaborative review groups"—teams of volunteers in each of many health care specialties who keep track of the latest findings in their fields, evaluate them, and incorporate them in systematic reviews and, when feasible and appropriate, meta-analyses. The original data and the pooled results are published electronically through The Cochrane Database of Systematic Reviews, available on disk, CD-ROM, and on-line. The system enables doctors to keep easily abreast of the current state of knowledge.

The Cochrane Collaboration and its products operate through Cochrane centers in several countries. The UK Cochrane Centre at Oxford is funded chiefly by the U.K.'s National Health Service Research and Development Programme; the Cochrane centers in other countries are funded by various public agencies and, to a limited extent, by foundations. Despite their diverse sources of funding, the centers in the United Kingdom, the United States, Canada, Italy, the Nordic countries, and Australasia are cooperatively linked in the Cochrane Collaboration. It may well become one of the chief mechanisms by which meta-analysis will play an increasingly important role in medicine.[7]

Envisioning the perfect study: At a 1986 workshop on meta-analysis, Donald Rubin felt that everyone was too much in agreement and set out to foment some dissension. He did so by telling his audience:

> Often, the right way to add provocative stimuli is to claim that everything everybody is doing is wrong. Even when this isn't true (and it certainly can't be in this context), it is often useful to take such an attitude and see how far it can be pushed. So I begin by claiming that everything everybody's been doing statistically for meta-analysis, including the things Bob Rosenthal and I have done and do, are irrelevant and have missed the point. We all should really be doing something else.[8]

Having thoroughly aroused his listeners, he then outlined his idea of the something else they should be doing. Instead of combining and summing up a batch of imperfect studies, they should be developing statistical methods of estimating what a perfect study would find. To do so, they should take a set of studies of some treatment and its effects, examine how a change in the value of each variable affects the outcome, and then, using curves plotted from those data, extrapolate to what a perfect study—all-embracing, free of sampling or other errors, and without any methodological uncertainties—would yield.

If, for instance, the effect size changes with the size of the sample, they would project statistically what the outcome would be if the sample included 100 percent of the individuals in the universe being studied. Or if the effect size varies with the experience of the researchers, they would project the findings of ideally experienced researchers, and if these results covaried with the size of the sample, they would calculate the interactions all along the sample-size curve by a second crisscrossing set of curves for the variable of experience. And so on for every conceivable variable that affects the outcome: time, place, method of treatment, characteristics of the one who is treated and of the one who is administering the treatment, and so forth.

The effects of all these relevant variables extrapolated to the theoretically perfect study, and the results of their interactions with every other variable, can be envisioned not as a set of curves on a two-dimensional graph but as a "response surface"—an undulating three-dimensional landscape of plains, valleys, and hills representing all the points of reality as revealed by the perfect study.

What is all wrong with meta-analysis, according to Rubin, is that it *interpolates*—looks for an answer inside a set of studies; what it should do is *extrapolate*—look for an answer beyond them by using their data to project the findings of an ideal study. These would be the "true" effects, not the probable effects yielded by present techniques.

"Standard statistical tools can be used to build and extrapolate this treatment-effect response surface," Rubin said, but thus far has offered only a few hints as to how that would be done. He admits that developing the necessary statistical tools and procedures would require "a relatively massive statistical effort in the context of real examples," and, being chairman of the statistics department at Harvard, he is too busy to do it; he hopes, though, that some graduate student will come along who will carry out the work under his guidance.

Reactions at the workshop and in the field to Rubin's vision have been mixed. His concept is dizzying and even alarming, and some meta-analysts and statisticians regard it as high-flown flapdoodle. Others, however, find it challenging, constructive, and a reasonable prediction of the future. A review of the book in which Rubin's presentation appeared concluded, "The chapter that truly speaks to the future of meta-analysis, and not to its distant and recent past, is the chapter by Donald B. Rubin entitled 'A New Perspective.'. . . [It is] an eminently sensible, indeed altogether wholesome, conceptualization of what research synthesis should be."[9]

The reviewer was Gene Glass.

A Parting Word

I have been a science writer nearly all my working life, and in the course of my work I have listened to and read the work of many bright and some brilliant men and women: mathematicians, physicists, chemists, physicians, geneticists, and, most of all, psychologists and sociologists. They have been a very varied lot, but the one trait they share is a pervasive and communicable enthusiasm about what they do. All serious and gifted scientists, I think, are adventurers—intellectual explorers making their way into terra incognita and enduring the dreadful tedium and innumerable travails and disappointments in the hope of achieving that transfiguring moment when at last they glimpse the truth and feel much like—

> stout Cortez when with eagle eyes
> He star'd at the Pacific—and all his men
> Look'd at each other with a wild surmise—
> Silent, upon a peak in Darien.
>   (John Keats, "On First Looking into Chapman's Homer")

That has most certainly been true of the fifty-odd men and women I met and interviewed for this book. Some were young, others not so young, and a few old; some were wonderful explainers and others hard to follow; many were ebullient and some sober; but all—truly, all—were enthusiastic about what they were doing and conveyed a sense of high intellectual adventure. I found it exciting and enriching to listen to them, read the fruits of their studies, and share their journeys and discoveries. I regret that I have come to the end of my travels with them. I can only hope that you do, too.

Some Finer Points in Meta-Analysis
Harris Cooper

The main body of the text introduced meta-analysis to the general reader, with a particular eye to underscoring the field's novel contribution to social science methods. As a consequence, it dealt with the actual mechanics of meta-analysis in a necessarily cursory way. This appendix aims to counter that deficiency, and much of the material in it requires an acquaintance with basic statistics. (Needless to say, even this amplifying discussion is somewhat simplified, however, and leaves many issues untouched. For the interested reader, the many excellent meta-analysis methods books mentioned in the text can provide a thorough picture of the field.)

This appendix is divided into three sections. Each section addresses a major issue in conducting a meta-analysis. The first section concerns how meta-analysts obtain effect sizes from individual studies in a form that is combinable across studies. The second section describes the mechanics of combining effect sizes and analyzing them for differences related to moderator variables. The third section deals with how meta-analysts interpret effect sizes, assigning degrees of "largeness" or "smallness" and of "importance" or "triviality" to the statistic.

Obtaining Effect Sizes in Combinable Form

Actually, about a dozen effect size metrics exist and are described in a book by Jacob Cohen (1988), entitled *Statistical Power Analysis for the Behavioral Sciences*. In practice, however, the three effect size metrics discussed in the text—the r-index, the d-index, and the odds ratio—nearly always do the trick. They are focused and informative, and one of the three fits just about every situation.

Each effect size metric accommodates relationships among variables with different measurement characteristics. The r-index is used to express the relationship between two continuous variables, such as when class size is related to achievement. The d-index relates one dichotomous variable to a continuous variable, such as comparing clients who do or do not receive psychotherapy (dichotomous) using subjective measures of well-being (continuous). The odds ratio is used when both variables are dichotomous, such as the effect of taking or not taking aspirin on the occurrence or nonoccurrence of heart attack. The choice of how to express the effect sizes, then, is determined by which metric best fits the measurement characteristics of the variables under consideration. A meta-analyst makes that choice by looking at the central relationship under consideration and at how the variables are measured.

A problem arises when the meta-analyst comes across separate studies that examine the same relationship but do so using different metrics. Suppose we are looking for studies on class size and academic achievement. We find one study that employed as data all the naturally occurring classes in a school district. Clearly, the r-index best fits this study because both class size and achievement vary over a continuous range of values. However, we find another study that used a large school district and compared only those classes with more than thirty students, labeled the "large class" group, with classes of fewer than twenty students, labeled the "small class" group. Classes with twenty-one to twenty-nine students were discarded from the data set. This study seems to fit the d-index best because the class size variable is measured as if it were dichotomous.

Which should the meta-analyst use? The r-index is still the metric of choice because the variables are *conceptually* continuous, even though the second study created two "artificial" extreme groups (with the probable intention of maximizing the chance that a significant difference would be found). So, for the second study we would calculate a d-index from the large-class and small-class means and standard deviations and then convert it to an r-index using a simple formula. Conversion formulas, and tables of equivalent values based on them, allow meta-analysts to move from one effect size metric to another. They are available in meta-analysis textbooks.

Suppose we find a study that compares three groups, say, a traditional psychotherapy versus a brief psychotherapy versus no treatment. How would we generate an effect size?

In this instance, we would most likely consider calculating two d-indexes, one comparing traditional psychotherapy to no treatment and another comparing brief psychotherapy to no treatment (we could also consider comparing traditional and brief therapies if this were the focus of our review).

The two d-indexes would not be statistically independent, since both rely on the means and standard deviations (sds) of the same no-treatment group. But this complicating factor (discussed below) is preferable to the alternative strategy of using yet a fourth effect size metric called percentage of variance (PV).

PV tells us how much of the variance in the dependent variable is explained by group membership. PV has the initially appealing characteristic of being usable regardless of the number of groups in the study (indeed, it can be used with two continuous measures as well). However, it has the unappealing characteristic of being relatively uninformative: The resulting effect size tells us nothing about which of the three treatments is most effective. Identical PVs can result from any rank ordering of the three group means. Thus, PV is an unfocused effect size metric that is rarely, if ever, used by meta-analysts.

Another problem facing meta-analysts is that many research reports do not contain the information needed to estimate an effect size. This is probably the most frustrating problem encountered by quantitative reviewers. To address this problem, the meta-analyst must comb a research report to find the data needed to make the calculation and sometimes make some assumptions.

Let's stick with the example of the effects of psychotherapy. In the best of all possible worlds, every research report that compared the well-being of psychotherapy patients with untreated controls would present either a d-index calculated by the primary researchers or a table that included the means, standard deviations, and sample sizes for each group.

Often, too often, that does not happen. Sometimes only the means associated with a significant difference are given. In this case, the meta-analyst first looks to see if the primary researchers reported the exact value of the statistical test associated with the psychotherapy comparison. In its simplest form, this will be a t-test, a test of the difference between two means. Say the researchers report that the comparison between final well-being indicated that clients receiving psychotherapy reported greater subjective well-being ($M = 52.4$) than the no-treatment controls ($M = 48.2$), where M signifies the mean, and that the t-value of 2.11, using sixty subjects, was significant at p < .05. No standard deviations are reported, so the d-index cannot be calculated directly. However, because the d index and t-test rely on much the same information (means, sds, and sample sizes), the meta-analyst can use a simple formula (also available in meta-analysis texts) to estimate the effect size from the value of the significance test. In this case, d = .55.

If the exact t-value is not given but the primary researchers do report a p level and sample size, the meta-analyst can estimate the t-value (by finding the two known quantities in a table of t-values) and plug it into the formula.

If a single-degree-of-freedom F-value from a one-factor analysis of variance is given, it can be converted to a t-value ($F = t^2$) and the formula used. However, if an F-value is based on a multiple-group comparison (say, traditional versus brief versus no therapy), or, if it comes from an analysis of variance with more than one factor (say, both treatment and sex of the client are part of the computations), then additional steps must be taken to make the F-value equivalent to the simple t-test. Sometimes these adjustments can be made, sometimes not.

Interestingly, studies that relate two continuous variables are quite likely to report the exact r-index associated with the result. If not, there is also a formula for converting a t-test to an r-index. Similarly, studies that relate two dichotomous variables are likely to present a table with the needed cross break of data. The odds ratio is then easily calculated.

Meta-analysts have invented lots of other seat-of-the-pants techniques that allow them to generate effect size estimates from incomplete reports. In nearly all cases, the meta-analyst is forced to make assumptions about the data that can be plausible or suspect. How plausible or suspect is for the users of the meta-analysis to decide.

For all effect size metrics, the biggest problem arises when primary researchers report that the comparison of interest was "not significant" and give no statistics whatsoever. Then, meta-analysts are really stuck. They can try to contact the researchers and ask for the data they need. This strategy meets with limited success. Alternatively, they can ignore the study, but this may upwardly bias the average effect size estimate. Or, they can assume the missing effect size is exactly zero, but this will likely bias their average estimate downward. Or, they can assume the effect size fell just below significance and calculate its largest possible nonsignificant value. If this value is assumed to be in the prevailing direction of other effect sizes, it will likely cause an overestimation of the average effect. If this value is assumed to be in the direction opposite to most other effect sizes, it will cause an underestimation.

Given all these possibilities, it is not unusual for meta-analysts to present multiple estimates of average effect sizes based on different assumptions about missing data. For example, a meta-analyst can present an average effect size based on the known data and an average based on very conservative assumptions about missing data, sort of stacking the deck against the hypothesis. If both approaches lead to a similar conclusion about the existence and importance of a relationship, the users of the meta-analysis can have greater confidence in its conclusion.

A bias in estimates of average effect sizes (and in comparisons between effect sizes) can result if missing data lead to the exclusion of the study. For this reason, meta-analysts are obligated to discuss how many data were missing from their reports, how the missing data were handled, and why they chose the methods they did.

A sample statistic—be it an effect size, a mean, or a standard deviation—is based on measurements of a small number of people drawn from a larger population. Sometimes these sample statistics will differ in known ways from the value obtained if every person in the population could be measured. Because effect size estimates based on samples are not always true reflections of their underlying populations, meta-analysts have devised ways to adjust for the bias.

A d-index based on small samples (less than ten people in each group) tends to overestimate the population value. So, a correction factor can be calculated to adjust small-sample d-indexes, making the values smaller but more accurate. Formulas and tables for calculating the adjustment are available. Some ways of calculating odds ratios also can lead to over- or underestimates, and similar adjustments may be needed.

In a related vein, r-indexes that estimate underlying population values very different from zero have nonnormal sampling distributions. This occurs because r-indexes are limited to values between $+1.00$ and -1.00. So, as a population value approaches either of these limits, the range of possible values for a sample estimate will be restricted toward the approached limit. Therefore, the distribution of sampled values will become more skewed away from normal. To use a visual image, if a set of sampled r-indexes centers around a value of, say, .40, then more positive values can range only from .41 to 1.00 while less positive values can range from .39 to -1.00. Thus, the distribution will appear to have its upper tail (the one at the $r = +1.00$ end) cut off.

To adjust for this, some meta-analysts convert r-indexes to their associated z scores, which have no limiting value and which will be normally distributed, before the estimates are combined. In essence, the transformation "stretches" the upper tail and restores the bell shape. Then, the z scores are combined and averaged. Once an average z score has been calculated, it can be converted back to an r-index.

If the r-index is close to zero, there is really no need to do the transformation. (Indeed, some meta-analysts eschew this transformation regardless of the r-index value.) An examination of the r-to-z transformation table reveals that the two values are near identical until $r = .25$. However, when the r-index equals .50 the associated z score equals .55, and when the r-index equals .8 the associated z score equals 1.1.

Another statistical problem arises when a single study contains multiple effect size estimates. This is most bothersome when more than one measure of the same construct is taken and the measures are analyzed separately.

Suppose we are conducting a meta-analysis comparing the effects of two workgroup structures on job satisfaction. We find a study that compared the two structures using both an attitude measure and a measure of absenteeism. Obviously, since the same workers are involved, these measures are not independent estimates of the effect. Thus, it would seem unfair to combine these two estimates plus a third from a separate study to arrive at an average effect. The first study would be given too much weight. Also, the assumption that effect size estimates are independent underlies the other meta-analysis procedures described below.

There are several approaches that meta-analysts use to handle dependent effect sizes. Some treat each effect size as independent, regardless of the number that come from the same sample of people, and assume that the effect of violating the independence assumption is not great. Other meta-analysts use the study as the unit of analysis. In this strategy, they calculate the mean effect size or take the median result and use this value to represent the study. So, if a study reports three nonindependent d-indexes of, say, .10, .15, and .35, the study might be represented by a single value of .20 if the mean is used, or .15 if the median of the several measures is used.

Recently, sophisticated statistical models have been suggested as a solution to the problem of dependent effect size estimates. However, the viability of these procedures lies in whether the meta-analyst can credibly estimate the actual degree of relation among dependent measurements. Because this approach is new and complex, and estimating dependencies is tricky, it has not been used much yet.

The issue of dependent estimates is not confined to the problem of multiple measures taken on the same sample. Results in the same study that are reported separately for different samples of people also share certain influencing factors. Suppose the effect of workgroup structure on job satisfaction is estimated separately for men and women within the same study. Then, the samples are independent but the type of work might not be, nor the quality of management, nor the study's design and execution. All these things will likely make these two effect sizes more similar than any two effects drawn at random. Taken a step further, a reviewer also might conclude that separate but related studies from the same group of investigators are not independent.

So when does it stop? In practice, most meta-analysts ignore the study-level interdependencies in effect sizes but not those based on shared samples.

Combining Effect Sizes Across Studies

State-of-the-art meta-analytic procedures call for the weighting of effect sizes by their sample size (or more accurately, by the inverse of their variance) when they are averaged across studies. The reason for doing so is that studies with larger samples yield more precise estimates and so should contribute more to the combined result. This weighting produces an estimated effect size that is closer to the population value.

As was mentioned in the text, a good meta-analysis will report the 95 percent confidence interval around an average weighted effect size estimate. The average estimate gives the most likely population value of the effect size, based in the known studies. The confidence interval gives the range of values that we can say with 95 percent certainty will contain the population value.

Also, the confidence interval can be used in place of the combined p level techniques. It can be used to reject the null hypothesis that the difference between two means, or the size of a correlation, is zero. If the 95 percent confidence interval does not include $d = 0$ or $r = 0$, then the null hypothesis can be rejected.

Having calculated an effect size for each study and then a weighted average of all the effects, a good meta-analyst will then want to calculate average effect sizes for subsets of studies. Often, a meta-analyst wants to compare separate estimates for studies that used different outcomes, different treatment implementations, or different types of subjects, to name just a few of the multitudinous ways studies can differ. If average effect sizes across subsets of studies are similar, then the meta-analyst can be more confident that the overall conclusion is generalizable across different situations. If the averages are not similar, then the meta-analyst has identified important qualifiers, or moderators, of the overall results.

The ability to raise questions about variables that moderate effects is one of the major contributions of meta-analysis. Even if no individual study has compared different outcomes, implementations, or types of subjects, the meta-analysis can give a first hint about whether these moderators are important. Suppose we are interested in whether brief psychotherapies are more effective with male or female clients. We might examine the literature and discover that no single study compares the effect of brief therapies on men and women. However, we might find some studies that compare brief therapies to no treatment that include just men and others that include just women. By calculating the average effect sizes across these two groups of studies and comparing them, we get a first indication of whether the sex of the patient moderates the effect of therapy.

We would not accept the conclusions of a primary research report if it did not formally test for the difference between two group means. Likewise, calculating average effect sizes for subsamples of studies and detailing the differences are not sufficient to claim that the estimates are truly different. Meta-analysts must formally test the difference between average effect sizes to determine if they are significant, or to rule out chance as an explanation for the difference.

Early on, meta-analysts used the familiar parametric inference tests, namely analysis of variance or multiple regression, that are used in primary research. The effect size served as the dependent variable and features of the study, such as treatment or sample differences, were used as "independent," or predictor, variables.

This approach was criticized, however, because meta-analytic data often do not meet the underlying assumptions of the familiar techniques. For example, the parametric inference procedures assume that each measurement of the dependent variable is influenced by a roughly equal amount of error (an assumption called "homoscedasticity of error"). However, it is unlikely this assumption is met when effect sizes are the dependent variables because the error in each effect size estimate is a function of its sample size (more error in smaller samples) and sample sizes can vary markedly from one estimate to another. For this reason, the familiar procedures have been largely abandoned in meta-analysis.

In their place, two approaches have gained acceptance. The first compares the variation in the observed effect sizes with the variation expected if only sampling error were making the effect size estimates differ. This approach involves calculating (1) the actual variance in the effect sizes that the meta-analyst obtains from studies and (2) the expected variance in these effects, given that all observed effects are estimating the same underlying population value. This expected value is a simple function of the average effect size estimate, the number of estimates, and the sample sizes. Sampling theory gives us quite precise estimates of how much sampling variation to expect in a group of effects.

The meta-analyst then compares the observed with the expected variance. Proponents of this procedure generally refrain from formal tests to judge whether a significant difference exists between the observed and expected variances. Instead, they establish an arbitrary criterion and use it. They might say that if the observed variance is twice as large as the expected sampling variance then they will assume the two are reliably different. Whatever the criterion, if the variance estimates are deemed similar, then sampling error is the simplest explanation for why the effect sizes differ. If they are deemed different, that is, if the observed variance is much greater than that expected from sampling error alone, then the search for systematic influences on effect sizes begins.

In addition, proponents of this approach often adjust effect size estimates to account for methodological artifacts that have calculable influences. For example, we know that social science measurements vary in reliability because they are influenced by factors extraneous to the construct they are meant to gauge: A measure of academic achievement is influenced not only by what students know but also by their health on the day of the test and the degree of commotion in the testing room. For some measures, the amount of unreliability can be estimated. With them, the effect sizes can be adjusted to tell us what the relationship among variables might be if the measures were pristine. When two variables are involved, these adjusted effect sizes are always larger than the observed ones. If the estimates are not available, the adjustments can be carried out using plausible assumed values or not done at all.

The second approach, called homogeneity analysis, provides the most complete guide to making inferences about a research literature. As just noted, effect sizes will vary somewhat, due to sampling error, even if they all estimate the same underlying population value. Like the first approach, a homogeneity analysis compares the observed variance to that expected from sampling error. It differs in that it includes a calculation of how probable it is that the variance exhibited by the effect sizes would be observed if sampling error alone was making them differ. In essence, the homogeneity test asks the question, "What are the chances of observing this much variance in a set of effect sizes if sampling error only is operating?"

Just as in a significance test of the difference between two means, if the probability of observing the variance is less than .05, we reject the notion that sampling error alone is the cause of differences in effect sizes. Suppose an analysis reveals a homogeneity statistic, typically called Q, that has an associated p value of .05. This means that only five times in a hundred would sampling error create this amount of variance in effect sizes. Thus, we would reject the (null) hypothesis that sampling error alone explains the variance in effect sizes and begin the search for additional influences.

The meta-analyst then tests whether study characteristics explain variation in effect sizes. Studies are grouped by features, and the average effect sizes for those groups are tested for homogeneity in the same way as the overall average effect size. In the *Handbook of Research Synthesis*, Larry Hedges gave a good example of how a homogeneity analysis is carried out. Hedges presented a table with data from ten studies examining whether a sex difference exists in the tendency to conform (see Cooper and Hedges 1994, table 19.2). The ten d-indexes were $-.33$, $.07$, $-.30$, $.35$, $.70$, $.85$, $.40$, $.48$, $.37$, $-.06$ (with positive values indicating females are more conforming). The weighted (by sample size) average of these d-indexes is $+.123$, indicating that females are more likely to conform than males. The overall homogeneity statistic for the set of effects is Q $= 31.799$, which is significant beyond $p < .005$. Therefore, Hedges could safely reject the hypothesis that the variance in this set of effect sizes was due *solely* to sampling error.

What else might be causing the effects to differ, or more precisely, which characteristics of the studies might be systematically associated with variance in effect sizes? As one possibility, Hedges decided to look at the sex of the authors of the research reports. He noted that the first two effect sizes came from studies for which 25 percent of the authors were male, the third effect size came from a study whose authors were 50 percent male, and the final seven effects came from studies for which all the authors were male. Is it possible that grouping studies in this manner accounts for some of the variance in effects?

First, Hedges calculated the average d-index for each of the three groups of studies. He found that the weighted average effect for the first two studies (25 percent male) was $d = -.15$. This indicates that studies with relatively few male authors find that males are more conforming than females. However, the 95 percent confidence interval includes values from $-.39$ to $+.09$. Therefore, because zero is contained in the interval, Hedges cannot reject the null hypothesis that this set of studies found no reliable sex difference in conformity. The single study whose authors were 50 percent male has an effect size of $d = -.30$, which is significantly different from zero; the confidence interval ranges from $-.59$ to $-.01$. Finally, the seven studies authored entirely by males reveal an average weighted effect of $d = +.34$, which is also significantly different from zero (the confidence interval is $.19$ to $.49$) but in the opposite direction. These studies indicate females are more conforming than males.

Apparently, Hedges was on to something. Whether a study found males or females more conforming appeared related to the gender composition of the authors: Studies authored exclusively by males found greater female conformity; studies with at least one female author did not. But, just looking at the average d-index in the three groups of studies does not tell us if they are reliably different. To do this, Hedges returned to homogeneity analysis. This time, however, he analyzed the variance in the three average effect sizes: $-.15$, $-.30$, and $+.34$. The associated Q statistic is 20.706, significant well beyond $p < .005$. So, Hedges could now say that grouping studies in this manner showed that some of the variance in effect sizes, beyond that expected by sampling error alone, could be accounted for by the gender composition of the team of authors.

In Hedges' meta-analysis, he assumed that the effect sizes coming from the separate studies were estimating a fixed population value rather than a random one. The distinction between fixed and random effects often baffles even sophisticated data analysts.

In essence, an effect size is said to be fixed when the sampling error discussed above is the only random factor affecting its estimation. Sometimes, however, other features of studies can be viewed as random variables. For example, in studies of class size and academic achievement, the effect of the teacher will differ from class to class in unsystematic ways. Might it therefore be appropriate to consider teachers to be randomly sampled from a population of teachers? Or to give another example, in a broad-based evaluation of Head Start, programs will differ in a multitude of ways from site to site. Should the included programs be considered a random sample of all programs? If the researcher answers "yes," then the statistical analysis must proceed in a fashion that takes this additional randomness into account.

In meta-analysis, the question is whether the effect sizes in a data set are affected by a large number of these uncontrollable influences—in the Head Start example, by, say, differences in teachers, facilities, community economics, state regulations, and so on. If they are, the meta-analyst must choose a statistical model that takes this random variance in effect sizes into account. If they are not, then random variance in effect sizes is ignored (or, more accurately, set to zero) and a fixed effects statistical model is used.

It is rarely clear-cut which assumption, fixed or random, is most appropriate for a particular set of effect sizes. In practice, most meta-analysts opt for the fixed effects assumption because it is analytically easier to manage. Some meta-analysts argue that fixed effects models are too often used when random-effects models are more appropriate (and conservative). Others counterargue that a fixed effect statistical model can be applied if a thorough, appropriate search for influences on effect sizes has been part of the analytic strategy, that is, if the meta-analyst looks at the systematic effects of influences such as teachers, facilities, community economics, and state regulations.

Interpretation of Effect Sizes

Effect size estimates are of little value unless users can understand their substantive, practical, and statistical significance. The first guides to interpreting effect sizes were provided by Jacob Cohen (1988), who proposed a set of values to serve as definitions of "small," "medium," and "large" effects. However, he recognized that judgments of "largeness" and "smallness" are relative, requiring a comparison between two items. Therefore, in defining these adjectives he compared the different average effect sizes he had encountered in the behavioral sciences.

Cohen defined a small effect as d = .2 or r = .1, which his experience suggested were typical of those found in personality, social, and clinical psychology research. A large effect of d = .8 or r = .5 was more likely to be found in sociology, economics, and experimental or physiological psychology. According to Cohen then, a clinical psychologist might interpret an effect size of r = .1 associated with the impact of psychotherapy to be "small" when compared to all behavioral sciences but "about average" when compared to other clinical psychology effects.

Because his contrasting elements were so broad, Cohen was careful to stress that his conventions were to be used as a last resort. At the time he was writing, comparing the effect of psychotherapy to "all behavioral science effects" might have been the best contrasting element available. Today, with so many meta-analytic estimates of effect available, other more meaningful contrasting effects can often be found.

Suppose we have just completed a meta-analysis of the effect of printed public service advertisements on adolescents' attitudes toward smoking. We find that the average effect is d = .2, indicating that teenagers exposed to print ads hold attitudes toward smoking that are two-tenths of a standard deviation more negative than teenagers not so exposed. Using Cohen's guide, we would label this effect "small." However, additional contrasting elements might be available to us. These might come from other meta-analyses that looked at entirely different ways to change smoking attitudes, like high school health classes. Or, they might come from meta-analyses of different but related treatments, such as the effect of television ads. Also, we might try to find meta-analyses that shared the same treatment or predictor but varied in outcome measure, for example, ones that examined actual smoking behavior or behavioral intentions rather than attitudes.

Effect sizes also need to be interpreted in relation to the methodology used in the primary research. Thus, studies with more extensive treatments (in our example, more frequent exposures to ads), more sensitive research designs (within-subject versus between-subject designs), and more trustworthy measures can be expected to reveal larger effect sizes, all else being equal. If we are comparing the results of a meta-analysis involving carefully controlled lab studies of print ads and attitudes with one involving field studies of TV ads and behavior, we have to consider the methodological differences before drawing a conclusion about the relative bigness or smallness of print and TV ad effects. In this instance, the deck is stacked against TV ads.

Judgments of size are not synonymous with judgments of importance or value. The relative merit of different treatments or explanations involves considerations in addition to the numerical size of a relationship. Most notable among these are the cost of particular treatments and the value placed on the changes the treatment is meant to foster.

Suppose we wanted to explore the relative cost effectiveness of decreasing class sizes from twenty-five to twenty students versus extending the school day by fifteen minutes. First, we would have to establish an estimate of the effect of each change. Assume that a meta-analysis finds the improvement in student achievement when class sizes decrease to be $d = .15$. Another (or the same) meta-analysis finds the improvement in achievement associated with the addition of fifteen minutes of instruction to be $d = .10$. So, reducing class size has a bigger effect.

But that is not enough. Next, we must calculate the cost per student of each change. We find that the new classrooms and teachers needed to reduce class size adds $200 to the cost of educating each child. The additional teacher salary needed to increase the length of the school day, plus building utilities and other expenses adds $100 per child. So, we would estimate a cost-effectiveness ratio by calculating the effect size gain per dollar spent. In this analysis, extending the school day yields more brains for the buck.

Conclusion

It is hoped that the reader has not been left with the impression that conducting a good meta-analysis presents a set of insurmountable practical problems. It does not. When social scientists first sought ways to measure variables or conduct experiments, the task must have seemed equally intimidating. However, the problems provide the challenges, not just in the search for new techniques but also in the refinement and application of the old ones. And it is the challenges, along with the clear understanding of the benefits that come with overcoming them, that provide the motivation for meta-analysts to continue work at the frontiers of scientific methods.

Notes

Unpublished quotations throughout the text are from personal interviews conducted by the author.

Chapter 1

1. Gina Koata. 1994. "New Study Finds Vitamins Are Not Cancer Preventers." *The New York Times*, July 21, 1994, p. A20.
2. Jane E. Brody. 1995. "Study Says Exercise Must Be Strenuous to Stretch Lifetime." *New York Times*, April 19, 1995, p. A1. The original study is Lee, Hsieh, and Paffenbarger (1995).
3. Jane E. Brody. 1995. "Trying to Reconcile Exercise Findings." *The New York Times*, April 19, 1995, p. A1.
4. Thompson (1994) fig. 2.
5. C. G. Moertel, "Improving the Efficiency of Clinical Trials," cited in Begg and Berlin (1988).
6. U.S. National Institutes of Health (1994).
7. Jerry E. Bishop. 1995. "Link Between EMF, Brain Cancer Is Suggested by Study at Five Utilities." *The Wall Street Journal*, Jan. 11, 1995, p. B6. The article refers to a study by David A. Savitz and Dana P. Loomis in *American Journal of Epidemiology*.
8. Joel Greenhouse and others, in a meta-analytic review of the aphasia treatment literature, in Wachter and Straf (1990) p. 31.
9. Becker (1990).
10. Mann (1994).
11. Light and Smith (1971).
12. Jeffrey Schneider, in an introduction to a set of meta-analyses of desegregation, in Wachter and Straf (1990) pp. 55–57.
13. Eagly and Johnson (1990) pp. 233–234.
14. The massive and influential review is Maccoby and Jacklin (1974). The later studies are summarized in Eagly and Wood (1991).
15. Fischer (1991).
16. Not all meta-analysts agree with this contention; see Hedges (1987).
17. Mulrow (1994).
18. The two 1984 studies: Buffler and others; Kabat and Wynder. The larger, later study: Janerich and others (1990).
19. Bunge (1991) pp. 553–554; Bunge (1992) pp. 72–73; Malcolm W. Brown. 1995. "Scientists Deplore Flight from Reason." *The New York Times*, June 6, 1995, pp. C1, C7. The article reports on a conference held at the New York Academy of Sciences.

20. Ibid.
21. White in Cooper and Hedges (1994) p. 42.
22. Goldfried, Greenberg, and Marmar (1990) p. 675.
23. Mulrow (1987).
24. T. Chalmers and Lau (1994).
25. Light and Pillemer (1984) pp. 3–4.
26. Pearson (1904) pp. 1243–1246.
27. Tippett (1931).
28. Cochran (1937) pp. 102–118.
29. For details, see Glass, McGaw, and Smith (1981); Light and Pillemer (1982); Sacks and others (1987); and Ingelfinger and others (1994).
30. Developments listed in the paragraph refer to Light and Pillemer (1984) and to brief summaries in Glass (1976) and in Glass, McGaw, and Smith (1981) pp. 24–25.
31. Glass (1976).
32. Some authorities divide them into six phases, some into many substages. See Cooper (1982); Durlak and Lipsey (1991); T. Chalmers and Lau (1993a); and Cooper and Hedges, in Cooper and Hedges (1994) pp. 8–13.
33. In Wachter and Straf (1990) p. 47.
34. Eysenck (1978). The peer review is from Cooper's personal files. Hall, interview with the author.
35. The figures are from my own search in late 1995. Higher ones have been reported for the three social science data bases between 1978 and 1989; see White in Cooper and Hedges (1994) p. 43, but this search did not eliminate duplications among the data bases. Another search reported five hundred listings for 1992 in MEDLINE alone, but included articles that mentioned or discussed meta-analysis and were not themselves meta-analysis (I. Chalmers and Haynes 1994).
36. Yusuf and others (1994).
37. Held, Yusuf, and Furberg (1989).
38. Baum and others (1981).
39. Hayashi and T. Chalmers (1993).
40. Lawrence K. Altman. 1992. "Tiny Cancer Risk in Chlorinated Water." *The New York Times*, July 1, 1992, p. A18. The report by Robert Morris and others appeared in *American Journal of Public Health* (July 1992).
41. Kranzler and Jensen (1989). For the statistically inquisitive, the figure $-.54$ is the measure of the regression of IQ on IT when both variables are scaled in standardized units. If two people differ by, say, twenty standardized units in IT, the slower person will be about ten units lower in IQ.
42. Ray (1993) p. 35.
43. Bushman and Cooper (1990).
44. Paik and Comstock (1994); Comstock and Paik (1990).
45. Lehman and Cordray (1993).
46. Greenberg and others (1992, 1994).
47. Olkin and Shaw (1994).
48. Sohn (1995).
49. In Wachter and Straf (1990) pp. 6–7.
50. Freeman Dyson. 1995. "The Scientist as Rebel." *New York Review of Books*, May 25, 1995, p. 33.

Chapter 2

1. "The talking cure" was what Anna O., a patient of Freud's early mentor and collaborator Josef Breuer, called Breuer's primitive form of psychotherapeutic treatment.
2. Luborsky (1972); Luborsky, Singer, and Luborsky (1975). The 93 percent improvement rate: Morton (1955).
3. Eysenck (1952) pp. 661–662.
4. Eysenck (1990).
5. Eysenck in Lindzey (1980) p. 165.
6. Reisman (1976) p. 352; Luborsky (1954).
7. The two studies: Bergin, summarized in Smith and Glass (1977), and Meltzoff and Kornreigh, cited in Luborsky, Singer, and Luborsky (1975).
8. Light and Smith (1971) p. 433.
9. National Task Force on the Prevention and Treatment of Obesity (1994).
10. Fisher (1926) p. 504.
11. Bailar and Mosteller (1992) p. 358; Rosenthal and Rubin (1979) p. 1165.
12. Glass, McGaw, and Smith (1981) p. 95.
13. Details in the section titled "Genesis of Meta-Analysis, Part I" are drawn from interviews with Glass and Smith; Glass (1976); and Smith and Glass (1977).
14. Smith and Glass (1977) p. 753.
15. Hunter and Schmidt (1990) p. 85. Also quoted in Cooper and Hedges (1994) p. 126.
16. Altick (1975) p. 13.
17. See Orwin in Cooper and Hedges (1994) p. 141.
18. Durlak and Lipsey (1991) pp. 311–313; Glaser and Olkin, in Cooper and Hedges (1994) pp. 340–341, 350.
19. Yeaton and Wortman (1993); Orwin in Cooper and Hedges (1994) pp. 145–153.
20. Orwin in Cooper and Hedges (1994).
21. Durlak and Lipsey (1991) p. 305.
22. Ibid., p. 310.
23. Rosenthal (1991a) pp. 97–98.
24. Becker in Cooper and Hedges (1994) p. 218.
25. Kraus (1995).
26. Draper and others (1992) pp. 178–180.
27. Bailar and Mosteller (1992) pp. 184–185.
28. Smith and Glass (1977) p. 753.
29. Gallo (1978) p. 516.
30. Eysenck (1978) p. 517.
31. Mary Lee Smith interview. For typical articles contesting Smith and Glass's findings, see Gallo (1978); Prioleau, Murdock, and Brody (1983); and Orwin and Cordray (1985). For typical articles confirming them, see Andrews and Harvey (1981); Landman and Dawes (1982); and Shapiro and Shapiro (1982).
32. Lipsey and Wilson (1993) p. 1200. Since many of the original studies appeared in more than one meta-analysis, the actual number of original studies is somewhat less than five thousand.

33. Cook and others (1992) p. 13.
34. Shadish and others (1993); also, Shadish and others (1995).
35. Eagly and Carli (1981).
36. Cook (1991) p. 264; Miller and Pollock (forthcoming).
37. Light (1984) p. 59.
38. Flather, Farkouh, and Yusuf (1994) p. 394.
39. Hedges in Cooper and Hedges (1994) p. 298; Hedges and Olkin (1985) pp. 11–12.
40. Shoham-Salomon and Rosenthal (1987); Shoham and Rohrbaugh (1994).
41. Shoham-Salomon and Rosenthal (1987) p. 27.
42. Shadish and Sweeney (1991). They are speaking of meta-analyses of psychotherapy, but their remarks apply to all forms of intervention.
43. Baron and Kenny (1986).
44. Shadish and Sweeney (1991).

Chapter 3

1. Hanushek (1989) p. 45.
2. Ibid., p. 47.
3. Memo to Larry Hedges from Laine and others, April 23, 1992.
4. Hedges in Cooper and Hedges (1994) p. 30.
5. Ibid., pp. 30–33.
6. Wachter and Straf (1990) p. 167.
7. Dickersin, Scherer, and LeFebvre (1994) p. 1290.
8. Knipschild (1994) p. 719.
9. Laine and others (1992) pp. 4–8.
10. Laine and others (1992) pp. 19–25. They give their results in other mathematical terms; I have used the p value given in Hedges, Greenwald, and Laine, (1994a) pp. 9–10.
11. Laine and others (1992) pp. 39–40.
12. Ibid., p. 38. The third technique, a correlation matrix analysis, yielded less impressive results than the two discussed here.
13. Eysenck (1994) p. 791.
14. Glass (1978).
15. Glass (1983) pp. 401, 404.
16. Hall and others, in Cooper and Hedges (1994) p. 20.
17. Matt and Cook, in Cooper and Hedges (1994) p. 515.
18. Hanushek (1989).
19. Hedges, Laine, and Greenwald (1994a) pp. 10, 11.
20. Ibid., p. 11.
21. That is, 0.7 times the sd of 34 percent.
22. Hanushek (1994) p. 5.
23. Ibid., pp. 7, 8.
24. Hedges, Laine, and Greenwald (1994b) p. 9; National Research Council (1992) p. 2, also cited in Draper and others (1992).
25. Hedges, Laine, and Greenwald (1994b) p. 10.

26. Hedges, Greenwald, and Laine (forthcoming).
27. Cooper (1989b) pp. 85–86.
28. Details that follow are drawn from Cooper (1989a); Cooper (1989b); and interviews with Cooper.
29. Cooper (1989a) p. 54.
30. Cooper (1989a) table 10.4; for the 60 percent figure, p. 163; and for homework and gender, pp. 74–75.
31. For published findings, see Cooper (1989a) p. 164, table 10.4.
32. Cooper (1989b).
33. I. Chalmers and others (1989).
34. Coplen and others (1990) and Hine and others (1989).
35. Hall and others, in Cooper and Hedges (1994) p. 18.
36. Cooper and Hedges (1994) p. 523.
37. Eagly and Carli (1981).
38. Eagly and Wood, in Cooper and Hedges (1994) p. 492.
39. Ingelfinger and others (1994) p. 123.
40. Wolf in Wachter and Straf (1990) p. 147.
41. Kippel (1981).
42. Becker in Cook and others (1992) p. 212.
43. The studies sponsored by the grants appear in Cook and others (1992).
44. Becker in Cook and others (1992) p. 215.
45. Cook and others (1992) p. 24.
46. Cook and Shadish (1994) p. 547 and almost all social psychology and sociology textbooks.
47. Cooper and Hedges (1994) p. 527.
48. Shadish in Cook and others (1992) p. 171. The "orientation effects" are those in his study, described earlier, of marital and family therapies, Shadish and others (1993); Shadish and others (1995).
49. Durlak and Lipsey (1991) p. 328.

Chapter 4

1. T. Chalmers (1994) p. 12.
2. "First major meta-analysis": Yusuf (1993) p. 3. The meta-analysis: T. Chalmers and others (1977).
3. "Of special interest": Lau and others (1992); "One of the most important papers": Iain Chalmers, interview, referring to Antman and others (1992).
4. Cook and others (1992) p. 285.
5. Bailar and Mosteller (1992) pp. 358, 372.
6. Lau, Schmid, and Chalmers (1995), items 1 through 15 in fig. 2.
7. Ibid., fig 3.
8. Colorectal surgery: Baum and others (1981); endoscopy: Sacks and others (1990).
9. T. Chalmers and Lau (1993a) pp. 164–165.
10. Glass (1976).
11. Emerson and others (1990) p. 339.

12. "Smaller effect sizes": Gilbert, McPeek, and Mosteller (1977) pp. 130–131; "results can always be improved": Hugo Muench, cited in U.S. General Accounting Office (1992a) p. 75; "larger effect sizes": Shadish, Heinsman, and Ragsdale (1993).
13. See items 12, 13, 16, and 18 in "References" in Lau and others (1992). The study giving the 22 percent figure: Yusuf and others (1985).
14. "268 randomized clinical trials"—Lau, interview. Previous meta-analyses: See "References" in Lau and others (1992).
15. Lau, Schmid, and T. Chalmers (1995).
16. Laird and Mosteller (1990).
17. Devine and Cook (1983); Devine, interview.
18. Greenhouse and others, in Wachter and Straf (1990) p. 34.
19. Lipsey in Cook and others (1992) p. 98.
20. Antman and others (1992).
21. Ibid., p. 243.
22. Ibid., p. 245.
23. Lau, Schmid, and T. Chalmers (1995).
24. T. Chalmers and Lau (1993a) p. 166.
25. T. Chalmers and Lau (1993b) p. 99.
26. Mosteller and T. Chalmers (1992).
27. The meta-analysis: Teo and others (1991); the ISIS-4 trial: ISIS-4 (1995). ISIS is a group that conducted one of the two very large trials of thrombolytic treatment alluded to earlier; the acronym stands for International Study of Infarct Survival. The other very large thrombolytic trial was conducted by GISSI—Gruppo italiano per lo studio della streptochinasi nell'infarto miocardico—which, like ISIS, conducts massive clinical trials.
28. Draper and others (1992) p. 186.
29. Flather, Farkouh, and Yusuf (1994) pp. 397–398.
30. Ibid., p. 404.
31. Collins and others (1995) pp. 20, 26.
32. Early Breast Cancer Trialists' Collaborative Group (1992).
33. Light and Pillemer (1984) p. 69.
34. Rosenthal and Rubin (1982a).
35. Law, Wald, and Thompson (1994).
36. Adapted from Moore and McCabe (1993) p. 189.
37. Cited in U.S. General Accounting Office (1992) pp. 75–76.
38. Laird in Wachter and Straf (1990) p. 51; Hine and others (1989).
39. Colditz (1994).
40. Ibid., tables 1 and 2.
41. Ibid., p. 701.
42. Ingelfinger and others (1994) pp. 349–351; Cooper and Hedges (1994) chapters 19 and 20.
43. Laird and Mosteller (1990) p. 15.
44. Hedges in Wachter and Straf (1990) p. 23.
45. Hedges (1982); Rosenthal and Rubin (1982a).

Chapter 5

1. Ambady and Rosenthal (1992).
2. Cooper in Wachter and Straf (1990) p. 90, citing Jacob Cohen, *Statistical Power Analysis for the Behavioral Sciences* (Hillsdale, N.J.: Erlbaum, 1988).
3. Lipsey in Cook and others (1992) pp. 86, 98.
4. Latané and Darley (1968).
5. Latané and Nida (1981).
6. The example is adapted from one in Cooper and Lemke (1991) p. 247.
7. Cooper and Lemke (1991) p. 250.
8. Ambady and Rosenthal (1992) pp. 267–269.
9. "Ten times": Greenwald (1975); "Two-thirds . . . one-third": Rosenthal (1991a) pp. 106–107; "55 percent . . . 22 percent": T. Chalmers and others (1987a); "Other studies": Begg in Cooper and Hedges (1994) p. 400.
10. Quoted in Hetherington and others (1989) p. 374.
11. Wachter (1988).
12. Shadish, Doherty, and Montgomery (1989).
13. Yusuf (1987) p. 285.
14. Durlak and Lipsey (1991) p. 323.
15. Rosenthal (1979).
16. Rosenthal and Rubin (1978) p. 381.
17. Begg in Cooper and Hedges (1994) p. 406.
18. Draper and others (1992) pp. 120–121; Begg in Cooper and Hedges (1994) pp. 406–407.
19. Rosenthal and Jacobson (1966).
20. Rosenthal and Jacobson (1968).
21. Rosenthal and Rubin (1978).
22. Cook and Campbell (1979).
23. The example is adapted from Matt and Cook, in Cooper and Hedges (1994) p. 513.
24. Cook and others (1992) p. 299; Matt and Cook, in Cooper and Hedges (1994) pp. 506–513.
25. Hunter and Schmidt, in Cooper and Hedges (1994) p. 326.
26. Ibid., p. 327.
27. Eagly and Wood, in Cooper and Hedges (1994) p. 486.
28. Quoted in Mann (1990).
29. The 1975 survey: Lipton, Martinson, and Wilks (1975); the 1977 update: Greenberg (1977) p. 141.
30. Details that follow are from Lipsey in Cook and others (1992) pp. 83–127; Lipsey (1995); and an interview with Lipsey.
31. Lipsey in Cook and others (1992) pp. 97–98. A similar way of assessing the real importance of what seem like small effects is the Binomial Effect Size Display of Rosenthal and Rubin. They appraise the effect of a treatment in terms of the *proportionate change* in the improvement or cure rate itself. A rise in cure rate from 40 percent to 60 percent thus is not a 20 percent rise but a *50 percent* rise (the 40 percent rate was increased by 20 points, or 50 percent). See Rosenthal and Rubin (1982c) and Rosenthal (1991a) pp. 132–135.

32. Lipsey (1995) p. 5.
33. Lipsey in Cook and others (1992) p. 98.
34. Lipsey (1995) pp. 11–13.
35. Ibid., p. 16.
36. Yeaton and Wortman (1993).

Chapter 6

1. U.S. General Accounting Office (1982) app., pp. 59–60.
2. Chelimsky (1994).
3. Ibid., pp. 4–5.
4. Chelimsky (1994).
5. National Academy of Public Administration (1994) pp. 14–15; Robert Pear. 1994. "U.S. Watchdog Gets Criticism on Objectivity." *The New York Times*, Oct. 17, 1994, A1, B10.
6. U.S. General Accounting Office (1995); see especially letter from DHHS.
7. U.S. General Accounting Office (1984) p. 6.
8. Ibid., pp. 7, 9.
9. Ibid., p. 16, footnote e.
10. Ibid., pp. ii, iv.
11. Ibid., pp. vi, vii.
12. Ibid., p. ii.
13. U.S. Senate Committee on Agriculture, Nutrition, and Forestry (1984) pp. 8, 16, 77.
14. Chelimsky (1994) p. 17.
15. Cordray in Wachter and Straf (1990) p. 111; see also Cook and others (1992) p. 338.
16. Lipsey (1993).
17. Letter of June 14, 1990, from Representative Dante Fascell to Eleanor Chelimsky (in PEMD's Bigeye bomb files). On the outcomes: Chelimsky (1994) pp. 13–14.
18. U.S. General Accounting Office (1991); Chelimsky (1994).
19. U.S. General Accounting Office (1987) p. 2; Chelimsky (1994).
20. U.S. General Accounting Office (1987) p. 3.
21. Chelimsky (1994).
22. Ibid., p. 21.
23. U.S. General Accounting Office (1992b).
24. U.S. General Accounting Office (1994) p. 9.
25. Ibid., p. 13.
26. Ibid., pp. 1–2.
27. Chelimsky (1991).
28. Ibid.
29. Ibid.
30. Centers for Disease Control (1991).
31. National Research Council (1986); U.S. Department of Health and Human Services (1986).

32. Wells (1988) p. 251, tables 1, 2.
33. Bayard is quoted to that effect in *Newsday*, Jan. 8, 1993, p. 5.
34. U.S. Environmental Protection Agency (1992) chapter 6: p. 16.
35. Ibid., chapter 6: pp. 17, 19.
36. Ibid., chapter 5: pp. 34, 35.
37. Ibid., chapter 1: p. 1.
38. Ibid., p. xv.
39. Philip J. Hilts. 1993. "U.S. Issues Guidelines to Protect Nonsmokers." *The New York Times*, July 22, 1993, p. A14.
40. Tom Kenworthy and David Brown. 1993. "Tobacco Firms Sue EPA on Cancer Ruling." *The Washington Post*, June 23, 1993, p. A1; John Schwartz. 1994. "Smoking Recast: From Sophistication to Sin." *The Washington Post*, May 29, 1994, p. A1.
41. Tom Kenworthy and David Brown. 1993. "Tobacco Firms Sue EPA on Cancer Ruling." *The Washington Post*, June 23, 1993, p. A1.
42. Gravelle and Zimmerman (1994a, 1994b).
43. Philip J. Hilts. 1994. "Danger of Tobacco Smoke Is Said to Be Underplayed." *The New York Times*, Dec. 21, 1994, p. D23.
44. Jacox and others (1994).
45. I. Chalmers and Haynes (1994).
46. Lawrence K. Altman. 1995. "Agency Issues Warning for Drug Wisely Used for Heart Disease." *The New York Times*, Sept. 1, 1995, pp. A1, A20. The meta-analysis was published in *Circulation*, September 1, 1995.
47. Lawrence K. Altman. 1995. "Agency Issues Warning for Drug Wisely Used for Heart Disease." *The New York Times*, Sept. 1, 1995, pp. A1, A20.
48. Dr. Robert Temple, FDA, interview.

Chapter 7

1. Draper and others (1992) p. 43.
2. Mann (1994).
3. Shapiro (1994) p. 771.
4. Sohn (1995); see chapter 1 for a fuller quote.
5. Cooper and Hedges (1994) p. 522.
6. Details are from Lau and others' proposal to the AHCPR (unpublished) and from two interviews with Lau.
7. I. Chalmers and Altman (1995) pp. 86–94; interview with I. Chalmers; and leaflet of February 12, 1995, from the Baltimore Cochrane Center.
8. Rubin in Wachter and Straf (1990) p. 155; see also Rubin (1992, 1993).
9. Glass (1991) pp. 1141–1142.

References

This is a list of sources cited in the text and in the Notes. It also includes a relatively small number of articles and books which, though not cited, are amplifications of those which are and may be of interest to readers who wish to pursue any of the matters discussed in this book.

Altick, Richard. 1975. *The Art of Literary Research*. New York: Norton.

Ambady, Nalini, and Robert Rosenthal. 1992. "Thin Slices of Expressive Behavior as Predictors of Interpersonal Consequences: A Meta-Analysis." *Psychological Bulletin* 111(2): 256–274.

———. 1993. "Half a Minute: Predicting Teacher Evaluations from Thin Slices of Nonverbal Behavior and Physical Attractiveness." *Journal of Personality and Social Psychology* 64(3): 431–441.

Andrews, Gavin, and Robin Harvey. 1981. "Does Psychotherapy Benefit Neurotic Patients? A Reanalysis of the Smith, Glass, and Miller Data." *Archives of General Psychiatry* 38: 1203–1208.

Antman, Elliott M., and others. 1992. "A Comparison of Results of Meta-Analyses of Randomized Control Trials and Recommendations of Clinical Experts. Treatments for Myocardial Infarction." *Journal of the American Medical Association* 268(2): 240–248.

Bailar, John C., and Frederick Mosteller. 1992. *Medical Uses of Statistics*. Boston: NEJM [New England Journal of Medicine] Books.

Bangert-Drowns, Robert L. 1986. "Review of Developments in Meta-Analytic Method." *Psychological Bulletin* 99(3): 388–399.

Baron, R. M., and D. A. Kenny. 1986. "The Moderator-Mediator Variable Distinction in Social Psychological Research." *Journal of Personality and Social Psychology* 51: 1173–1182.

Baum, Mark, and others. 1981. "A Survey of Clinical Trials of Antibiotic Prophylaxis in Colon Surgery: Evidence Against Further Use of No-Treatment Controls." *New England Journal of Medicine* 305: 795–799.

Becker, Betsy Jane. 1990. "Coaching for the Scholastic Aptitude Test: Further Synthesis and Appraisal." *Review of Educational Research* 60(3): 373–417.

Begg, Colin B., and Jesse A. Berlin. 1988. "Publication Bias: A Problem in Interpreting Medical Data." *Journal of the Royal Statistical Society* 151(3): 419–463.

Buffler, P. A., and others. 1984. "The Causes of Lung Cancer in Texas." In M. Mizell and P. Correa, eds., *Lung Cancer: Causes and Prevention*. New York: Verlag Chemie International.

Bunge, Mario. 1991. "A Critical Examination of the New Sociology of Science. Part 1." *Philosophy of the Social Sciences* 21(4): 524–560.

———. 1992. "A Critical Examination of the New Sociology of Science. Part 2." *Philosophy of the Social Sciences* 22(1): 46–76.

Bushman, Brad J., and Harris M. Cooper. 1990. "Effects of Alcohol on Human Aggression: An Integrative Research Review." *Psychological Bulletin* 107(3): 341–354.

Centers for Disease Control, U.S. Department of Health and Human Services. 1991. "Smoking-Attributable Mortality and Years of Potential Life." *Morbidity and Mortality Weekly Report* 40: 62–71.

Chalmers, Iain, and Douglas G. Altman. 1995. *Systematic Reviews*. London: BMJ Publishing Group.

Chalmers, Iain, and Brian Haynes. 1994. "Reporting, Updating, and Correcting Systematic Reviews of the Effects of Health Care." *British Medical Journal* 309: 862–865.

Chalmers, Iain, and others. 1989. *Effective Care in Pregnancy and Childbirth*. Oxford: Oxford University Press.

Chalmers, Thomas. 1994. "Meta-Analysis and Its Role in Evaluating Endoscopic Therapies for Bleeding Peptic Ulcer." *Masters in Gastroenterology* 6(2): 12–17.

Chalmers, Thomas C., and Joseph Lau. 1993a. "Meta-Analytic Stimulus for Changes in Clinical Trials." *Statistical Methods in Medical Research* 2: 161–172.

———. 1993b. "Randomized Control Trials and Meta-Analyses in Gastroenterology: Major Achievements and Future Potential." In Kenneth S. Warren and Frederick Mosteller, eds., *Doing More Good Than Harm: The Evaluation of Health Care Interventions*. New York: New York Academy of Sciences.

———. 1994. "What Is Meta-Analysis?" *Emergency Care Research Institute* 12: 1–5.

Chalmers, Thomas C., and others. 1977. "Evidence Favoring the Use of Anticoagulants in the Hospital Phase of Acute Myocardial Infarction." *New England Journal of Medicine* 297: 1091–1096.

———. 1981. "A Method for Assessing the Quality of a Randomized Clinical Trial." *Controlled Clinical Trials* 2: 31–49.

———. 1987a. "Meta-Analysis of Clinical Trials as a Scientific Discipline. I: Control of Bias and Comparison with Large Co-operative Trials." *Statistics in Medicine* 6: 315–325.

———. 1987b. "Meta-Analysis of Clinical Trials as a Scientific Discipline. II: Replicate Variability and Comparisons of Studies That Agree and Disagree." *Statistics in Medicine* 6: 733–744.

Chelimsky, Eleanor. 1984. "Statement on Evaluations of WIC's Effectiveness, before the Committee on Agriculture, Nutrition, and Forestry, United States Senate. Washington, DC: U.S. General Accounting Office. Unpublished.

———. 1991. "On the Social Science Contribution to Governmental Decision-Making." *Science* 254: 226–231.

———. 1994. "Politics, Policy, and Research Synthesis." Keynote address, Russell Sage Foundation National Conference on Research Synthesis, Washington, D.C., June 21.

Cochran, William G. 1937. "Problems Arising in the Analysis of a Series of Similar Experiments." *Journal of the Royal Statistic Society* 4(suppl.): 102–118.

Cohen, Jacob. 1988. *Statistical Power Analysis in the Behavioral Sciences*. Hillsdale, NJ: Erlbaum.

Colditz, Graham A. and others 1993. *The Efficacy of BCG in the Prevention of Tuberculosis: Meta-Analyses of the Published Literature*. Boston: Technology Assessment Group, Harvard School of Public Health.

———. 1994. "Efficacy of BCG Vaccine in the Prevention of Tuberculosis." *Journal of the American Medical Association* 271(9): 698–702.

Collins, R., and others. 1995. "2.4: Large-scale Randomized Evidence: Trials and Overviews." In D. Weatherall, J. G. G. Ledingham, and D. A. Warrell, eds., *Oxford Textbook of Medicine*. Oxford: Oxford University Press.

Committee on Undergraduate Education. 1994. *CUE 1994–95: Harvard University Course Evaluation Guide*. [Cambridge, MA]: Harvard College.

Comstock, George, and Haejung Paik. 1990 "The Effects of Television Violence on Aggressive Behavior: A Meta-Analysis." Paper prepared for the National Research Council Panel on the Understanding and Control of Violent Behavior. S. I. Newhouse School of Public Communication, Syracuse University.

Cook, Thomas D. 1991. "Meta-Analysis: Its Potential for Causal Description and Causal Explanation Within Program Evaluation." In Günther Albrecht and Hans-Uwe Otto, eds., *Social Prevention and the Social Sciences*. Berlin: Walter de Gruyter.

Cook, Thomas D., and D. T. Campbell. 1979. *Quasi-Experimentation: Design and Analysis Issues for Field Settings*. Boston: Houghton Mifflin.

Cook, Thomas D., and William R. Shadish. 1994. "Social Experiments: Some Developments over the Past Fifteen Years." *Annual Review of Psychology* 45: 545–580.

Cook, Thomas D., and others. 1984. *School Desegregation and Black Achievement*. Unpublished report. Washington, DC: National institute of Education. ERIC no. ED 241 671.

———. 1992. *Meta-Analysis for Explanation: A Casebook*. New York: Russell Sage Foundation.

Cooper, Harris M. 1982. "Scientific Guidelines for Conducting Integrative Research Reviews." *Review of Educational Research* 53(2): 291–302.

———. 1989a. *Homework*. New York: Longman.

———. 1989b. "Synthesis of Research on Homework." *Educational Leadership* (November): 85–91.

———. 1989c. *Integrating Research: A Guide for Literature Reviews*, 2nd ed. Newbury Park, CA: Sage Publications.

Cooper, Harris, and Larry V. Hedges, eds. 1994. *The Handbook of Research Synthesis*. New York: Russell Sage Foundation.

Cooper, Harris M., and Kevin Lemke, 1991. "On the Role of Meta-Analysis in Personality and Social Psychology." *Personality and Social Psychology Bulletin* 17(3): 245–251.

Coplen, S. E., and others. 1990. "Efficacy and Safety of Quinidine Therapy for Maintenance of Sinus Rhythm After Cardioversion. A Meta-Analysis of Randomized Control Trials." *Circulation*, 82: 1106–1116.

Cordray, David S., and Robert T. Fischer. 1994. "Job Training and Welfare Reform: A Policy-Driven Synthesis." Paper presented at Russell Sage Foundation National Conference on Research Synthesis, June 1994, Washington, D.C. Unpublished.

Devine, Elizabeth C. 1992. "Effects of Psychoeducational Care for Adult Surgical Patients: A Meta-Analysis of 191 Studies." *Patient Education and Counseling* 19: 129–142.

Devine, Elizabeth C., and Thomas D. Cook. 1983. "A Meta-Analytic Analysis of Effects of Psychoeducational Interventions on Length of Postsurgical Hospital Stay." *Nursing Research* 32(5): 267–274.

———. 1986. "Clinical and Cost-Saving Effects of Psychoeducational Interventions with Surgical Patients: A Meta-Analysis." *Research in Nursing & Health* 9: 89–105.

Dickersin, Kay, Roberta Scherer, and Carol LeFebvre. 1994. "Identifying Relevant Studies for Systematic Reviews." *British Medical Journal* 309: 1286–1291.

Draper, David, and others. 1992. *Contemporary Statistics, Number 1: Combining Information. Statistical Issues and Opportunities for Research.* Washington: National Academy Press, for the American Statistical Association.

Druckman, Daniel. 1993. "The Situational Levers of Negotiating Flexibility." *Journal of Conflict Resolution* 37(2): 236–276.

———. 1994. "Determinants of Compromising Behavior in Negotiation." *Journal of Conflict Resolution* 38(3): 507–556.

Durlak, Joseph A., and Mark W. Lipsey. 1991. "A Practitioner's Guide to Meta-Analysis." *American Journal of Community Psychology* 19(3): 291–332.

Eagly, Alice H., and Linda L. Carli. 1981. "Sex of Researchers and Sex-Typed Communications as Determinants of Sex Differences in Influenceability: A Meta-Analysis of Social Influence Studies." *Psychological Bulletin* 90(1): 1–20.

Eagly, Alice H., and Blair T. Johnson. 1990. "Gender and Leadership Style: A Meta-Analysis." *Psychological Bulletin* 108(2): 232–256.

Eagly, Alice H., and Wendy Wood. 1991. "Explaining Sex Differences in Social Behavior: A Meta-Analytic Perspective." *Personality and Social Psychology Bulletin* 17(3): 306–315.

Early Breast Cancer Trialists' Collaborative Group. 1992. "Systematic Treatment of Early Breast Cancer by Hormonal, Cytotoxic, or Immune Therapy." *The Lancet* 339: 1–15, 71–85.

Emerson, John D., and others. 1990. "An Empirical Study of the Possible Relation of Treatment Differences to Quality Scores in Controlled Randomized Clinical Trials." *Controlled Clinical Trials* 11: 339–352.

Epstein, William. 1995. *The Illusion of Psychotherapy.* New Brunswick, NJ: Transaction Publishers.

Eysenck, H. J. 1952. "The Effects of Psychotherapy: An Evaluation." *Journal of Consulting Psychology* 16: 319–324.

———. 1978. "An Exercise in Mega-Silliness." *American Psychologist* 33: 517.

———. 1990. *Rebel with a Cause.* London: W. H. Allen.

———. 1992. "Meta-Analysis, Sense or Nonsense?" *Pharmaceutical Medicine* 6: 113–119.

———. 1994. "Meta-Analysis and Its Problems." *British Medical Journal* 309: 789–792.

Fischer, P. J. 1991. *Alcohol, Drug Abuse and Mental Health Problems Among Homeless Persons: A Review of the Literature.* Washington: U.S. Department of Health and Human Services.

Fisher, R. A. 1926. "The Arrangement of Field Experiments." *Journal of the Ministry of Agriculture of Great Britain* 33: 505–513.

Flather, M. D., M. E. Farkouh, and S. Yusuf. 1994. "Meta-Analysis in the Evaluation of Therapies." In Desmond G. Julian and Eugene Braunwald, eds., *Management of Acute Myocardial Infarction*. London: W. B. Saunders Company, Ltd.

Gallo, Philip S. 1978. "Meta-Analysis—A Mixed Metaphor?" *American Psychologist* 33(5): 515–517.

Gilbert, John P., Bucknam McPeek, and Frederick Mosteller. 1977. "Progress in Surgery and Anesthesia: Benefits and Risks of Innovative Therapy." In John P. Bunker, Benjamin A. Barnes, and Frederick Mosteller, eds., *Costs, Risks, and Benefits of Surgery*. New York: Oxford University Press.

Glass, Gene V. 1976. "Primary, Secondary, and Meta-Analysis of Research." *The Educational Researcher* 10: 3–8.

———. 1978. "In Defense of Generalization." *The Behavioral and Brain Sciences* 3: 394–395.

———. 1983. "Synthesizing Empirical Research: Meta-Analysis." In S. A. Ward and L. J. Reed, eds., *Knowledge Structure and Use*. Philadelphia: Temple University Press.

———. 1991. "Review of *The Future of Meta-Analysis* [Wachter and Straf (1990)]." *Journal of the American Statistical Association* 86(416): 1141.

Glass, Gene V, Barry McGaw, and Mary Lee Smith. 1981. *Meta-Analysis in Social Research*. Beverly Hills, CA: Sage Publications.

Goldfried, Marvin R., Leslie S. Greenberg, and Charles Marmar. 1990. "Individual Psychotherapy: Process and Outcome." *Annual Review of Psychology* 41: 659–688.

Gravelle, Jane G., and Dennis Zimmerman. 1994a. *CRS Report for Congress. Cigarette Taxes to Fund Health Care Reform: An Economic Analysis*. Washington: Congressional Research Service, Library of Congress.

———. 1994b. Statement on Environmental Tobacco Smoke before the Subcommittee on Clean Air and Nuclear Regulation, Committee on Environment and Public Works, U.S. Senate, May 11, 1994. Washington: Congressional Research Service.

Greenberg, D. F. 1977. "The Correctional Effects of Corrections: A Survey of Evaluations." In D. F. Greenberg, ed., *Corrections and Punishment*. Newbury Park, CA: Sage Publications.

Greenberg, Roger P., and others. 1992. "A Meta-Analysis of Antidepressant Outcome Under 'Blinder' Conditions." *Journal of Consulting and Clinical Psychology* 60(5): 664–669.

———. 1994. "A Meta-Analysis of Fluoxetine Outcome in the Treatment of Depression." *Journal of Nervous and Mental Disease* 182(10): 547–551.

Greenwald, A. G. 1975. "Consequences of Prejudice Against the Null Hypothesis." *Psychological Bulletin* 85: 845–857.

Hall, Judith A. 1978. "Gender Effects in Decoding Nonverbal Cues." *Psychological Bulletin* 85(4): 845–857.

Hanushek, Eric A. 1981. "Throwing Money at Schools." *Journal of Policy Analysis and Management* 1: 19–41.

———. 1989. "The Impact of Differential Expenditures on School Performance." *Educational Researcher* 18(4): 45–62.

———. 1994. "Money Might Matter Somewhere: A Response to Hedges, Laine, and Greenwald." *Educational Researcher* 23(4): 5–8.

Hayashi, K., and T. C. Chalmers. 1993. "Famotidine in the Treatment of Duodenal Ulcer: A Meta-Analysis of Randomized Control Trials." *Gastroenterology International* 6(1): 19–25.

Hedges, Larry V. 1982. "Estimation of Effect Size from a Series of Independent Experiments." *Psychological Bulletin* 92: 490–499.

———. 1987. "How Hard Is Hard Science, How Soft Is Soft Science? The Empirical Cumulativeness of Research." *American Psychologist* 42: 443–455.

Hedges, Larry V., Rob Greenwald, and Richard D. Laine. 1996. "The Effect of School Resources on Student Achievement." *Review of Educational Research* 66:361–396.

Hedges, Larry V., Richard D. Laine and Rob Greenwald. 1994a. "Does Money Matter? A Meta-Analysis of Studies of the Effects of Differential School Inputs on Student Outcomes." *Educational Researcher* 23(3): 5–14.

———. 1994b. "Money Does Matter Somewhere: A Reply to Hanushek." *Educational Researcher* 23(4): 9–10.

Hedges, Larry V., and Ingram Olkin. 1985. *Statistical Methods for Meta-Analysis*. Orlando, FL: Academic Press.

Held, Peter H., Salim Yusuf, and Curt D. Furberg. 1989. "Calcium Channel Blockers in Acute Myocardial Infarction and Unstable Angina: An Overview." *British Medical Journal* 299: 1187–1192.

Hetherington, Jini, and others. 1989. "Retrospective and Prospective Identification of Unpublished Controlled Trials: Lessons from a Survey of Obstetricians and Pediatricians." *Pediatrics* 84(2): 374–380.

Hine, L. K., and others. 1989. "Meta-Analytic Evidence Against Prophylactic Use of Lidocaine in Acute Myocardial Infraction." *Archives of Internal Medicine* 149: 2694–2698.

Hunter, John E., and Frank L. Schmidt. 1990. *Methods of Meta-Analysis: Correcting Error and Bias in Research Findings*. Newbury Park, CA: Sage Publications.

Ingelfinger, Joseph A., and others. 1994. *Biostatistics in Clinical Medicine*, 3rd ed. New York: McGraw-Hill, Inc.

ISIS-4 [Fourth International Study of Infarct Survival] Collaborative Group. 1995. "ISIS-4: A Randomised Factorial Trial Assessing Early Oral Captopril, Oral Mononitrate, and Intravenous Magnesium Sulphate in 58,050 Patients with Suspected Acute Myocardial Infarction." *The Lancet* 345: 669–685.

Jacox, A., and others. 1994. *Management of Cancer Pain: Clinical Practice Guideline No. 9*. Washington: U.S. Department of Health and Human Services, Public Health Service.

Janerich, D. T., and others 1990. "Lung Cancer and Exposure to Tobacco Smoke in the Household." *New England Journal of Medicine* 323: 632–636.

Kabat, G. C., and E. L. Wynder. 1984. "Lung Cancer in Nonsmokers." *Cancer* 53: 1214–1221.

Kippel, G. 1981. "Identifying Exceptional Schools." *New Directions for Program Evaluation* 11: 83–100.

Knipschild, Paul. 1994 "Some Examples." *British Medical Journal* 309: 719–721.

Kranzler, John H., and Arthur Jensen. 1989. "Inspection Time and Intelligence: A Meta-Anaylsis." *Intelligence* 13: 329–347.

Kraus, Stephen J. 1995. "Attitudes and the Prediction of Behavior: A Meta-Analysis of the Empirical Literature." *Personality and Social Psychology Bulletin* 21(1): 58–75.

Laine, Richard, and others. 1992. "Dollars and Sense: Reassessing Hanushek." Unpublished paper submitted in Education 411, University of Chicago School of Education, June 16, 1992.

Laird, Nan M., and Frederick Mosteller. 1990. "Some Statistical Methods for Combining Experimental Results." *International Journal of Technology Assessment in Health Care* 6: 5–30.

Landman, Janet Tracy, and Robyn M. Dawes. 1982. "Psychotherapy Outcome: Smith and Glass' Conclusions Stand Up Under Scrutiny." *American Psychologist* 37(5): 504–516.

Latané, Bibb, and John Darley. 1968. "Group Inhibition of Bystander Intervention in Emergencies." *Journal of Personality and Social Psychology* 10(31): 215–221.

Latané, Bibb, and Steve Nida. 1981. "Ten Years of Research on Group Size and Helping." *Psychological Bulletin* 89(2): 308–324.

Lau, Joseph, Christopher H. Schmid, and Thomas C. Chalmers. 1995. "Cumulative Meta-Analysis of Clinical Trials Builds Evidence for Exemplary Medical Care." *Journal of Clinical Epidemiology* 48(1): 45–57.

Lau, Joseph, and others. 1992. "Cumulative Meta-Analysis of Therapeutic Trials for Myocardial Infarction." *New England Journal of Medicine* 327: 248–254.

Law, M. R., N. J. Wald, and S. G. Thompson. 1994. "By How Much and How Quickly Does Reduction in Serum Cholesterol Concentration Lower Risk of Ischaemic Heart Disease?" *British Medical Journal* 308: 367–373.

Lee, I.M., C. C. Hsieh, and R. S. Paffenbarger, Jr. 1995. "Exercise Intensity and Longevity in Men. The Harvard Alumni Health Study." *Journal of the American Medical Association* 273(15): 1179–1184.

Lehman, Anthony F., and David S. Cordray. 1993. "Prevalence of Alcohol, Drug, and Mental Disorders Among the Homeless: One More Time." *Contemporary Drug Problems* (Fall): 355–383.

Light, Richard. 1984. "Six Evaluation Issues That Synthesis Can Resolve Better than Single Studies." In W. H. Yeaton and P. M. Wortman, eds., *Issues in Data Synthesis*. New Directions for Program Evaluation, no. 24. San Francisco: Jossey-Bass.

Light, Richard J., and David B. Pillemer. 1982. "Numbers and Narrative: Combining Their Strengths in Research Reviews." *Harvard Educational Review* 52(1): 1–26.

———. 1984. *Summing Up: The Science of Reviewing Research*. Cambridge, MA: Harvard University Press.

Light, Richard, and Paul V. Smith. 1971. "Accumulating Evidence: Procedures for Resolving Contradictions Among Different Research Studies." *Harvard Educational Review* 41(4): 429–471.

Lindzey, Gardner, ed. 1980. *A History of Psychology in Autobiography*, Vol. VII. San Francisco: W. H. Freeman.

Lipsey, Mark W. 1993. "Using Linked Meta-Analysis to Build Policy Models." Paper prepared for National Institute of Drug Abuse Technical Review, Bethesda, MD.
———. 1995. "What Do We Learn from 400 Research Studies on the Effectiveness of Treatment with Juvenile Delinquents?" In J. McGuire, ed., *What Works: Effective Methods to Reduce Re-Offending*. New York: John Wiley.

Lipsey, Mark. W., and David B. Wilson. 1993. "The Efficacy of Psychological, Educational, and Behavioral Treatment: Confirmation from Meta-Analysis." *American Psychologist* 48(12): 1181–1209.

Lipton, D., R. Martinson, and J. Wilks. 1975. *The Effectiveness of Correctional Treatment: A Survey of Treatment Evaluation Studies*. New York: Praeger.

Luborsky, Lester. 1954. "A Note on Eysenck's Article, 'The Effects of Psychotherapy: An Evaluation.'" *British Journal of Psychology* 45: 129–131.

———. 1972. "Another Reply to Eysenck." *Psychological Bulletin* 78(5): 406–408.

Luborsky, Lester, Barbara Singer, and Lisa Luborsky. 1975. "Comparative Studies of Psychotherapies: Is It True That 'Everyone Has Won and All Must Have Prizes'?" *Archives of General Psychiatry* 32: 995–1008.

Luborsky, Lester, and others. 1993. "The Effect of Dynamic Psychotherapies: Is It True That 'Everyone Has Won and All Must Have Prizes'?" In N. Miller, L. Luborsky, and others, eds., *Psychodynamic Treatment Research: A Handbook for Clinical Practice*. New York: Basic Books.

Maccoby, Eleanor E., and Carol N. Jacklin. 1974. *The Psychology of Sex Differences*. Standford: Stanford University Press.

Mann, Charles C. 1990. "Meta-Analysis in the Breech." *Science* 249: 476–478.

———. 1994. "Can Meta-Analysis Make Policy?" *Science* 266(11): 960–962.

Miller, Norman, and Vicki Pollock. Forthcoming. "Use of Meta-Analysis for Testing Theory." In *Evaluation and the Health Professions*.

Moore, David S., and George P. McCabe. 1993. *Introduction to the Practice of Statistics*, 2nd ed. New York: W. H. Freeman.

Morton, R.B. 1955. "An Experiment in Brief Psychotherapy." *Pscyhological Monographs* 69 (386).

Mosteller, Frederick, and Thomas C. Chalmers. 1992. "Some Progress and Problems in Meta-Analysis of Clinical Trials." *Statistical Science* 7(2): 227–236.

Mulrow, Cynthia D. 1987. "The Medical Review Article: State of the Science." *Annals of International Medicine* 106: 485–488.

———. 1994. "Rationale for Systematic Reviews." *British Medical Journal* 309: 597–599.

National Academy of Public Administration. 1994. *The Roles, Mission and Operation of the U.S. General Accounting Office*. Report Prepared for the Committee on Governmental Affairs, United States Senate, Washington: National Academy of Public Administration.

National Research Council. 1986. *Environmental Tobacco Smoke: Measuring Exposures and Assessing Health Effects*. Washington: National Academy Press.

National Task Force on the Prevention and Treatment of Obesity. 1994. "Weight Cycling." *Journal of the American Medical Association* 272(15): 1196–1202.

Olkin, Ingram, and Douglas V. Shaw. 1994. "Meta-Analysis and Its Applications in Horticultural Science." Stanford University; University of California, Davis. Unpublished paper.

Orwin, Robert G., and David S. Cordray. 1985. "Effects of Deficient Reporting on Meta-Analysis: A Conceptual Framework and Reanalysis." *Psychological Bulletin* 97(1): 134–147.

Paik, Haejung, and George Comstock. 1994. "The Effects of Television Violence on Antisocial Behavior: A Meta-Analysis." *Communication Research* 21(4): 516–546.

Pearson, Karl. 1904. "Report on Certain Enteric Fever Inoculation Statistics." *British Medical Journal* 3: 1243–1246.

Prioleau, Leslie, Martha Murdock, and Nathan Brody. 1983. "An Analysis of Psychotherapy Versus Placebo Studies." *Behavioral and Brain Sciences* 6: 275–310.

Ray, William J. 1993. *Methods: Toward a Science of Behavior and Experience*. Pacific Grove, CA: Brooks/Cole Publishing Company.

Reisman, John M. 1976. *A History of Clinical Psychology*. New York: Irvington.

Rosenthal, Robert. 1979. "The 'File-Drawer Problem' and Tolerance for Null Results." *Psychological Bulletin* 86: 638–641.

———. 1991a. *Meta-Analytic Procedures for Social Research*, rev. ed. Newbury Park, CA: Sage Publications.

———. 1991b. "Teacher Expectancy Effects: A Brief Update 25 Years After the Pygmalion Experiment." *Journal of Research in Education* 1(3): 3–12.

Rosenthal, Robert, and Lenore Jacobson. 1966. "Teachers' Expectancies: Determinants of Pupils' IQ Gains." *Psychological Reports* 19: 115–118.

———. 1968. *Pygmalion in the Classroom*. New York: Holt, Rinehart & Winston.

Rosenthal, Robert, and Donald. B. Rubin. 1978. "Interpersonal Expectancy Effects: The First 345 Studies." *Behavioral and Brain Sciences* 3: 377–415.

———. 1979. "Comparing Significance Levels of Independent Studies." *Psychological Bulletin* 86(5): 1165–1168.

———. 1982a. "Comparing Effect Sizes of Independent Studies." *Psychological Bulletin* 92: 500–504.

———. 1982b. "Further Meta-Analytic Procedures for Assessing Cognitive Gender Differences." *Journal of Educational Psychology* 74(5): 708–712.

———. 1982c. "A Simple, General Purpose Display of Magnitude of Experimental Effect." *Journal of Educational Psychology* 74(2): 166–169.

Rubin, Donald B. 1992. "Meta-Analysis: Literature Synthesis or Effect-Size Surface Estimation?" *Journal of Educational Statistics* 17(4): 363–374.

———. 1993. "Statistical Tools for Meta-Analysis: From Straightforward to Esoteric." In Peter David Blanck, ed., *Interpersonal Expectations: Theory, Research, and Applications*. Cambridge: Cambridge University Press.

Sacks, Henry S., and others. 1987. "Meta-Analysis of Randomized Controlled Trials." *New England Journal of Medicine* 316: 450–455.

———. 1990. "Endoscopic Hemostasis: An Effective Therapy for Bleeding Peptic Ulcers." *Journal of the American Medical Association* 264(4): 494–499.

Shadish, William R., Jr., Maria Doherty, and Linda M. Montgomery. 1989. "How Many Studies Are in the File Drawer? An Estimate from the Family/Marital Psychotherapy Literature." *Clinical Psychology Review* 9: 589–603.

Shadish, William R., Jr., Donna T. Heinsman, and Kevin Ragsdale. 1993. "Comparing Experiments and Quasi-Experiments Using Meta-Analysis." Paper presented at Annual Convention of the American Psychological Association, Dallas, TX, November 4.

Shadish, William R., Jr., and Rebecca R. Sweeney. 1991. "Mediators and Moderators in Meta-Analysis: There's a Reason We Don't Let Dodo Birds Tell Us Which Psychotherapies Should Have Prizes." *Journal of Counseling and Clinical Psychology* 59(6): 883–893.

Shadish, William R., Jr., and others. 1993. "Effects of Family and Marital Psychotherapies: A Meta-Analysis." *Journal of Counseling and Clinical Psychology* 61(6): 992–1002.

———. 1995. "The Efficacy and Effectiveness of Marital and Family Therapy: A Perspective from Meta-Analysis." *Journal of Marital and Family Therapy* 21: 343–358.

Shapiro, David A., and Diana Shapiro. 1982. "Meta-Analysis of Comparative Therapy Outcomes: A Reply to Wilson." *Behavioural Psychology* 10: 307–310.

Shapiro, Samuel. 1994. "Point/Counterpoint: Meta-Analysis of Observational Studies. Meta-Analysis/Shmeta-analysis." *American Journal of Epidemiology* 140(9): 771–778.

Shoham, Varda, and Michael Rohrbaugh. 1994. "Paradoxical Intervention." *Encyclopedia of Psychology* 3: 5–8.

Shoham-Salomon, Varda, Ruth Avner, and Rivka Neeman. 1989. "You're Changed If You Do and Changed If You Don't: Mechanisms Underlying Paradoxical Interventions." *Journal of Consulting and Clinical Psychology* 57(3): 590–598.

Shoham-Salomon, Varda, and Robert Rosenthal. 1987. "Paradoxical Interventions: A Meta-Analysis." *Journal of Consulting and Clinical Psychology* 55(1): 22–28.

Smith, Mary Lee, and Gene V Glass. 1977. "Meta-Analysis of Psychotherapy Outcome Studies." *American Psychologist* 32(9): 752–760.

———. 1987. *Research and Evaluation in Education and the Social Sciences.* Beverly Hills: Sage Publications.

Sohn, David. 1995. "Meta-Analysis as a Means of Discovery." *American Psychologist* (February): 108–110.

Teo, K. K., and others. 1991. "Effects of Intravenous Magnesium in Suspected Acute Myocardial Infarction." *British Medical Journal* 303: 1499–1503.

Thompson, Simon G. 1994. "Why Sources of Heterogeneity in Meta-Analysis Should Be Investigated." *British Medical Journal* 309: 1351–1355.

Tippett, Leonard H. C. 1931. *The Methods of Statistics.* London: Williams & Norgate.

U.S. Department of Health and Human Services. 1986. *The Health Consequences of Involuntary Smoking: A Report of the Surgeon General.* DHHS Pub. No. (PHS) 87-8398. Washington: U.S. Department of Health and Human Services.

U.S. Environmental Protection Agency, Office of Research and Development. 1992. *Respiratory Health Effects of Passive Smoking: Lung Cancer and Other Disorders.* Washington: U.S. Environmental Protection Agency.

U.S. General Accounting Office. 1984. *Report to the Committee on Agriculture, Nutrition, and Forestry, United States Senate.* GAO/PEMD-84-4 [Evaluation of the Special Supplemental Program for Women, Infants, and Children]. Washington: U.S. General Accounting Office.

———. 1987. *Drinking-Age Laws: An Evaluation Synthesis of Their Impact on Highway Safety*. GAO/PEMD-87-10. Washington: U.S. General Accounting Office.

———. 1991. *Rental Housing: Implementing the New Federal Incentives to Deter Prepayments of HUD Mortgages*. GAO/PEMD-91-2. Washington: U.S. General Accounting Office.

———. 1992a. *The Evaluation Synthesis*. GAO/PEMD-10.1.2. Washington: U.S. General Accounting Office.

———. 1992b. *Cross Design Synthesis: A New Strategy for Medical Effectiveness Research*. GAO/PEMD-92-18. Washington: U.S. General Accounting Office.

———. 1992c. *Hispanic Access to Health Care: Significant Gaps Exist*. GAO-PEMD-92-6. Washington, DC: U.S. General Accounting Office.

———. 1994. *Breast Conservation Versus Mastectomy: Patient Survival in Day-to-Day Medical Practice and in Randomized Studies*. GAO/PEMD-95-9. Washington: U.S. General Accounting Office.

———. 1995. *Welfare to Work: State Programs Have Tested Some of the Proposed Reforms*. GAO/HEHS-95-93. Washington: U.S. General Accounting Office.

U.S. National Institutes of Health, National Task Force on the Prevention and Treatment of Obesity. 1994. "Weight Cycling." *Journal of the American Medical Association* 272: 1196–1202.

U.S. Senate Committee on Agriculture, Nutrition, and Forestry. 1984. Hearings of March 15 and April 9, 1984, on Evaluation and Reauthorization of the Special Supplemental Food Program for Women, Infants, and Children [WIC]. Washington: U.S. Government Printing Office.

Wachter, Kenneth W. 1988. "Disturbed by Meta-Analysis?" *Science* 241: 1407–1408.

Wachter, Kenneth W., and Miron Straf, eds. 1990. *The Future of Meta-Analysis*. New York: Russell Sage Foundation.

Wells, A. Judson. 1988. "An Estimate of Adult Mortality in the United States from Passive Smoking." *Environment International* 14: 249–265.

Wolf, F. W. 1986. *Meta-Analysis: Quantitative Methods for Research Synthesis*. Newbury Park, CA: Sage Publications.

Wortman, Paul M. 1992. "Lessons from the Meta-Analysis of Quasi-Experiments." In Fred B. Bryant and others, eds., *Methodological Issues in Applied Social Psychology*. New York: Plenum.

Yeaton, William H., and Paul M. Wortman. 1993. "On the Reliability of Meta-Analytic Reviews." *Evaluation Review* 17(3): 292–309.

Yusuf, Salim. 1987. "Obtaining Medically Meaningful Answers from an Overview of Randomized Clinical Trials." *Statistics in Medicine* 6: 281–286.

———. 1993. "Cardiologist Salim Yusuf Gets to the Heart of Meta-Analysis." [Interview with Yusuf.] *Science Watch* 4(8): 3–4, Sept./Oct.

Yusuf, Salim, and others. 1985. "Intravenous and Intracoronary Fibrinolytic Therapy in Acute Myocardial Infarction: Overview of Results on Mortality, Reinfarction and Side-Effects from 33 Randomized Controlled Trials." *European Heart Journal* 6: 556–585.

———. 1994. "Effect of Coronary Artery Bypass Graft Surgery on Survival: Overview of 10-Year Results from Randomised Trials by the Coronary Artery Bypass Graft Surgery Trialists Collaboration." *The Lancet*, 344(8922): 563–570.

Index

Agency for Health Care Policy and Research (AHCPR), 158–59
agreement rate (AR), 37
Altick, Richard, 35
Ambady, Nalini, 109–12, 115–18
American Psychological Association, 41
American Statistical Association: on combined p values, 39; potential of meta-analysis, 161
Antman, Elliott, 94
"apples and oranges" issue, 61–63
artifacts, 131–34
Ascher, Michael, 50
averaging: effect sizes, 31–33; meta-analysis, 9–10, 51; Pearson's, 8

Bacille Calmette-Guérin (BCG), 104–8
Barber, Theodore X., 122, 125
Battle over Homework, The (Cooper), 70
Bayard, Steven, 155–56
Becker, Betsy Jane, 24n, 71, 73–74, 77
Bergin, Allen, 26
biases: in effect size estimates and samples, 172–73; errors resulting from, 58; publication, 118–21, 132
Boschwitz, Rudy, 145
breast cancer meta-analyses, 99–101, 149–54
Breton, André, 9, 20
Bright, Ivey, 46
Bushman, Brad, 16

Calmette, Léon, 104
Carli, Linda, 72
causality: explanations of, 77–80; using meta-analysis to establish, 74–77

Centers for Disease Control (CDC), 104–7
Chalmers, Iain, 83, 86, 94, 98–99
Chalmers, Thomas, 7, 81–82, 84, 86–89, 92, 94–96, 103, 164
Chelimsky, Eleanor, 135–39, 142, 145–46, 149, 153
clinical trials: meta-analysis of acute myocardial infarction treatment using streptokinase, 86–99; meta-analysis of large, 99–101; question of small versus large, 96–99; results of meta-analyses of, 84; using RTMAS to hasten, 164
Cochran, Thad, 145
Cochran, William G., 11
Cochrane Collaboration: funding of, 165; U.K. Centre, 83; use of meta-analysis, 164; work of, 98
Cochrane Database of Systematic Reviews, 164
coding: of data for meta-analysis, 29, 35–37, 45–46; decision making and compatibility in, 36–37; for effect size, 33, 36–37; form used in meta-analysis, 40; task of, 35
Cohen, Jacob, 33, 169, 180
Colditz, Graham, 104–8
Collins, Rory, 97–101
colon cancer meta-analysis, 2; 2,
confidence interval: around weighted effect size estimate, 175; as range of real value, 24–25; substitute for p level techniques, 175
Cook, Thomas, 79
Cooper, Harris, 13, 16, 24n, 55, 68–71, 114, 163, 177–78
Cordray, David, 16, 128, 139, 141

205